TRANSPLANTED INTO UNACCUSTOMED EARTH

LONG-TERM PERSPECTIVES ON BEING ADOPTED AS OLDER CHILDREN

John Y. Powell, Ph.D.

John Y. Powell, Ph.D., Author
Illustrations by Patsy Faires, MFA

*To ensure privacy of the individuals who participated in this study, all
identifiable information—names, places and family details—have been altered.
In all other respects, the life stories in this book are transcriptions of tape-
recorded interviews with adults who were adopted older children. Because of
the universality of feelings related to adoption, some readers may believe they
recognize individuals. However, this book represents not only a limited number
of those in the study group, but the common feelings that are expressed by
older children who move into foster, institutional and adoptive placements.*

Book design by PenworthyLLC

ISBN: 978-0-578-71883-5

Dedicated to my Dear Wife Betsy

Whose love, understanding and support over many years have made *Transplanted into Unaccustomed Earth* possible!

John Powell, 2020

TABLE OF CONTENTS

FOREWORD

Forty years ago at the dawn of what would become landmark child welfare legislation (Public Law 96-272, The Adoption Assistance and Child Welfare Act of 1980), Kermit Wiltse, noted child welfare scholar at UC Berkeley, captured at least in part the challenge of translating our knowledge of child well-being into public policy and professional practice:

> When we speak of every child's right to permanency and continuity of care...we are endeavoring to express a very subtle kind of right and one not easily reduced to statutory expression or articulated in an agency manual. It is more a concept of what every child needs to grow and develop as a human being .[1]

Today we are in the early stages of launching a major new child welfare legislative effort--The Family First Prevention Services Act of 2018 (Public Law 115-123)--where efforts to achieve permanency for children in the child welfare system continue with new emphasis and a sense of urgency. Present day efforts are both enriched and made more complex with insights garnered from 40 years of research efforts and practice innovation in such areas as: guardianship arrangements, intensive family preservation strategies, the use of concurrent planning, family reunification, kinship foster care, family finding strategies, and strategies designed to build upon and honor strengths in indigenous communities and communities of color.[2]

To this present effort, Dr. Powell brings a fascinating glimpse into the lived experience of a small group of older children placed for adoption in earlier times and in a specific regional context.

To me, the value of this work lies in its unadorned rendering of the lived experience of such children viewed by them at two points in time. The author is to be commended for giving voice to narratives that are often not easy to read or assimilate. The book offers the reader –whether parent, professional, adult adoptee, or simply concerned citizen- something truly rare in our fast paced society: the opportunity to simply listen intently and reflect as did the author.

Dr. Powell's present work will be helpful to child welfare professionals, parents, policy makers as well as adult adoptees and young people in the care system who both struggle to make meaning of their own life course, as well as to gently assist others in the continuing search for that subtle right of permanency. I commend this book to all who labor in or are touched by the modern child welfare system.

James K. Whittaker, Ph.D.
Charles O. Cressey Endowed Professor Emeritus
School of Social Work
The University of Washington
Seattle, WA

INTRODUCTION:
How this Book Came To Be

In 1983, I selected "older child adoptions" as the topic of my University of North Carolina at Greensboro (UNC-G) doctoral (Ph.D.) dissertation.[1] The words "older-child adoptions" at first seemed to describe a straightforward process, but I have become intrigued by what these three words can represent. This volume, *Transplanted into Unaccustomed Earth*, grew out of an off-and-on over-35-years quest to better understand, better utilize, and help improve the complex, life-changing phenomenon of school-age child adoptions. [2]

Over the years since my choice, many adults have shared how thankful they were to have been adopted as older children. One person, who was adopted as a teenager, said he opened telephone conversations with his adoptive parents by saying, "You saved my life!" Unfortunately, I have also witnessed children dealing with broken hearts after their dreams for new "forever families" were shattered. Other older child adoption veterans recalled maltreatment, abuse and isolation. Some parents would not allow their adopted children to discuss or contact birth sib-lings and other people who had been important in their pre-adoption lives—often for a decade or more.

Whether the participants of this study categorize their older child adoptions as being positive, negative or in between, they believe that their adoptions helped set the courses of their lives in more positive directions. My older-child adoption research has changed my life as well. Over time, I have come to realize that the choice of "school-age child adoptions" as the topic of my dissertation has become more of a "calling" than a "choice."

After the 1983 dissertation was completed and a Ph.D. was awarded, an academic friend thoughtfully, without my knowing, shared a copy of the dissertation with her editor/publisher. Soon the editor wrote that her firm wished to publish it if it were rewritten for a wider variety of

9

readers. In 1985, a revision of the dissertation was published as *Whose Child Am I? Adults' Recollections of Being Adopted*.[3] The book was positively reviewed in the USA and Great Britain, and it was available in hardcover for 10 years.

Older-child adoptions continued to intrigue me even after I retired as an East Carolina University (ECU) professor emeritus. I worried and wondered about "Angela," "Benny," "Dana," "Jason," "Joanne," "Lee," "Madelyn," "Marshall," "Maynard" and the other participants of my study. How were their school-age adoptions impacting the later portions of their lives? With my dear wife's blessings, this time in my 70s and 80s, I embarked on my final research adventure to find out—with Dr. Alan Keith-Lucas' words echoing in recesses of my mind:

> We have very little first-hand knowledge of what our well-intentioned (adoption) plans for a child mean to him—what a child has to cope with when he becomes 'somebody else,' changes his name, 'belongs' to a new family, and is still the same person she (or he) has always been.[4]

Transplanted into Unaccustomed Earth was written to help fill the lack of systematically collected "first-hand knowledge" about school-age adoptions. The nine largely verbatim adoption stories (Chapters 4 to 9) are fascinating and inspiring, but at times emotionally painful to read. A friend, professional colleague, and adoptive father said these unique biographical accounts are "Not easy to forget; they stick with you!"[5]

John Y. Powell, Ph.D.
2020

PART ONE

BEGINNINGS

CHAPTER ONE

A QUEST TO BETTER UNDERSTAND AND IMPROVE OLDER CHILD ADOPTIONS

> "The only advice I would give to
> somebody I was counseling about
> adoption is this: Don't give up on an
> older child with a difficult past-- like
> Marshall (who was adopted at age 14). He (or
> she) can turn out just as great as Marshall has!"
> *(Marshall's wife, Chapter 9)*

There are more than 100,000 children and youth in the United States waiting to be adopted, and many are age 6 or older.[1] Numerous improvements have been made in adoption practices and policies since 1983 when this long-term research study began as my doctoral dissertation project. Yet almost four decades later, many school-age adoptable children continue to be vulnerable and face uncertain futures.

This book's nine participants volunteered to go beyond telling about the older-child, adoption-related experiences that occurred during their childhoods, teenage years and young adulthoods. They told the "rest" of their adoption stories with the desire that others might better understand school-age adoptions for their lifelong and life-changing potentials. They also hoped to make future older-child adoptions easier for children and families.

Adopted (give or take) a half-century ago, they have "lived" the older-child experience, they helped usher in the modern older-child movement, and they have made (and continue to make) important suggestions for further improving school-age adoptions. They serve as excellent guides for those of us who desire to better understand and improve such adoptions.

Most older child adoptions succeed. They can positively and powerfully change lives—not only during childhoods, but throughout the lifetimes of adopted people. As the biographical stories in this volume disclose, the positives effects of older child adoptions often are carried forward in the lives of the participants' children, grandchildren and later descendants.

At the same time, school-age adoptions can also enhance the lives of the members of host adoptive families. Successful older child adoptions, like good marriages, are mutually beneficial. Madelyn (Chapter Four) expressed the process well: "It was like I educated my (adoptive) parents and they educated me. I was there to help them, too."

When older adoptions do not succeed, however, both children and altruistic host adoptive families suffer negative effects, often feeling like "total failures." Birth family members, if involved, may struggle with guilt and shame for "giving away" their children to somebody else (or "having" their children "freed" for adoptions by court decrees), only to discover that their birth children are once more adrift in the welfare system. Social workers and other helpers who have guided adoptions that have failed may feel depressed and wonder what they might have done to prevent such disruptions from occurring.

"Billy's" Shattered Dream

It is desired that "Billy's" story and the other disguised adoption experiences shared in this volume, both positive and negative, may be viewed as learning opportunities that help advance the practice of older child adoptions, increase their use, and indirectly lead to more enlightened adoption policies.

Billy's ordeal exemplifies how painful it is for a child to meet, to become excited about and emotionally prepare to live with an adoptive family, only to have his or her dreams shattered. I worked in a children's residential center where Billy had been placed by a department of social services. His initial adoption experience was upsetting to witness. I asked myself, "What can be done to make older child adoptions more likely to succeed and at the same time be less stressful for adoptable children, adoptive and birth families and all who are involved?"

§ § §

At the age of 10, after returning from a pre-adoption visit, Billy jubilantly made the rounds of the staff at the children's center to tell about the family he hoped would adopt him. Their beautiful home and their exciting lifestyle seemed magical to him. After early parental abuse and multiple moves from foster home to foster home to institution, he had been admitted into our residential children's center to be "cured." Indeed, he had made many gains. He and our staff had diligently worked to modify the frantic excitability of his younger years. While he no longer acted out his feelings in destructive and violent ways, Billy continued to carry emotional scars from his unfortunate early life.

He was quite different now, but to be a part of the stable, middle-class family who was considering adopting him, he had to leap into a new world. It was a world where he would be expected to act politely, demonstrate appropriate affection toward his new parents, and learn to give and take with the family's birth children.

Several visits with the prospective adoptive family had gone well: the first on our campus, another during an overnight at a nearby motel, and a third for which Billy took his first airplane ride to the family's out-of-state home. After these visits, his county department of social services worker asked the family if they desired to adopt Billy. When they answered, "Yes," she asked Billy if he wished to be adopted by the family. He jumped at the chance. It was planned for Billy's placement to occur at the end of the school term.

The parents invited Billy to accompany them and their biological children, who were about Billy's age, on an extended hiking, camping trip during Spring Break. On the day he was leaving for this final visit, he was quite nervous, as was the staff. His childcare workers had carefully prepared him. For days they had been shopping, packing his bags, and giving him tips on how to respond in different situations.

Still, he looked quite anxious as he paced about our lobby awaiting his family. When he recognized their car, he ran to greet them, and his new family reciprocated with warm hugs. Several staff members helped him carry his luggage and some of his favorite toys and games to the car. We waved goodbye, hoping that he was adequately prepared.

Shortly after our office opened on the morning he was to return, the prospective adoptive parents telephoned Billy's social worker to say some problems had developed. Billy returned with the family a few minutes before noon. His prospective adoptive parents, the county adoption worker, and one of our staff social worker held a hasty conference.

That day, there was a campus-wide picnic lunch on the center's lawn. Soon staff heard the news, whispered ear-to-ear at the picnic. Billy's hoped-for adoptive family had decided, "after much crying, praying, and soul-searching," that Billy did not "fit" into their family's lifestyle. They thought he would be "better off" with another family. Some months before, a court had legally freed Billy for adoption, severing the remaining frail ties with his birth family. He had been preparing to have a better life with a new family, but now he had no one.

Billy was teary-eyed as he joined the picnic. He went from staff member to staff member asking the same question. When he found me talking to a sensitive and skilled special education teacher, Billy blurted out to the two of us, "Were you ever adopted?" I answered, "No," but to my surprise, the teacher nodded her head. She opened her arms, and the two warmly embraced. Weeping, Billy clung to her, having found someone who had also been initiated into the adoptive experience-- hoping she could thereby understand how devastated he felt.

A Desire to Learn More About Older Child Adoptions

Witnessing Billy's experience and several events similar to his changed my professional goals. I began a long-term quest to better understand, and I hoped, in small ways, to help improve the intricate and complex phenomenon of older child adoptions.

While continuing to work full time, I was a Ph.D. student in the

Department of Human Development and Family Studies at the University of North Carolina-Greensboro (UNC-G). This was during the first part of the modern older-child adoption era. As I became more aware of post-placement difficulties that some school-age children and their adoptive families were experiencing, I decided to seek permission from my dissertation committee to conduct a qualitative, exploratory study to learn more about the unique dynamics of school-age child adoptions.

In addition to gaining my doctoral dissertation committee's approval, I needed to resolve another important issue: Where could I locate a sample of adults who had been adopted as older children? By chance, I raised this question with Cliff Sanford, a friend and professional colleague. To my surprise, he told me that in the late 1950s he had helped to pioneer an older child adoption program in an out-of-state children's home where he had been employed as director of social work (Chapter Three).

Cliff thoughtfully contacted his former employer, who invited Cliff and me to meet with him and his associates to explain the proposed research study. Believing the project had the potential to help improve older- child adoption practices and policies, the CEO and his staff courageously approved the plan. About the same time, the UNC-G dissertation committee approved my proposal.

The initial goal was to find adults who had been adopted through the agency's older-child adoption program. Approximately 75 people met that criterion, but since neither they nor their adoptive parents were legally required to stay in touch with the agency, it was difficult to find many potential participants.

Eventually, with the gracious assistance of the agency's CEO and staff, 21 potential adult participants were located. All but four agreed to tell their adoption stories as part of my Ph.D. dissertation study.

The adoption stories provided data for my qualitative exploratory dissertation, *Adults Who Were Adopted as Older Children.*[2] The dissertation was approved and I received my doctoral degree in 1983. Two years

19

later, as a means of providing older child adoption information for the general public, I wrote a book based upon the dissertation that was entitled *Whose Child Am I? Adults' recollections of being adopted.*[3]

In 1987, I was offered a faculty appointment in the School of Social Work at East Carolina University (ECU), a position that provided many opportunities to continue the quest to better understand and help improve older child adoptions. For example, there were a number of workshops and presentations for which many of the people in the audiences had either been adopted or had helped facilitate adoptions. I hope they learned from the presentations, and I, in turn, gained a great deal of knowledge from them in the discussions that followed — invaluable, practice-centered and personal-experience knowledge.

Also, the research formed a basis for a number of articles. In 1988, I helped organize and lead a well-attended ECU symposium: "Permanence for Troubled Children Through Adoption." The proceedings were published and distributed to a number of adoption agencies and universities. Finally, I enjoyed teaching an elective graduate-level course on child adoptions, using my 1985 book, *Whose Child Am I?*[4] as one of the assigned readings.

From these activities, I was regularly reminded of the 1983 interviews, my adoption-centered dissertation, and what had been learned. About this time, ideas for a follow-up study began to develop because I believed it could provide important information on the long-term effects of older child adoptions.

Beginnings of the 2007-2020 Follow-Up Study

After retiring from ECU as Professor Emeritus of Social Work, I began the follow-up study. Fortunately, several of the original participants were located, and they volunteered to participate once again, this time by focusing on how their adoptions had affected their lives since the 1983 interviews. A ninth person who had not been previously interviewed, "Benny," a brother of Joanne and Maynard, volunteered to add his story to those of his sister and brother (Chapter Six). Nine adoption stories are therefore included in this volume.

I looked forward to talking with the participants, but wondered how I might be received after a quarter-century absence. My fears were unfounded. I was warmly greeted like a long-lost friend.

Rarely do we hear from nine older child adoption veterans regarding how childhood adoptive experiences have impacted their lives for about half a century. Those experiences include events such as: (1) being "tricked" into finalizing an adoption; (2) being adopted by a family, and after the adoption was finalized, not being allowed to communicate with siblings and other birth relatives—sometimes for a decade or more.

Surviving such adversities is but one part of these compelling stories. Readers will also learn about and ponder how some older adopted children managed to bounce back from dangerous, chaotic childhoods to become caring, loving parents and grandparents.

The Structure of This Book

As new information was acquired from the 2007-2020 follow-up interviews and contacts, the following outline was developed:

Part I: Beginnings explains the reasons for seeking to better understand and improve older child adoptions. It also describes how a traditional children's home broke with its past to help pioneer older-child adoptions.

Part II: Adoption Stories allow readers to "see" older child adoptions "from the inside out" through the "eyes" of adults who have lived the experience.

Part III: Observations & Conclusions contains observations, conclusions and recommendations as well as an appendix. The appendix includes acknowledgments, research notes and references.

The most important portions of this book are the adoption stories that appear in Part II, wherein participants tell in their own words how their adoptions have impacted their lives for about 50 years.

The 1983 and 2007-2020 Interviews and Conclusions

This book brings together, in one volume, information that has been acquired from 37 years of research and thinking about older child adoptions—beginning with the original research in 1983 and culminating with the 2007-2020 interviews and contacts.

The 1983 adoption research was unique in several ways. At that time, I could find no qualitative research that systematically sought the viewpoints of adults who had been adopted as older children. For those early interviews, I followed an approach pioneered by cultural anthropologists. I imagined myself as a stranger trying to learn from a group of diverse people who had several things in common. These commonalities included:

1. At the time of their adoptions, they were older adopted children (ages 6 - 14).

2. The adoptions were arranged by the same agency (the children's home where Cliff Sanford had worked).

3. Growing up in their adoptive homes, they had to cope with living in the "two different worlds"—their adoptive family and their birth family worlds.

4. They had experienced uncertainty, unpredictability and danger in their childhoods, and learned to survive such obstacles, often alone.

5. They appeared to have abilities to quickly "size people up" and determine if strangers were trustworthy or not.

As readers will discover, the participants are thoughtful, insightful guides. In both 1983 and 2007-2020, our conversations were constructed to let them recall, with minimal input from me, the events they remembered about their adoptions and how these unique experiences had impacted their lives. Using a broad-based outline, the interviews were audio recorded, transcribed and then edited into easy-to-understand adoption stories. The participants reviewed the drafts, and I worked with each person to check for accuracy and confidentiality—being sure all names, places and events had been disguised. These extensive contacts had the effect of making each participant a coauthor of his or her story.

The 2007-2020 interviews and contacts focus on the personal and family changes that occurred in the quarter of a century after the dissertation interviews were conducted. They reveal important and very useful information concerning how relationships and levels of contacts changed over time with both adoptive and birth families. The ability of the participants to bounce back is impressive. Comparing the circumstances they endured as children with the way they have matured into responsible adults caused me to think anew about resiliency.

Readers can observe that significant information is woven into the adoption stories. This includes biographical information, cultural contexts, and family dynamics. In addition, these stories reveal the emotions of the adopted participants during critical times in their lives such as:

1. when birth parents or courts "gave" the participants to "strangers" (their new, previously unknown adoptive parents);
2. when their birth family ties were severed or contacts with them were greatly reduced;
3. when they had to accommodate to new and different environments as they grew up in their adopted homes;
4. when many were separated from their birth siblings and other birth relatives for a decade or more; and
5. how they reacted when they were reunited with siblings and other birth family members, often after many years of separation.

The participants' memories and thoughts about being adopted as older children were recorded during interviews at two different periods in their lives: 1983 and 2007-2020 In 1983, their ages ranged from late teens through the late 30s, and in 2020, the year that this book is being completed, their ages vary from the late 40s to the early 70s.

§ § §

This book, *Transplanted into Unaccustomed Earth,* was written for a wide variety of readers. I hope it may be of interest to: (1) those who have been adopted as older children and their families, and those who are considering such involvement; and (2) students (social work, family therapy, counselors, etc.), practicing professionals, researchers, policy makers and volunteers—in effect, all people who desire to better understand and improve the processes, regulations, and laws that guide older-child adoptions. To that end, I have tried to refrain from using professional jargon and to write in ways that maintain interest, provide useful information and also connect with the inner feelings of readers.

The approach used for notes and references identifies items numerically in the primary text. Readers can then locate the author's notes and the sources of references in the "Notes" section of the Appendix. This method, allows for uninterrupted reading and at the same time permits readers to easily locate additional information as desired.

Using "Transplanted" as Part of the Book's Title

In my Professor-of-Social-Work days, several Master of Social Work (MSW) students requested that an elective course be offered on the practice and policies of child adoptions. I was asked if I would be interested in developing and teaching it. I readily agreed.

Several sessions of each course focused on older-child adoptions. As an introduction to that topic, I assigned the Master of Social Work (MSW) students to read the adoption stories in *Whose Child Am I?*[5] Then they participated in classroom discussions that explored and contrasted similarities and differences between infant/young-child adoptions and older-child adoptions. These discussions stimulated creative thoughts and interesting observations. Frequently, MSW students commented that the word "placement" tended to be used for both groups, but they did not think the word "placement" appropriately described older-child adoptions. They believed that adoptions of older children should be child-paced, more open, negotiated processes that allow older children to participate in helping select their new families.

As I was preparing for one of the class discussions that compared the similarities and differences of infant/young child and older child adoptions, a new term for "placement," came to mind. I thought to myself that the word "transplanted" would more accurately describe the older child adoption process.

In the next class session, I suggested that the word "transplanted" as an alternative to "placement." The MSW students' responses were generally positive. Several observed that "transplanted" represents a continuous, on-going, more dynamic process—not a single, passive event. Others noted that occasionally using "transplanted" might help reinforce the reality that older adopted children have memories of their birth families and other pre-adoption caregivers that need to be acknowledged and discussed.

Some MSW students suggested that adoptions of children could be compared, in some ways, to transplanting trees. Somewhat like young seedlings, infants and young children tend to adapt more readily to their new environments. Older child adoptions are similar to transplanting larger and more mature trees in that they require: (1) extreme care in removing them from familiar environments; (2) thoughtful and careful selection of their new "homes"; and (3) careful placement into their new "unaccustomed earth" settings. Regular TLC (Tender Loving Care), maintenance and support are needed for both older and younger adopted children.

§ § §

I had not thought of the classroom discussion that compared older adoptions to transplanting trees for several years. As a draft of this introductory chapter was being written one spring morning, our dog, Penny, nudged me to take her for a walk outside. She meandered underneath a tree in our front yard that was in full bloom with gorgeous pink flowers. With leash in hand, I stooped to follow her, and the long forgotten "transplanted" metaphor came to mind.

My wife and I had selected our retirement home, in part, because of its attractive landscaping, and we especially admired a pink flowering tree in our front yard. Since the original owners planted the tree, we do not know whether it was young and small or more mature at the time of transplantation. It really doesn't matter, because either way we greatly enjoyed the tree's beautiful flowers each spring. Others also enjoy its beauty. In fact, a next-door neighbor used the tree, in full bloom, as a backdrop when he photographed his daughter in her high school graduation cap and gown.

When one compares adopting children to transplanting trees, it is important to know that adopted children can be loved, cherished and become lifelong gifts to families regardless of whether they are older or younger at the time of their adoptions. In return, adoptive families can become enduring, loving, wonderful gifts to their "transplanted" children.

Using "transplanted" rather than "placed" for older-child adoptions implies a new start and new growth opportunities. Carefully planned, implemented and supported adoptions tend to succeed just as do carefully transplanted trees. Wisely considered and skillfully implemented adoptions can be a blessing to all concerned: children, families, and the communities in which they live. Adoptions that derive from selfishness, misguided beliefs, emotional instability or poor planning and management can be lifelong destructive events for adopted children and all who are involved.

§ § §

The word "transplanted" that is part of the title of this book reinforces the reality that older adopted children have histories and conscious memories that need to be recognized. Yet "transplanted," used as a replacement for "placed," does not fully capture the dynamic, interactive and complex processes of adoptions for school-aged children.

Lee, in Chapter 7, opens up another way of thinking about adoptions of older children and youth. He believes that older child adoptions are similar to marriages. He explained:

> [Getting married,] that's about as close as I can get [to being adopted as an older child]. You just have to pick them out. Both parties have to have the freedom to choose and to feel good about their choice for it to work. I'm not much on advice, but I knew when I met my adoptive family that we clicked. I knew that it would work out okay.
>
> Don't make children go live with a family unless the child fits right in with them. When things, fit, it can be wonderful, but when they don't, it can be a living hell.

26

Considering the word "transplanted" as a possible replacement for "placed," although it is an imperfect description, may help readers think anew about what happens to older children when they are moved from one environment to another. Perhaps reading the adoption stories in this volume may stimulate readers to think about and suggest more accurate, more action-centered words than either "transplanted" or "placed."

Using Nathaniel Hawthorne's Phrase "Unaccustomed Earth" in the Title

The previous pages explain how the word "transplanted" came to be used in the title, but the phrase "unaccustomed earth" was a stroke of luck. Sometimes I absentmindedly forget to turn off our car's radio when I park. Later when the car is restarted, I listen to whatever is being featured at that moment, music or news. Such was the case one morning years ago when I heard a book critic remark that "unaccustomed earth" was one of his favorite phrases. A Google search revealed that Nathaniel Hawthorne was perhaps the first to use the phrase about a century and a half ago.

"Unaccustomed earth" somehow clicked in my mind with the word "transplanted." As a result, I carefully considered Hawthorne's words and later chose to use *Transplanted into Unaccustomed Earth* as the book's title. Readers may wish to consider that "unaccustomed earth" can refer to different soil environments, ranging from fertile to toxic. Nathaniel Hawthorne, however, used "unaccustomed earth" to convey positive, new-life opportunities:

> Human nature will not flourish, any more than a potato, if it be planted and replanted, for too long a series of generations, in the same worn-out soil. My children have had other birthplaces, and, so far as their fortunes may be within my control, shall strike their roots into unaccustomed earth.[6]

As the adoption memoirs in this book indicate, older children who were transplanted into adoptive homes tend to confirm Hawthorne's belief that "strike[ing] their roots into unaccustomed earth" somehow opened up and enriched their lives. The transplanted children in my study were afforded new growth and new opportunities. This held true even when some were transplanted (adopted) into unhealthy environments.

Advantages and Limitations of the Study

A comprehensive 1983 literature review revealed that one source of important data was missing. No cited studies indicated that adult "veterans" of school-aged child adoptions had been interviewed in systematic ways to gain firsthand knowledge regarding how they had coped with being "transplanted" (adopted) into "unaccustomed earth" (new, previously unknown families). In addition, no cited studies sought advice from the "veterans" of ways to improve the practices of older-child adoptions. This lack of specific knowledge led to the qualitative research study described in this volume. The goals of the study were to better understand school-age adoptions from the "inside out," and to help improve the practices and policies of such adoptions.

The participants were pioneers of the modern older-child adoption movement. Their stories give readers firsthand accounts of how adopted children, their new adoptive families, and their birth families perceive and cope with such new practice concepts.

Some readers might conclude that this study should be considered an historical account of the beginnings of the modern older-child movement, rather than as a study of relevant, contemporary adoption issues. Such arguments could be based on the fact that the study's participants were adopted approximately 50 years ago. Still, anecdotal evidence indicates that many issues these participants encountered continue to be troublesome today. One such issue is separating biological siblings and denying their freedom to communicate with each other for long periods of time. The interviews of participants for this book revealed they express great concern about this issue. Clearly, further research using larger and more diverse samples could discover if, indeed, this issue and others are still of concern.

This study should not be used to generalize to all older-child adoptions. It does provide new, significant knowledge but it is limited by factors such as:

1. The participants were pioneers of the modern older child adoption movement.

2. The study sample is small and represents only white, older-adopted children who were placed by one agency, a children's home located in the southern United States. (These adoptions occurred before the home was racially integrated.)

3. The study relies on only one source of data: the childhood and adult memories of the participants. Having worked as a social worker for a half-century with people who have been adopted, interested in or involved with older child adoptions leads me to believe that the feelings and thoughts expressed by the participants will resonate with many readers.

Disguised Information

All identifying information referring to the participants, their families, friends, former caregivers and other persons in this book has been changed. Names of places and institutions, as well dates and other identifying information have also been changed—in an effort to help keep the participants of this study anonymous and undisturbed. Any similarities with actual people, places, dates or events are coincidental, unintentional and accidental.

Although the identities of the participants have been protected since 1983, it is difficult to keep them from being identified in today's social media environment.

Selecting an anonymous name for the residential agency that placed the older adopted children was difficult, and as a result, the agency is being referred to by generic names such as the "home," the "agency," the "children's home" or the "institution."

CHAPTER TWO

TRANSPLANTING OLDER CHILDREN INTO UNACCUSTOMED EARTH IS NOT NEW

"Orphan Trains" were used from the
mid-1800s until the first part of the
20th century to "transplant" as many as
250,000 homeless, out-of-control children
and youth from Northeastern cities into
new environments, often with Midwestern
farm families.[1]

Adopting older children is not a new or uniquely American concept. The Bible and the ancient "legal codes of the Chinese, Hindus, Babylonians, Romans and Egyptians" contain references to adopting children—both younger and older. The "purposes [of adoptions] have varied considerably by country and by period—for example, to make possible the continuance of family religious traditions, to provide an heir, to overcome difficulties in recognizing an out-of-wedlock child, or, more recently, to provide permanent homes for children in need of them." [2]

One of the oldest known legal documents is the Babylonian Code of Hammurabi. A provision in this 4,000-year-old document makes it clear that adoptions were irreversible: "If a man takes a son in his name, adopts and rears him as a son, the grown man may not be demanded back" by the birth family. [3]

Ancient adoptions were often related to the adopter's political and economic interest. Rome's ruling aristocracy had laws and procedures for adoptions, and they often used adoption of older children and youth to strengthen political and economic ties. Even some of Rome's emperors were adopted to allow peaceful transitions of power. Abandoned or captured children, however, would often be enslaved. [4]

There are also periods in America's history when children were forcibly moved from their native, "accustomed earth" settings. (1) One horrific example was the enslavement of children and adults. It is difficult to comprehend that children of African ancestry were bought and sold as commodities only a little over five generations (150 years) ago. In addition to the terrible practice of enslaving fellow human beings, often there was little regard for keeping children with their parents, brothers and sisters, and other relatives. [5] (2) A second example was Native American children who were separated from their families and culture by placing them into boarding schools where they were taught English, European history, and other aspects of western civilization, while at the same time their native language, history, culture and traditions were belittled. Also Native American children were routinely moved into Caucasian foster and adoptive homes. By the 1970s, "surveys indicated that between 25-35 percent of all Indian children were separated from their (birth) families and either institutionalized, adopted or placed in foster homes." The Indian Child Welfare Act of 1978 was enacted to help end such practices. [6]

Mass Movements of Children and Youth into Unaccustomed Earth

One way to consider how the modern older child movement began, gained momentum and revolutionized adoption practices is to consider how societies have found ways to care for large numbers of children and youth without adequate, safe and dependable places to live. Two examples of moving large numbers of children into safer environments are: (1) Great Britain's World War II "Pied Piper" program, and (2) America's "Orphan Train" experiments.

During World II, Great Britain evacuated thousands of children from its cities, industrial and urban areas. These children were temporarily moved ("transplanted") into less populated areas in an effort to protect them from Nazi bombs and possible invasions.[7] Years ago, a British professional colleague Spencer Millham (1932--2015) shared his personal

34

experience of boarding a train in London as a young boy with his sister. They wore labels placed around their necks by their parents, giving the children's names and the names and address of their parents. He recalled arriving many hours later at a Welsh railway station with the label still around his neck, waiting to be taken in "by strangers." While south Wales is only a few hundred miles from the East End of London, the move was both an emotional and a cultural shock.

Spencer never forgot this terrifying experience. He became an internationally respected researcher and advocate for children who were separated from their homes and families and placed into "unaccustomed earth" settings (i.e., boarding schools, residential children's centers, foster homes, adoptive homes, etc.). Upon his retirement, Spencer was appointed Officer of the Order of the British Empire (OBE) in recognition of his important contributions on behalf of children.[8]

§ § §

In America, from 1853 through 1929 a number of Northeastern children's agencies used "Placing Out"/ "Orphan Train" concepts to "transplant" about a quarter of a million (250,000) homeless and/or out-of-control children and youth into new environments, usually with farm families.[9]

In an influential 1859 book, Charles Loring Brace made reference to the "horrors" of reformatories and orphanages. In their place, he touted the merits of placing children in private homes, as "families are God's reformatories."[10]

At first, children and youth found unattended in New York, Boston and other Eastern cities were placed with local families. The supply of available families was soon exhausted, and many of the remaining children were first transported to rural areas of New York, Massachusetts and neighboring states. Later, trains often referred to as "Orphan Trains" transported children to the vast Midwest. Usually the children were taken from town to town, where families selected children at train-side meetings.

35

> Bewildered "orphan train" children—lined up at railroad stations across the heartland of America—were selected or rejected by prospective frontier farm families. The children would "watch in all directions, scanning closely every wagon that came in sight, and deciding from the appearance of the driver and horses, more often from the latter, whether they would go for that farmer." [11]

Often families signed agreements to keep the children until they were 18, and the children, in turn, were expected to help with the farm and housework. At 18 they were "to be provided with a Bible, two suits of clothing, and $50 in cash." After that, these young people often had to quickly learn to take care of themselves, without birth family support. Many of these "placed out" children, however, developed into responsible, dependable adults—becoming successful parents, businessmen and businesswomen, doctors, farmers, lawyers, ministers, and government officials—a few rose to positions of prominence.[12]

However there were dark aspects of "placing out:"

> Charles Loring Brace and the New York Children's Aid Society were the best known but not the first or only sponsors of this movement. They aimed to personally separate children geographically or culturally from their Catholic parents and communities by placing them in worthy Anglo-Protestant families that would Americanize them and salvage their civic potential while simultaneously reducing urban poverty and crime. Such disregard for natal ties was unusual, illustrating bias against immigrant groups (Irish or Italian) whose ethnoracial identities although in flux were considered inferior. Even so, the architects of the orphan trains often failed to achieve their goal. Poor parents had no intention of losing their children and they usually did not, even in the case of very young children placed permanently for "adoption." [13]

The social conditions of the past 60 years have parallels to "Orphan Train" times. In both periods many school age children and youth did not or do not currently have parents (or parent-like caretakers) who are able to provide love, adequate care, supervision and a sense of permanency for their children. Concerned citizens, then and now, sought and continue to seek answers and find remedies. In the 1850s "placing out" was considered by Charles Loring Brace to be (like the title of his 1859 book), "the best method of disposing of our pauper and vagrant children." [14] Beginning in the 1960s and continuing to the present, modern day older child/special needs adoptions have offered thousands of older children and youth opportunities for permanence and more hopeful futures.

Adoptions in the First Part of the Twentieth Century

Massachusetts, in 1851, was the first state to enact a modern adoption law. There judges had to be satisfied that adoptions were "fit and proper" before adoption decrees were entered.[15] Later, a "Progressive Movement" gained momentum. One of its goals was to end the use of orphanages and institutions for long-term care of children. The movement's efforts led to President Theodore Roosevelt's call for the first White House Conference on the Care of Dependent Children in 1909. The Conference issued a statement saying that the nuclear family represented "the highest and finest product of civilization" and therefore it was best able to serve abandoned and orphaned children.[16] The impact of the Conference led to a gradual increase in adoptions. As late as the 1920s, however, a number of adoptions continued to be casually arranged by newspaper advertisements and usually involved an infant given up at birth by the mother. Many adoptions continued to be registered by deed--but not approved by a court.[17]

The goals of the 1909 and later White House Conferences slowly gained momentum, and by the early 1940s, some states had enacted legislation to regulate and professionalize children's adoptions. Often such laws required social workers and other professionals to conduct initial investigations to verify the fitness of adoptive homes. Until final court decrees were granted, children's placements were often supervised by public and private welfare agencies. Therefore, professionally supervised adoptions became a part of the child welfare system.[18]

Historically, many societies have used institutions to help care for homeless children. In America, until the middle of the last century, when birth relatives were unable or unwilling to provide appropriate care, many orphans, half-orphans (children with one parent deceased), and other dependent children and youth were often placed in orphanages or children's residential programs for long-term care. [19]

Were the experiences of growing up in an orphanage mostly negative as some contend, or were there positive aspects of institutional care? In an East Carolina University lecture, a colleague and friend James Campbell, described his experience of growing up in an orphanage from 1939 until 1956 as a mix of hardships and benefits.

Professor James Campbell's Story

While it was called an "orphanage", the institution that "raised" Jim had only a small minority of "full" orphans—the majority of the children had at least one living parent. After Jim's parents died, an older sister and grandmother struggled to keep the nine siblings together, but they were unable to do so. The five youngest children were placed in an orphanage to keep them together—Jim was 3 at the time. As was the custom in such facilities of that day, they were segregated into large dormitories, called "cottages," by age and sex. "I was never able to stay with or be raised around any of my siblings who accompanied me there. This has resulted in a quasi-alienation from my siblings, and I am closer to some of the boys I was raised with than my own family."

Because he was so young, Jim doesn't remember his parents or being placed in the institution, but an older sister told about the first day of their arrival. At dinner in the central dining hall:

> She heard me crying at my table and heard the matron in charge of me saying if I did not stop crying I would get no food. My sister left her table, went over to me, picked me up and took me to her table and held and fed me. Of course this was serious breach of regulations and she was punished for it.

Despite such personal harshness and disregard for family ties, Jim received a number of benefits: a fine elementary and high school education, good work habits, and an extended-like-family of friends who supported one another as children in care, and now stay in touch with one another as adults.

The orphanage was Jim's home until he graduated from high school and simultaneously joined the US Air Force. Professor Campbell recalled his dilemma in leaving the children's home:

> Try to imagine, if you will, where you were and how you processed the world when you were only 17. Now try to imagine yourself at that age with no safety net beneath you, no home to go to, no job, no skills except that of a farm laborer, no older and wiser parent or adult advisor to whom you could turn, and the understanding that as of graduation day you were expected to leave the only home you had known since you were 3. That was me at age 17.

In the concluding remarks, he added:

> [While living at the orphanage,] I was surrounded by caring individuals, almost to a person, who provided for me and sheltered me from the temptations, pushes and pulls of society. And I have come to believe that the next best substitute for my biological family was [the children's home] that reared me. And I will ever be grateful for my home. [20]

However, he also noted in his lecture: "I believe that this slice of Americana is no longer with us . . . (and) in my opinion, it will never return—as we knew it." [21]

Unfortunately, not all people who lived in long-term-care children's residential centers were able to remain in their agencies until they finished high school or left their institutional homes in an orderly process. Cliff Sanford, in the next chapter (Chapter 3), dramatically describes how he and his wife, Anne, informally and almost instantly adopted 12-year-old twin brothers who were being quickly discharged from an orphanage for a trivial infraction of the rules. As readers will discover, their adopted sons grew up to become responsible and successful people. One has since died, but the remaining adopted son often told Cliff and Anne, "You saved my life!"

Older and Younger Child Adoptions Differ

The basic concept of adoption is that a child not born into a family is incorporated into and becomes a full family member, but such a general definition does not distinguish between "young child" and "older child" adoptions. A rough distinction between the two terms, I feel, derives from the ability of individuals who were adopted as older children to be able to recall a number of events surrounding their adoptions on a long-term basis. This would typically include remembering people and situations such as: (1) their birth family members, (2) separations from their birth parents/families, (3) interim caretakers (foster parents, extended family members, etc.), (4) meeting and, one hopes, helping to choose potential adoptive parents, (5) placements with persons who wish to adopt them, and (6) adjusting to their new adoptive environments. Individuals, who were adopted as infants and young children, usually, cannot clearly recall pre-adoption people and the pre-adoption events.

Even using the above guidelines, it is difficult to set an age when children should be considered "older adopted children." While interviewing adopted people for my 1983 doctoral dissertation study, I came to believe that individuals who were adopted at age six and older tend to remember many more events surrounding their adoptions than do younger children.[22] Children in the public child welfare system who are eligible for adoption are often not considered to be "older adoptable children" until they are age 9 and older.[23] The age of 6 may be more reasonable than 9 as a general dividing line between young and older child adoptions, but using a selected age brings up other issues.

Can Traumatic Early Childhood Events Be Remembered? A Story of Two Young Children

Infants and pre-school children have few, if any, long-term conscious memories of their adoptions and pre-adoption lives. Still, is it possible that they may carry some significant events in sub-conscious ways into adulthood? Can some traumatic events be "etched" into one's memory at ages earlier than might be expected? The following story illustrates the significance of memory even in the adoption of young children.

40

A man I once sat beside on an airplane noticed that I was reading a book about adoptions. An adoptive father, he asked about the book, and this started a conversation that led him to share a thought-provoking story.

§ § §

After seeking various medical opinions, he and his wife accepted the fact that they would likely not have children born to them and decided to adopt. With the waiting list so long in their home state, they chose to adopt a foreign-born son and daughter.

Their first child, a boy, arrived when he was seven weeks old. The father told of how they had received an airmail letter and photographs prior to the boy's journey to America. He and his wife felt that the letter describing their son, the photos of him, and their own preparation activities, such as painting and decorating his nursery, helped them begin "bonding" with their son even before he arrived. After the couple picked up the infant at an international airport, he went to sleep in his new mother's arms during the auto trip back to their home, and thereafter easily accepted his new parents and his "transplantation" into a vastly different cultural environment.

A year or so later, they adopted a second foreign-born child from the same country when she was 2 ½ years old. The birth mother had released this child to an orphanage soon after she was born, and she lived there until her move to America. When her adoptive parents met their daughter in the airport, she was crying and kicking her escort. She continued to be unsettled during the auto trip home. At bedtime, she frantically ran around her bedroom. Attempts to soothe her were unsuccessful. Finally her new parents decided to leave her alone, but they sat just outside her bedroom door. When she became quiet and fell asleep, they peeked into her room. She had taken all the toys and clothes that she could carry and placed them in a pile and laid on top of her collection, spread eagle-like, with her arms and legs extended— trying to cover her newly acquired possessions as best she could. The parents surmised that their daughter's chaotic early life and living in an orphanage caused her to fear that someone would snatch away her new gifts if she did not protect them.

41

My airplane flight companion said that he and his wife dearly love both of their children, but they wisely recognized that their daughter came into their lives with a longer pre-adoption history than did their son. To emphasize this point, the father shared an interesting and informative event related to his daughter's pre-adoptive memories. Several months after she became part of their family, the parents decided that she had settled down enough to take her and her brother to visit relatives in a cosmopolitan city. While there, they went sightseeing in a popular historic area. As they walked about, a gentleman from the children's native country saw the children, and guessed that they were born in his home country. He introduced himself, and politely asked the parents if he could say "Hello" to them in their original language. Their son took this in stride, but their daughter became upset. They had trouble calming her down during the rest of the visit, but on returning home, she went immediately to her room and systematically touched all her toys, furniture and clothes. After checking everything, she came out with a big smile. The parents doubted that their daughter was upset by the words the foreign gentleman said to her, but instead they believe just hearing the sounds of her native language may have frightened her and caused her to think that she might be returned to the orphanage.

Whose Child Am I? A Dilemma for Adopted People

Adoption laws and practices are concerned with the question of who "owns" an adopted child? In the past, the biological parents' ownership of their children approached the absolute. In America today, for adoptions to occur, either birth parents voluntarily relinquish their rights or courts legally free children for adoption. Adoptive parents, in turn, become legally responsible for their adopted children.[24]

In the United States, individual states determine the openness of adoption records, and applicable state laws vary considerably—from open to closed records. Some states allow for openness only when both birth parent(s) and their biological children consent. For decades however, many countries such as Scotland and Finland have had adoption records open for public search by adults.[25] Regardless of laws, open adoptions are occurring because in today's more open society, many birth parents want to be a part of the selection process—helping to choose their child's new parents. Additionally, many wish to negotiate ways that they might be able to communicate with and perhaps visit their birth children after adoptions have been finalized.

Sandy Cook (Chapter 10) contends that older child adoptions are already "open," because people adopted at age 6 and older can usually remember where they were born, the names of relatives and other details of their birth families. Noted adoption scholar, David Kirk, believed that adopted people are denied a basic freedom by not being allowed to have information about their birth family. Further, he thought that adoptive parents who acknowledged, discussed and mutually shared adoption-related feelings, issues and concerns with their children could help facilitate shared empathy and understanding. While David Kirk's book, *Shared Fate*, focused on secrecy issues of infant and young child adoptions, many of his concepts also apply to older child adoptions.[26]

As the adoption stories in this book reveal, people who have been adopted as older children struggle with the question *Whose Child Am I?* The older adopted people in my study have had to live in what some call "several different worlds"—their adopted world, their birth family world, and also the world they developed for themselves—marriage, children, vocation, etc. For some, this has been a difficult struggle.

The Modern Older-Child Adoption Movement

Beginning in the 1960s, social changes occurred which had a major effect on adoption services—such as:

(1) widespread use of improved birth control methods (the "pill");

(2) changing societal mores that make it easier for unmarried mothers to rear their own children; and

(3) the liberalization of abortion laws in some states resulted in a decrease in the number of infants available for adoption.

At the same time, the widespread extent of child abuse began to be recognized in the early 1960s, and as a result, there has been an increase in the number of older children who were placed in foster homes and group care. A number of these placed children were later freed by court action for adoption.[27] In a sense "the tables turned"—the number of adoptable infants and young children had diminished while the number of older adoptable children had swelled.

As a result, there was a concerted effort to make the public aware that older children were available for adoption, and a variety of prospective parents applied. Some were motivated to adopt older, hard-to-place children for religious and humanitarian reasons. Others who desired to adopt babies but could not because of the limited supply often were willing to consider older children. A paradigm shift began to occur on two levels: (1) among prospective adoptive parents, and (2) among professionals, child advocates, and government and civic leaders. Many of the latter group had long realized that the foster care system left much to be desired, and they began to rethink the position that only small, healthy children were suitable for adoption. As a result, policy and laws changed to promote the adoption of older children. Two examples were: (1) foster parents began to be encouraged (rather than discouraged) to adopt foster children who were already in their care; and (2) the Adoption Assistance and Child Welfare Act of 1980 (PL-96-272) was enacted. This was a statute that provided federal funds (for the first time) to support the adoption of special-needs children, including some older children as well. [28]

Arguments such as those Goldstein, Freud, and Solnit advanced in their 1973 book, *Beyond the Best Interest of the Child*, were instrumental in bringing about changes in adoption practices. They (and others) reasoned that children who drift through foster care, moving from placement to placement, would be better served if their interests were of paramount concern. They pointed out that (1) time has different meanings for children, (2) that several months of delay can be devastating to a child's sense of well-being, (3) that a lack of consistent parenting or a loss of parental figures often leads to feelings of helplessness and profound deprivation, and (4) that children whose parents seemed unable to look after them adequately would fare better with an early decision for adoption or other care arrangements that provided long-term, stable parenting.[29] Persuaded by this reasoning, social workers, courts, and agencies have become vigorous in freeing older children for adoption. As a result, the number of older child adoptive placements has increased and the options for dependent children have broadened.

Older adopted children carry early memories, pleasant and unpleasant, forward with them in their feelings and loyalties, regardless of legal decrees. Transplanting them into adoptive families can create problems that require more than simplistic approaches. Many questions need to be thoughtfully considered in order to make older child adoptions more meaningful—such as how can difficult-to-place children be prepared for adoption so that their chances for successful outcomes will be increased? How can such children, before and after adoptions, be helped to deal with painful and haunting past memories so that strong attachments can be formed with their adoptive families? What types of training and support systems are necessary to prepare and undergird adoptive families? The above questions are not to argue that adoptions of older children should be avoided, because as this book demonstrates, such adoptions can be of great benefit to many children—powerfully changing their lives.

Making Older Child Adoptions Simpler and More Visible

At the time of its publication in 1979, the authors of an influential adoption book, *No Child Is Unadoptable*, believed that we had begun to experience "a tremendous revolution" in the way we think about and conduct the adoption of children. They contended that all children, including older and special-needs children, are adoptable.[30] History has proven them to have been correct. A revolution has occurred, and this has led to a broadening of options for adoptable children and youth.

Older child adoption advocates called for more openness and simplicity in the selection and placement of children and youth. For example, in 1982 Soule observed, "I think all too often we make the whole process so unnecessarily complicated. Make all of the waiting children visible. Let families see the children and let their worker mail out their adoption study on any child they desire. I bet we would place a lot more children." [31]

45

Soule's 36-year-old desire "to make all of the waiting children visible" has been partly fulfilled. There are now extensive photo-listings of "waiting children" readily available on the internet. Yet unfortunately, even with the current degree of openness, many children that have been freed for and desire to be adopted languish in the foster care system (foster family homes and various forms of group care).

As of September 30, 2016, an estimated 117,794 children in the US were waiting to be adopted, and about 59 percent were ages 6 and older.[32] While progress is being made in providing adoption opportunities for older children and youth, one tends to feel sad perusing older adoptable children's websites and seeing photographs of and reading brief descriptions about numerous waiting children and youth who desire permanent families.

Summary

Historian and adoptive parent, Ellen Herman, author of *Kinship by Design*, observed:

> Adoption tells uncommon stories about how children, adults, and families navigate the common experiences of love and loss, identity and belonging. This combination of uniqueness and universality makes adoption historically interesting and important. Before states passed adoption laws in the mid-nineteenth century, an assortment of private, largely unregulated arrangements transferred children between adults and households for reasons of love, labor, and inheritance. After 1900, adoption was re-imagined as a delicate process requiring skilled management and specialized knowledge. Who surrendered children and why? Were children who need new parents normal enough to qualify for adoption? Were adults who were willing to raise other people's children up to the tasks?
>
> How should these adults and children be brought together? I call the operation that answered these questions 'kinship by design.' Its historically unprecedented and ambitious goal was to conquer chance and vanquish uncertainty.[33]

CHAPTER THREE

Clifford Weldon Sanford, Jr. died on July 27, 2017, at age 89. Cliff and his wife, Anne Leah Register Sanford, were pioneers in the older child adoption movement. As a young married couple and expecting the first of four biological children, they adopted, "almost instantly," twin adolescent brothers. Their newly acquired sons were being "shipped" for a minor infraction from an orphanage-like children's residential facility to uncertain futures. Cliff, the "orphanage's" farm manager, and Anne informally adopted the teenagers and raised them along with their four biological children. All six of their children became successful, caring and responsible adults.

Professionally: The experience of adopting two of his sons and witnessing other similar events led Cliff to earn a Master of Social Work degree. He became an innovative, creative leader, teacher, author and consultant in the field of child/family social work services. One of Cliff's many accomplishments was to help establish an older child adoption program that gave alternatives to children and youth who were "stuck" in foster and institutional care. He wanted children and youth in such settings to have opportunities, if they desired, to become a part of new families.

In the chapter that follows, Cliff told about adopting their teenage sons and establishing the older child adoption program. His interview was audiotaped and later transcribed into a typed narrative, which Cliff then read, edited and approved. To his credit, he did not "sugarcoat" any portion. He asked me to truthfully report both the joys and difficulties inherent in school-aged adoptions. A few days before he died, Cliff urged me to finish this book so that others might learn from his and Anne's adoption experiences and from the experiences and advice of the participants of this research study. Ultimately Cliff hoped that this book (and the research that undergirds it) might help improve the practices of older child adoptions for present and future adoptable children.

Thank you Cliff and Anne!

John Powell, Author

PS: To honor Cliff and Anne's leadership in the older child adoption movement, their "real" names appear in this volume.

CLIFF SANFORD:
ORIGINS OF A PIONEERING
OLDER CHILD ADOPTION PROGRAM

Anne, Cliff's wife, was expecting their first biological child when they, almost instantly, informally adopted 12-year-old twin brothers who were being "shipped" from an "orphanage." The illustration that opens this chapter depicts Anne welcoming the boys into their new family. One of the boys died as an adult, but the surviving one (now retirement age) often reminded Cliff and Anne of the importance of their extraordinary kindness by beginning telephone calls to them by exclaiming, "You saved my life!"

As I began the final phase of writing this book, I realized that one important aspect still had not been explained: Why and how did a children's home break with the status quo and begin an innovative adoption project? To obtain this important and interesting history, I contacted Cliff Sanford, who graciously agreed to be interviewed. Cliff's words, while edited for ease in reading, were taken verbatim from interview transcriptions.

Cliff made this older-child adoption study possible. In the 1950s, he worked as the director of social work in a residential children's center that developed a pioneering older-child adoption program. The agency had begun as an orphanage and needed, in the last part of the 20th century, to move into a new era of modern services for children and families.

Note: To protect their privacy, the names of and other identifying information about the Sanfords' adopted sons have been changed, but their adoption stories are true.

49

Older-child adoptions were not just an academic and theoretical concept for Cliff and his wife, Anne. They had adopted twin brothers from another children's institution where Cliff had previously worked. The unique events surrounding this "unofficial" adoption were seared into their memories.

According to Cliff, when he and Anne met in college, he was an "agriculture major, motorcycle-riding, drum major, GI student who was smitten by a beautiful, popular, blonde co-ed." They both liked working with children and shared deeply held religious beliefs grounded in serving others. They married after graduation, and Cliff began work at a traditional Southern children's institution near the Mississippi River, which like many in that era had begun as an orphanage after the Civil War, but by the early 1950s served few orphans. They considered his new employment to be a missionary-like commitment, but they quickly realized that even church-related children's homes were subject to capricious, self-protective decision-making. Cliff recalled:

> The adoption of our twin sons occurred during my first job in group child care as the farm manager of a children's home in the Deep South, That was eight years before I was employed as a social worker at a children's home in another state.

> Soon after moving into the farm manager's home, five miles from town and campus, we realized that everyone, around, in church and on campus called it "the orphanage." That name should have warned us of what we faced, but what did we know?

> How did the adoptions occur? One of the brothers had gotten into an argument with his dormitory matron (who now would be called a "housemother" or "childcare worker"). They were screaming at each other, and he lost his temper and cursed at her, using a few derogatory words that today are commonly heard on TV. The brothers were good boys, and the incident should have ended with counseling and a mild reprimand. Instead, the matron, responsible for a dormitory of 40 boys, insisted on severe punishment. Perhaps she did so out of the need for self-protection and the need for control of the situation. Arbitrary and quick dismissals, (in cases such as misbehavior) or as the children called them, "being shipped," were common practices

50

of children's homes and orphanages of that era. In these instances children were usually sent to Departments of Public Welfare in counties where they had lived prior to entering the children's home.

I had gone to see the director about a farm-related matter. His door was ajar, and I overheard him talking with some staff members about Frank and Tommy: "We're going to have to ship them out of here right away, but don't tell them. In the morning, have their matron keep them out of school, and have her put whatever belongings they have in a cardboard box. Then we'll have somebody take them back to the county where they came from."

The word "ship" was commonly used by staff members of many residential institutions. It described how dependent children were considered as commodities who could be moved around without much thought or planning, instead of being seen as vulnerable children who need our protection and love. Brought to the orphanage when they were only 4 and 5 years old by their grandparents, the brothers had been living there for eight years, almost 70 percent of their lives. On top of that, since the staff discouraged family visiting, their frail birth family bonds had withered. The orphanage was the only home they knew, one that in spite of its shortcomings had helped them become excellent students and taught them how to live a disciplined life with good work habits. Now, suddenly, they were being returned in a chaotic way to the Department of Public Welfare in their home county, an agency that had no role in their lives, past or present.

It was troubling to see children like these two, who didn't own anything—not even their own clothes. In the orphanage, they were clothed out of a common closet, Every morning you would hear comments like, "You got the red shirt today. I'll trade you!" The orphanage and many other such organizations were started with noble intentions, but tended over time to focus on maintaining order and obedience rather than meeting the needs of the children in their care.

Frank and Tommy had worked for me on the farm, and I knew what fine boys they were—and what great potential they had. I was stunned. I went back out to the truck, drove home and told my wife, who was four months pregnant, what I had overheard. We agreed we needed to intervene.

I drove back to the office, told the director I had overheard the conversation about "shipping" Frank and Tommy, and said as calmly as I could: "Anne and I would like for them to come live with us and become part of our family."

At that time, children were often moved about informally and people, like directors of children's residential institutions, wielded great power and authority. Taking it upon himself to make such life-changing decisions, the orphanage director responded, "If you take them, I'm not going to give you any more money; you're the farm manager—that's all you'll be paid. You can't change your mind later if it doesn't work out—I'm not going to take them back."

When I agreed to his terms, he persisted. "Are you sure you want to do this?"

After I emphasized that Anne and I wanted to raise Frank and Tommy as though they were our sons, he confirmed in a judicial-like tone "They are yours."

That was all there was to the process. The newly adopted brothers moved into our home that afternoon.

How did they react? As I walked out of the administration building, I looked out across the campus where all the boys were raking leaves. I walked over to Frank and said, "I'm going to ask you an unexpected question, and I'm very serious about it. Anne and I would like for you to come live with us and be a part of our family."

Startled, he replied, "When and for how long?"

I said, "Right now, and forever."

"What about Tommy?" he asked.

"I'm going right now to ask Tommy the same question--you were the first one I saw."

He wanted to know when they were to come, and when I responded

52

"Right now," his only question was if he had time to "get my stuff."

I told him to get his things and meet me at the truck, then I found Tommy and had the same conversation. Thank goodness it worked out beautifully. Anne and I have been blessed with six children, including Frank and Tommy. Tommy died a few years ago, but we stay in touch with his widow, child, and grandchildren. Our adopted sons have been an integral part of our family since we adopted them, but remember there is only a ten-year age difference between us. Maybe we became more like older siblings to them as they became adults.

The adoption of the boys profoundly changed and enriched our lives in many ways—including vocationally. When I started my career in children's homes as the farm manager, my intent was to eventually become an agricultural missionary in an undeveloped country. After serving four years as the farm manager, I moved to another institution and served two years in a general management position. As I learned more about the plight of children living in institutions like these, my whole life was turned around and I wanted to do something to make the lives of the children and their families better. Anne supported my decision, and we moved next to a university setting, because I wanted to learn more effective ways to help children and their families. That was a time of big change for us. I enrolled in a Master of Social Work program, and Frank and Tommy were in college—attending different schools in different states.

Frank Expresses Immense Gratitude to Anne and Cliff Sanford

Cliff suggested I call his surviving adopted son, Frank, to gain another perspective. From the very beginning, Frank was forthright in his account.

Cliff and Anne saved our lives. When we were taken to the orphanage by our grandparents, we were scared to death. The older boys constantly teased and bullied us, and the staff did little to stop them. I couldn't stop crying, and the older boys and the staff colluded to teach me a lesson. The boys shut me up, along with a mouse they had caught, in a large paper barrel that had held detergent. That's the type of treatment I had.

Still, Tommy and I did benefit from our orphanage experiences. It was a hard way to grow up—we learned to work hard—and most of all, we learned how to survive and take care of ourselves. If Cliff hadn't intervened, we would have gone back into the chaos of our birth family or been moved about into the welfare system. There's no telling what would have happened to us.

In recent years, I've called Cliff and Anne every so often, and before they can say anything but "Hello" I start the conversation with, *"YOU SAVED MY LIFE!"* I literally mean that.

Cliff and Anne have always treated Tommy and me like we were born to them. They still consider Tommy's widow, his children and his grandchildren to be part of their family.

They were ideal adopted parents and very understanding. When we wanted to visit with our birth family, they let us. I met my birth mother on one of those visits, but I was turned off by her and haven't desired to see her since.

We identified with Cliff and Anne's values and lifestyles and tried to become the kind of good citizens they are. In fact, I chose to attend the university from which Cliff and Anne graduated, and it has led to a successful business career.

What more can I say? Our experience is like the title of your book, *Transplanted into Unaccustomed Earth*. Being transplanted into Cliff and Anne's family transformed our lives. They gave us new opportunities for growth and development and they encouraged us. I still feel their love and support!

Tommy's Widow Shares Her Perspective

Tommy, Cliff and Anne's other adopted son, died a few years ago, but I spoke with his widow to gain yet another perspective. Tommy's widow was eager to describe how much she values her own relationship with Cliff and Anne. She made the following comments:

> Tommy and Frank both immediately said yes to the invitation to live with Cliff and Anne. They knew Cliff was a good man, because they worked for him on the orphanage's farm. Tommy was all for it, and the adoption made a big impact on his life. He insisted that had Anne and Cliff not taken them, they would surely have gotten into trouble. Tommy and Frank had never enjoyed Christmas until they moved in with Anne and Cliff, who gave the boys their first Easter baskets, their first bicycles and even helped them purchase and fix up their first cars. When the boys graduated from high school, Anne and Cliff moved to another state for Cliff to attend graduate school, and their relatives invited Tommy and Frank to live with them prior to starting college.

> Tommy went to college for two years before he joined the Navy. He served four years and then worked at different sales jobs. Finally, he settled on a major company where he stayed for 30 years.

> I am Tommy's second wife. He died 30 years after we were married, but Anne and Cliff consider me and my daughter part of their family. Our only child, a daughter now in her 30s, looks upon them as her grandparents. She and I are very thankful they are in our lives.

Cliff Continues to Reflect on the Beginnings of the Older Child Adoptions Program

In his interview, Cliff remembered:

> After I completed my graduate degree, I was employed as a social worker at the home. A short while later, the director of social services accepted a position with another agency, and the CEO offered me the position. My passion for trying to change things for the children there led to the idea of starting the older-child adoption project.

Often in the 1950s and 1960s, children either stayed in institutional settings long enough to grow up and graduate from high school, or, if they engaged in common teenage behaviors and messed up, out they would go—"shipped." Where they went wasn't much of a concern.

Institutions were focused on: "Let's get other children in to fill beds." The Home was, in some ways, like other children's homes all across the country, but its CEO and I were ready to change things. I had gone back to school to learn how to serve children and their families in new and better ways rather than remaining stuck in the mode of "how not to do it," or "let's do it today like we did it yesterday." I knew there were a lot of older children for whom adoption was a logical option, but only a few such adoptions were actually occurring—and even those were random. Generally, people would say either, "These children are too old; they will not adapt to family living"; or "No families are going to want to adopt older children; they want infants and babies."

At the Home, we believed that school-aged child adoptions were an option, but we had to find people who were interested in adopting them. We advertised to let families know this was a possibility. Then, we went through a process of helping children accept and prepare for adoption, and got them together with a family to create a melding. A child in the welfare system might have been placed in a foster home, but that was considered a temporary situation with no assurance of permanency. Neither a foster family nor an institution was a resource for young people beyond age 18 or graduation from high school.

Although some children's institutions had "baby cottages," the leaders of the Home knew young children did not belong in residential group care, and placed them with foster families. As a result, with rare exceptions, there were only school-age children on our campus. When I began working there, approximately 175 children were in group care on the campus, and about 75 were in foster homes located within a reasonable driving distance. Having just completed my graduate work, I thought I knew of all the possibilities for assisting children and families, but I soon learned about a new service that allowed children to return to their birth families. In fact, about 85 children were with a birth parent or with a close relative. The Home was subsidizing these families financially, but generally surreptitiously, so that county welfare departments would not subtract that amount of money from the family's public assistance payments. At that time assistance payments totaled 75 percent of what the county had determined a specific family needed, but people turned their heads and pretended not to know that additional help was being provided. When I agreed to take the director of social services position, I made it clear to the CEO that we would work aggressively and without apology with the biological family—not just the child—to allow them to "own" their family plans. They were to be in the driver's seat. We would not participate in a family situation that simply "rocked along" in limbo.

What I proposed was not threatening to the CEO. When he came to the Home, he had been in a masters-degree social work program for a year and had new visions for the agency. In fact, he showed respect and support for the initiative. He simply asked, "How are you going to do that? How will it work? How much will it cost? Can the same social workers be used?"

I responded that the four social workers currently on staff sat in their offices, where children came to "see" them, either on their own or because the social worker had summoned them. These professionals were doing a lot of good, but touching only the tip of the iceberg. I proposed that we divide the state into four areas plus a smaller area for me to handle on a part-time basis, and assign a social worker to each area so that they would be out in the field, at least 50 percent of the time. Having an assigned area would make travel more efficient, and encourage them to make more frequent contacts with the children's families and the referring agencies with whom we worked. The counseling with the children on campus would become far more relevant and productive.

To help minimize transportation costs, I had talked with the local Volkswagen dealer, who had agreed to sell us VW "bugs" at a low price and "throw in" maintenance service.

At that point, I became a salesman: "How can you miss?" The CEO saw the wisdom and agreed, but queried me on how I planned to get things started. I admitted that the hardest part would to be to help our social workers transition to a new way of practicing—leaving a child-centered concept and adopting a "family as client system" concept. I anticipated there would be some "smoke," and I might need back up. He assured me that I'd have his support.

That was the start of a robust program to help families establish a plan, and stay with them through an intensive development process. Our first objective was to help families meet their goals, but if that wasn't possible, we would move to another alternative that might work for the sake of the child. So we got our VW bugs, and we sent the social workers out into the field two weeks each month. After two years this had become the standard way of operating. In the field, the social workers handled new requests for admission, supervised foster home placements and subsidized family placements, followed-up on children who had returned home, and worked intensively with families who had children in care at the Home.

When it came to caring for children living in two of the Home's service areas—group/campus care and foster family care—the concept of turnover rate was very important. Keeping track of how they left (planned or unplanned), when (age, grade or graduation), and where they went after they left us (to their biological family, to another group care placement, to independent living, etc.) revealed a great deal. Did they graduate from high school, or did they leave care abruptly and in an unexpected way—such as being over 18 (aging-out), being "shipped" for behavior, or being a runaway? Reviewing the facts can be an unpleasant, but necessary exercise. Questions like these helped us to conceptualize our policies for working with families and their children. Even good outcomes, such as seeing families reach their goals of re-unification, resulted in children leaving campus or foster home care, and that caused turnover. When we began to look at our annual rates of turnover and carefully examined where the children went, the results helped us evaluate what kind of program we were running and look ahead at what we wanted the program to be.

We decided we did not want to have "raising children" as a general-ized goal. As we were developing our family-centered policies, we invited the late Dr. Alan Keith-Lucas, from the University of NC-Chapel Hill (UNC-CH), to come to the Home as a consultant. One morning as they were walking to school he joined three of our high school students on campus to learn about their plans for the future. One told him that her social worker was working with her and her mother on a plan "to see if we can't get our act together and live together again—so I'm moving back home at the end of the school term." Another described meetings with a foster home family "to see if we can get along together." The last one said: "Haven't you heard about us—the Jones children? We'll be here until the last bell rings. . . and move out on our own." Dr. Keith-Lucas was impressed that the children knew as much about what was going on as did the staff members. We were glad to receive that feedback. Individualized family planning was happening.

The first paper I delivered as a social worker, entitled, "The Role of the Child at Intake," focused on the child's participation in what was going on regarding her/his welfare. What does this have to do with adoptions? Certain children at the Home were what I would call "stagnant in care," meaning they lived in our campus group care program without understanding why they were in care and what the plan was for their future. I believed the intake process set the stage for what ultimately happened to children after they were admitted into programs like ours.

We started using consultants annually from UNC-CH. Dr. Keith-Lucas was the first, and the next year Hank Hollingsworth came. When he and I carefully examined the case files, reading the detailed notes that we required our social workers to dictate, we found cases where we had missed "golden opportunities." The child's family wasn't a resource—it just wasn't there. There were human beings involved, but no family. These children, often subconsciously, were looking for a family. Some had no family visitors, and others had a parent or another family member who every month said things like, "We'll come and get you next month," and seldom came. These were children truly in limbo.

We began to realize we could go beyond foster care to help these children find permanent, lifelong relationships in adoptive families. The Home had already made policy decisions not to continue with an orphanage mind-set, so why not help children without viable families find new families? Also, we had 75 or so children in foster family care, and several of those families wanted to adopt the children in their care. We soon realized, however, that we didn't have enough families who were ready, able and eager to adopt children at the Home who needed viable families.

To get the older child adoption process flowing, I set up a group meeting with our social workers, and said, "You carefully go over the dictation in the files of the children we have in care, and when you see an "ah hah moment" that's when we missed it. That's the time we should have started talking about adoption."

As they began to analyze the case notes, they became excited. I took this information to the CEO, suggested it was time to move toward older-child adoption, and offered some illustrations. One was a boy who had been in care for about three years since his family had disappeared. A foster home for him would mean temporary care—that's the language of the profession. He needed something permanent.

The staff was reluctant: "It's unlikely that we can find families that want to adopt someone this old. It's just not in the thought processes of families to consider such a thing." In the face of such questions, the CEO asked what I proposed to do and I proposed a campaign among all the churches that supported the Home, asking the pastors and church leaders to talk with their congregations about older child adoptions. This would enable us to find out if there were families in their churches and communities who would consider or at least talk with us about adopting. To me, we had to complete that step before we raised hope among the children in our care.

The CEO approved our plan. We moved forward and received an unbelievable number of positive responses from families. That brought up a whole new "hornet's nest" of problems for the four social workers. How can you tell if a family is really ready to adopt an older child, and how do you go about making such decisions? That is very complex, very hard work even for social workers experienced in working with families at various levels of psycho-social functioning.

Enter the personal biases of social workers. Does one accept only adoptive families who share a social worker's values or what we would now call "world views"? Today we know that with appropriate support and help, adoptive parents can come from a wide variety of backgrounds and lifestyles, but in the 1950s and 1960s some of the Home's social workers had narrow views of what constituted acceptable candidates. How far could our social workers stretch their cultural selves in working with families outside their preconceived notions? Of course, many such issues could be worked through with training and supervision, but some of their beliefs were deeply ingrained.

The issue of studying families for adoptive placement was new and formidable. The work we were doing with the children's biological families to move toward reunification contained elements of family studies. Studying families for foster care gave us additional experience to build upon. As we struggled with such issues, we continued to receive inquiries from families all over the state. We asked our social workers to make appointments and go by to see the families in their territories to talk with them on the surface about their interest in adopting an older child.

As we began to plan how best to conduct family studies, we posed questions such as: What are the strengths and weaknesses of the family? What are their motivations? What are their expectations of and for the child?

In one case, for example, a family wanted to adopt an 8-year-old boy—preferably a blond-headed boy. After meeting with the family, one of our social workers discovered that a year before their 8-year-old son had been killed in the corn mill that the father operated, and they were looking for a replacement. The parents' grief was real and you could empathize with the family, but such an adoption would be far from healthy.

Our goal was to find emotionally healthy families who could truly accept and love our school-age adoptable children: children who had been traumatized and children who had lived in chaos and poverty. Most of the inquiring families were childless. Occasionally others would have birth children, most commonly a single birth child and no ability to bear additional children. They desired an adopted child or children so their birth child would have a sibling(s).

At the Home we came to realize that although infant and young child adoptions required skilled social work services, our older child adoption project would be far more complex and tougher work. It would require more time, dedication, and willingness to provide on-going support to children and their families, and not everyone would be happy with the outcomes. We had a choice: we could choose not to proceed because we were scared, or we could forge ahead with this challenging project.

In the USA, there are about a million children in foster care now, and many linger in limbo partly because both individual social workers and departments of social services across the country are scared to death of older child adoptions. Most counties do not provide the funds to allow the departments to employ trained child welfare staff To the credit of the Home, we decided we were not going to give in to "fear." We were going to take on the project.

The next step was to determine which children in our case loads were really ready or past ready to discuss being adopted. It took about two years to prepare for the first older child adoptions. For the most part, children began to be placed in adoptive homes in about 1960.

There was a two-part process: (1) selecting children ready for adoption and working with them and their biological families to reach a unified adoption decision as the plan for the child, and (2) determining potentially qualified and "ready" adoptive families.

Surveying the number of children was not difficult. We had only to analyze each file to determine if a child or a sibling group should be moving toward adoption. As families sent in inquiries, we selected those we deemed appropriate, and set about training them to meet the needs of older children. Dr. Alan Keith-Lucas beautifully expressed the plight of older adopted children in the foreword of your 1985 book. John, you used Keith's thoughts in the introduction to this volume:

> What (do) our well-intentioned plans for a child really mean to him--what has a child to cope with when he becomes 'somebody else,' changes his name, 'belongs' to a new family and is still the same person he or she has always been.

To help our children cope with this dilemma, we wanted them to participate in both the "decision thinking" and the "decision making." Such a process may go on for months. We were not there to sell them on the idea, but we wanted their involvement. Yes, this is hard for a child to do, but it's also hard to know that there is no hope of returning to your biological family and that you may live five, six or seven more years at the Home. Adoption was a brand new thought for these children, who needed to know what they would really be risking. We began to work on that, child by child.

County public welfare systems around the state placed most of the youmger children, and neither the Home nor the families had custody. When we began our older child adoption program in the 1960s, the juvenile and domestic relations courts had little, if any, experience in ruling on petitions for permanent custody with the right to place for adoption. To help county judges experience our older-child adoption procedures, we asked significant relative(s) to appear in court with their soon-to-be-adopted child(ren). It is one thing to say, "I've talked to your mother and she thinks this is the right thing to do." It is another for the child to hear a birth mother or other significant relatives say, "This is the right thing to do." For social workers, that's not easy. They may believe such direct statements are hurting children. The point of clarifying is to show that the birth family is behind the adoption. Getting that message out made a real difference.

Good older-child adoptions require hard, gutsy social work. Dr. Alan Keith-Lucas served as a consultant. He described a helping process as consisting of three parts: "reality, empathy and support."

The toughest part is helping children in care deal with the "stark reality" that their biological families would not be a resource for them in the future. It was difficult work for the five of us social workers. As the director I carried half a load, so I wasn't asking my colleagues to do something I wasn't doing myself.

As the participants in your study recalled childhood memories of being adopted during their school-age years, some remembered feelings of surprise and shock when the subject of adoption was introduced. They believed they were not at the Home to be adopted, and as the process proceeded they felt they were being "bought and sold" like livestock or commodities. Others, like Lee, recalled being allowed to help select their adoptive families. The critical question is how this important initial interface was engineered and carried out. What was it like for them? We did not have a blueprint for this process. Like pioneers, we had to figure that out. We experimented with different models, but considered it essential to allow both the child and the prospective family to be able to "psyche out" what was going on. We wanted that initial phase to be done in steps. The first step was an introductory meeting—going out to get an ice cream cone or something like that— for each to see what the other looked like, how they talked, etc. The social worker would then follow up with the child and the prospective adoptive parents to talk through what they were thinking and feeling.

Social workers can be tempted to think they know how to make these selections themselves. We tried to guard against playing God, lest the child or the family believe we were playing games. Although we decided which families and which children were most likely to be attracted to each other and form a bond, the "choosing" was theirs not ours.

When you begin this process, you must help the child understand his /her fantasies of being "rescued" by his biological family, and of course, this is done best by simultaneously helping the biological family members come to terms with their true intentions and capabilities. We first had to sit down with the biological parent(s) and/or important relatives and help them face the decision. Unfortunately, in a lot of case records from county welfare departments, we would find the names of the parents followed by two words: "Whereabouts Unknown." Those words turned our social workers into detectives. We had to find the parent(s), let them know what was going on, and make them a part of the decision-making process.

In the infrequent instance when a parent, usually the father, was in prison, we arranged contact through the warden. I remember meeting with a father who was serving a life sentence for murdering his wife. I laid it out for him: "You are in here for the rest of your life. I know you love your kids, and I know they love you. You will never be able to be a parent to them, but they can continue to be thinking about you and loving you. They do not understand why you did what you did, but they need to move on with their lives. To be really free to become part of an adoptive family, they need to hear you say that's what you want for them. If you decide that you can say that, I'll bring them here so you can tell them. They do not need to hear me saying, 'Your daddy said so and so.' They need to hear you say that." This father did indeed tell his children he believed having them adopted by another family was the best thing for them.

This illustrates how serious we were about helping children and their biological families face the reality that decisions had to be made. The option so often chosen in the past was to simply leave children in limbo.

For the same reason, we always had a parent or significant relative and the child or children in the courtroom, so that the judge could hear everyone say what they wished before awarding custody (with the right to place for adoption) to the Home.

Of course, children will never completely finish dealing with the idea of adoption, and some of the stories in this book point that out, but being a part of the court's decision-making process may be a starting point for finding new, permanent families.

Events leading up to the adoptions so severely traumatized some of the children and their birth families in your study that they could not consciously take in or remember what was happening, a reaction we now refer to as Post Traumatic Stress Disorder (PTSD).

It may be wise in some cases to make videos or audio recordings of important adoption-related meetings and events. Children need accurate historical records of their childhoods. A recording of a birth parent saying, "I think adoption is the best plan for you" is especially important to make available to an adopted child as he or she grows older.

After we started placing children in adoptive families, (although the state did not require it) we stayed with the adoption for a year and conducted visits at least quarterly and more often in cases requiring closer attention. We sometimes had to use "Plan B." One example was nine-year-old Billy, who had become very protective of his two younger brothers after their father murdered their mother. We wanted to place the three of them in an adoptive home together, but no family would agree to accept all of them. Instead, we identified a family who seemed to meet Billy's needs, and another that appeared to be a good fit for the younger boys. We explained the situation to the families, asking them if they wanted to meet these children as a way to begin—without commitments. We didn't want to begin an adoption process unless they were willing to form an extended family relationship between the two families--so that these siblings could stay in contact with one another. Both families were delighted. They went through the yearlong process together.

At his first visit with our social worker, Billy said: "My new daddy takes me hunting. I have my shotgun now. If my new daddy puts his shotgun on his shoulder, I put my shotgun on my shoulder. If he stops to listen to what he hears in the woods, I stop to listen to what I hear in the woods. If he spits on a stump, I spit on a stump."

The two families got together the first time for a cookout at the younger brothers' adoptive home. The social worker attended. A few weeks later the social worker visited Billy's adopted home and asked if Billy felt okay about the arrangement. His adoptive mother responded there was no question he was "doing fine," and elaborated: "Whenever we go someplace, Billy wants to ride shotgun. I have to ride in the middle of the seat of our pickup truck. When the cookout-visit with his brothers was over, we got into the truck, he leaned over and put his head on my shoulder and gave out a big sigh, 'Ahhhh!' He went to sleep leaning against me on the way home."

The children's home was now firmly established in the adoption of older children. A number of children were in the yearlong adoption trial phase, and we provided follow-up counseling as well as monitoring. After the year was over, if everyone agreed, we asked the court to finalize the adoption. Once that happened, we might call them up to ask, as friends, how the child and family were doing, but the adoptive parents knew that we no longer had any right to get involved. Now I wonder if a longer structured relationship between the social workers/children and the adoptive parents might have been helpful. From the beginning of the program in 1960 to the time I left the Home in December of 1965, we had placed approximately 75 children from our group care (institutional) and foster family care population, within which the average age was 9.6.

In some cases problems developed after placement. A few adoptive parents got really upset about it. When this happened, our goal was to get them under the care of competent professionals who could provide counseling and treatment--such as psychiatrists, clinical social workers, psychologists, family therapists, etc.

Sometimes social workers returned upset from field visits with families in the midst of the adoption process. They would ask what they should do when they sensed a glitch in the adoption match. When this happened, I responded with questions like: "Do they (the child and the adopting family) want it to work? If I sent you out to do a community survey, it wouldn't be hard to find families in which the children and the parents were having problems, but would you accept a response like, 'Let's end the arguments and acting out by dissolving the family--sending the child away?' Or would you advocate for a range of helping efforts to assist the family and the child so that they could learn better how to relate and live together?"

As the initial stage unfolds, a child begins to realize this is a momentous time in her or his life and might start thinking, "Maybe I would be better off staying here on the campus." Similar doubts may arise for the potential adoptive family, who finally sees an older adoptable child for the first time. For social workers there is an urge to step in and take over, but the adoptable child and the potential adoptive family own the process at this point. One of the participants, Lee, beautifully put it into perspective: "It's like a marriage. You just got to pick them out."

The social worker's job is to make sure that both parties are thinking and feeling it through, and that they are talking out loud about what they are thinking and feeling. A social work degree does not automatically provide an understanding of one's psychological makeup and how that influences a working relationship with a client, or how one's own life experiences affect the ability to be a helping person. The five social workers at the children's home were very diverse people, with different life experiences that brought varied convictions into the dynamics of the adoption process.

What other options did the 75 or so older children we placed for adoption have? They could have remained in the institution, or lived in "temporary" foster home care. All of the people whose stories appear in this volume said they were glad that they had been adopted, although many of the adoptions had serious shortcomings. I am sad that some of them did not work out very well, but biological families also experience difficulties. Go to a nearby town, randomly select 75 families, and I can guarantee that some will be dysfunctional, and these families would likely be biological.

The CEO of the Home gets a lot of credit for his courage and willingness to stick with the older adoption program through thick and thin times. Most directors of children's agencies would have been scared to death to let a pioneering, untraditional program like this happen. There are about a million children in the US who are living today in some type of "temporary" out-of-home foster care placement. How many of them have social workers who are willing and courageous enough to help them and their biological families honestly face the reality of getting their act together with timely concrete actions or setting their children free to become a part of another family? Or for that matter, how many organizations caring for some of today's approximately one million "in limbo" children have administrators who would allow the formulation of such programs or Boards who would appropriate the necessary funds? That's tough work, that's hard work, and that's the kind of work that the children's home was all about as we initiated and carried out our older-child adoption program.

It's easy to blame biological parents for being irresponsible, but some of the citizens in our society, the politicians that represent them, and even some of the public social workers they employ poison the atmosphere for honest, courageous social work. For example, I was asked by a supposedly forward-thinking County Department of Social Services to conduct a series of workshops on working with families. As I began my presentation at the initial meeting with social workers and supervisors, quickly one of the supervisors interrupted to say, "I don't think you realize that we are working with the scum of the earth." No one in the room spoke up and said, "I don't feel that way." That's a heck of a place to start, but unfortunately too many people responsible for working with families come from such perspectives.

A year or two after the older adoption project was started, we, the social workers, developed a uniform process for helping families regardless of their situations. These instances included: families independently coming to us for help, Departments of Public Welfare with temporary custody seeking placement, or churches wanting to help families place children. Our new process required meeting with the children and parent or the significant relative, at which time the social worker would say: "We are not going to take these children and work with this family unless everyone in this room agrees that such a move is in the child's best interest—and believes this is what should take place. Furthermore, everyone must agree to work with us to develop and carry out realistic, long-term plans for the future of these children so they will not get lost in placement."

Of course, we got a lot of grief from the Departments of Public Welfare, because their notion was that the case was theirs and was considered "handled" if a child was placed. Some of the parents also liked not having plans, because they did not have any responsibilities. They could come occasionally to see their children without being expected to really be a parent. We knew that we needed to have intentional plans for children: plans that were not static; plans that were reviewed and revised with a goal of striving to meet a child's needs.

We social workers had our hands full: to implement our new helping process, to look after the needs of the children in institutional and foster home programs, to manage the counseling and financial assistance program for children living in their own homes, to do foster home and adoption studies, to help children move toward adoption and to supervise adoption placements during the yearlong adoption process. The social workers were as busy as a "stump full of ants," quite different from the image of sitting in their offices "seeing" children.

They felt good and proud of what had been accomplished, and that's the way it should have been.

By 1965, we were seeing a turnover rate of 30 percent plus in the group care/foster family care population, due in large part to our "family as client" process. Children were going back to live with parents or relatives, and our social workers were actively following up on these reunifications or they were moving into other permanency outcomes.

With all the population we had in care, we made generous use of community resources, such as the Child Guidance Clinic and the Speech Clinic. We almost always had at least one child receiving therapy from some source, and some of these children were being prepared for adoption. Special services would occasionally be needed, and we felt that if we could help straighten that out before an adoptive placement was made, it would help make the adjustment easier. So, indirectly the word got out to the area's professional community that we had an older-child adoption program. The Home was recognized for its leadership.

While I had no official relationship with the Board, that of course was the CEO's role, I wrote an annual report designed to give Board Members a clear picture of what we were doing. It included statistics on how many of the children entered, left to return to their biological families, graduated from high school, were placed for adoption and so forth. In addition, I wrote a narrative that incorporated several anonymous case summaries, and the CEO used them to describe what the Home had accomplished that year. They were also published in our newsletter. These efforts enabled the constituency of the Home to conceptualize what our program entailed.

Cliff's account of the development of the Home's older-child adoption program tells a remarkable story of courage and determination—a story of how a non-profit, century-old, church-related agency strove to serve children and their families with a quest for excellence and relevance. Led by Cliff Sanford with the support of its CEO, the Home defied the stereotype of institutions remaining stagnant and rigid. In fact, it became a pioneer in diverting school-age children from long-term institutional and foster care and into adoptive homes. Their efforts helped spawn a national movement that has greatly expanded the options for children in the child welfare system.

In 1983, the CEO of the children's home told me that their older-child adoption program had been Cliff's idea. As the CEO put it: "Cliff was the right person at the right time, and he helped us change direction."

Clifford W. Sanford, Jr., died in the summer of 2017. While he was unable to see the published version of this book, he reviewed and approved the final draft of his story.

PART TWO

ADOPTION STORIES

A Guide for Reading the Adoption Stories

The adoption stories are organized by chapters. Chapters Six and Eight present adoption stories of siblings who were adopted by different families: Chapter Six tells the stories of Joanne, Maynard and Benny; and Chapter Eight presents Dana and Jason's stories. In both chapters, sisters and brothers were separated from one another for more than a decade. The remaining chapters, presenting the stories of Madelyn, Angela, Lee and Marshall, primarily describe one person's adoption experience.

The varied life experiences of the nine participants, considered individually, provide interesting and important information about school-age adoptions. Considering their stories collectively, readers can observe similarities and patterns in how the participants coped with their adoptions as older children and how they continue to cope with the impact of their adoptions decades later.

Section I of each chapter is based on the 1983 interviews and describes the first portion of the participants' lives: their pre-adoption, post-adoption and young-adult memories and experiences.

The contents of the second portion (Section II) derive from interviews, emails and other contacts from 2007 through 2020. In Section II, the focus is on how being adopted as older children has impacted their lives and viewpoints over time.

Readers, therefore, have the opportunity to compare and contrast some long-term effects of older child adoptions.

Chapter Four

Adopted at age six

Birth, Adoptive and Adult Family Structures

Birth Family: Madelyn's birth mother died of a heart attack at 22 years of age. At that time, her birth father was age 46 (24 years older than his wife). Madelyn was almost 6, and her two younger sisters were 2 and 4 years of age. Her father had worked in construction, and due to declining health, he became a convenience store clerk. Soon after the mother's death, the father was diagnosed with a terminal illness. As a result, he contacted the children's home for assistance, and a social worker there suggested the possibility of adoption. The father agreed.

Adoptive Family: Madelyn was the first sibling to be adopted. Her adoptive parents were childless. The younger children were placed in foster care, but soon Madelyn's adoptive parents adopted the two younger children as well. The adoptive father was a church choir director and noted singer, and the adoptive mother worked as a legal secretary. Later, she changed careers, and started her own real estate business. While Madelyn was in college, her adoptive parents divorced.

Madelyn's Family as an Adult: Madelyn and her husband, Greg, (a CPA) were married soon after they graduated from college. They have three sons, the younger two being twins. a daughter-in-law and grandchildren. Their elder son is married, and he and his wife have several children.

Madelyn has been recognized for her skill as an artist, and has her own studio and gallery. She and Greg are community leaders in the small coastal village where they live.

MADELYN

As Madelyn told her adoption story, she paused for a
moment and declared: "My whole life was in a little box."
She was referring to the memory of her birth father giving
a cardboard box containing her meager possessions to her
new adoptive parents. She explained: "I was frightened
and uncertain about what was happening and fought this
momentous change in her life."

SECTION I

Childhood to Age 22

Madelyn was age 22 at the time of this interview.

Madelyn responded positively to a letter from the director of the
children's home asking if she would consider participating in
my doctoral dissertation study, *Adults Who Were Adopted as Older
Children*. I knew little about her except that she was newly married, had
recently earned a fine arts degree and desired to become a professional
artist.

Madelyn and her husband, whom she had asked to have "listen in"
during our interview, lived on the outskirts of a large metropolitan
area. When I arrived at their duplex apartment, Madelyn, an attractive,
neatly dressed young woman, warmly welcomed me and introduced
me to her husband, Greg. Also a recent college graduate, Greg had
found employment in a large accounting firm, and was preparing to
take his CPA exam. The furniture was arranged so that Greg could
be an active participant in our interview, and Madelyn thoughtfully
served lemonade on this hot summer evening.

As we were getting settled, she apologized for the appearance of their apartment, explaining that, as newlyweds, they had few possessions. When I commented on several beautiful paintings, Greg proudly pointed out that they were Madelyn's work. Along with several refurbished, distinctive accent pieces that I suspected Madelyn had carefully selected from relatives' attics or garage sales, the paintings gave the sparsely furnished apartment a sense of style and grace.

Noting they had been married only a month, Madelyn began by saying she was in the midst of a job search, hoping to work for an advertising firm or other organization where she could further develop her drawing and painting skills. The couple was in the process of joining a church, which Madelyn explained was prompted by her having developed a religious faith under the tutelage of her adoptive father, who served as choir director of a large church. In summary, she said, "Things are going well for me. If I can find a job, I'll feel more useful than I do in this housewife business. Then things will be better."

The Years Before and After Her Adoption at Age 6

Madelyn chose to begin our discussion with a description of her birth family, which she characterized as "dirt poor" and a "family in a mess."

> I was five years old when my mother died of a heart attack at age 22. Our daddy, who was 24 years older than Mother, realized that he, too, was dying. He passed away about a year and a half after Mother died. He was in and out of the hospital. At times, I was left to look after my younger sisters. After my birth mother died, I felt like I was a little mother to my sisters. I was changing my youngest sister's diapers, but I didn't really know how to do that. I remember taking her diapers off and throwing them in the corner, and that's where they stayed.

Seeking to make arrangements for his children while he was still able to do so, her father contacted the children's home and spoke with a social worker, who suggested that he consider adoption. At essentially the same time, Madelyn's future adoptive parents applied to the children's home, hoping to adopt a girl. She does not clearly recall the events leading up to her adoption, but she vividly remembers the day her birth father transferred her to the adoptive parents:

> I was so young that I didn't realize I was being adopted or even what the word adoption meant, but I distinctly remember the day my birth father gave me to my new (adoptive) parents. I believe that was the first time we had ever met.
>
> The events of that day are kind of seared in my brain. My birth father and I were sitting in a room at the children's home, and he was telling me good-bye. I don't remember all that was said except that he promised to visit me. Then, he took me out on the front porch, and we walked down the stairs toward a blue car. A grinning lady and man were standing by it, but I didn't know that they were going to be my new parents. When we got to the car, my birth dad handed me to my new father, and I just took a hunk out of the strange man's arm. I bit him. Then, I hauled off and kicked him. I slapped him and started screaming and crying.

She continued to fight as her adoptive father "forced" her into the car. Her adoptive mother tried to hold Madelyn on her lap:

> I was fighting so hard that I kicked the dashboard out. My mother tried to calm me down by saying, "We've got this nice little doll at home for you and this beautiful little umbrella." I screamed back at her, "I don't want your stupid old umbrella." I was just going crazy because I was leaving all that I had ever known.
>
> Before we drove off, my birth father gave my adopted father a little pasteboard box. It contained all the possessions I owned—a few clothes and a couple of toys. My whole life was in just a little box.
>
> My bride doll was at the top of the box. After my birth dad gave the little box to my new dad and before we drove away, my new dad handed my bride doll to me through the open car window. I grabbed it and held onto it as tightly as I could.

As she and her adoptive parents drove away, she remembered struggling to look back: "I saw my old dad waving goodbye." She continued:

> The difference between my birth family's home and that of my adoptive parents was like the difference between night and day. My birth family was so poor that all five of us slept in one room in a very old house that was falling down. So, when my adoptive parents showed me around my new home, I just couldn't believe it. I had a bedroom all to myself, and everything in it matched. It had all this wonderful furniture. I didn't think it was real. I had clothes in the closet. I had never owned a toothbrush, I had never had a hairbrush or anything. It was all there and I just couldn't believe it.

Madelyn's adjustment was made easier by the fact that she was able to stay in touch with her two sisters, who were nearby in foster homes.

> Since my adoptive parents regularly saw my sisters, my father said, "Well, I just love that little one. She's just so cute—let's just get her, too." Then my parents thought, "We might as well get them all." They came into the family about a month or so apart. It was a joyful experience when we got back together again. I still feel a special closeness to them, but we don't see each other very often now because of various circumstances.

The girls' terminally ill birth father was healthy enough to visit his daughters once in their adoptive home. When he became quite sick and was hospitalized, the adoptive parents took the girls to visit him. "They knew he was dying," Madelyn explained, "and didn't want to deprive him of seeing us."

Madelyn's visits with her dying birth father "were weird." As she described that time: "It was a strange experience, kind of like saying hello and goodbye at the same time, and that's hard for anyone—especially at a young age."

Daily life changed radically for Madelyn in her new home. She went from a helter-skelter existence to an orderly life as the daughter of the minister of music of a large Protestant church, and she is thankful for the "good moral upbringing" she received.

82

I've got a couple of friends that were adopted, and they're not like me. They may have been given more (material) things and more money, but their morals are a lot different. So, I think I was lucky to have been adopted by a Christian choir director and his wife. The adoption was mutually beneficial—it was like I educated my parents and they educated me. I was there to help them, too. They couldn't have any children of their own. They were in their late 30s when they adopted us. They had been trying for years but they couldn't have kids.

Also, I felt like God put me there because He knew there was potential in my life. Being adopted allowed me to develop my art talent. Because of their economic situation and their lack of awareness, I would not have had an opportunity to do that with my real family. Perhaps I tried to express myself artistically even as an infant. I don't know, but as far back as I can remember, I loved creating and making things. I enjoyed the praise that I got at home, at school and at church.

Growing Up in Her Adoptive Home

During the early years, the adoptive home provided a loving environment for all three girls. In the years immediately preceding our initial interview, however, Madelyn's adoptive parents divorced.

I just couldn't believe it. At first it was like, "Oh no, another family is falling apart. I just can't get through this. I can't believe it's happening again." It's been easier on me than on my sisters because they were at home living through the turmoil.

After the divorce, her adoptive father married his childhood girlfriend. Turning to the subject of her adoptive mother, Madelyn chose her words carefully:

I don't know how to say this kindly, but it's hard to relate to her. She's distant, but we do stay in touch with each other. She would tell me as I was growing up that I was too much like her and that's why we argued and fussed so much. I hated her for saying that. I would think to myself, "I'm not your blood child," and sometimes I would say out loud, "I don't really think you wanted me as a daughter anyway." I

83

know it was mean and cruel to say such things to her, but those were the feelings that came out. We were often bitter to one another. I tended to rebel against her.

I think she wanted us when we were young. She seemed to enjoy us as little kids. However, when we got to those teenage years, things got rough and with the pressures of money and college--she didn't seem to want the responsibility anymore. I went through college totally on student loans, grants, art scholarships, part-time jobs, and a little bit of everything. I'm proud of that and I'm still paying for it. There is a loan of $10,000 that is coming due any time.

Notwithstanding these memories, Madelyn was working hard to heal old wounds and form a better relationship with her adoptive mother.

Greg commented that such conflicts are "normal for a teenage girl and her mother." He suggested that perhaps they might now be forming a closer relationship than Madelyn wanted to admit.

Madelyn's adoptive mother had made some drastic changes in her life, going from working as a legal secretary to starting her own real estate business. Madelyn explained: "She's now in the business world, and she's learned to be really competitive. By nature, she's really strong-willed and will not let anybody walk over her."

During her teenage years, Madelyn thought of her adoptive father as an "authority figure." It was not until the divorce occurred that she began to feel differently about him.

I felt really sorry for him because I felt nothing was his fault. So, I started siding with him and began talking with him. I realized once I was beyond the teenage stuff I could relate to him as a friend. We're a whole lot closer now. We really understand each other and can talk about the difficult times when I was growing up. It feels like we have filled in the rough places of the past--and, strangely, it feels like it has been that way all the time I've known him.

Discovering Her Extended Birth Family

Madelyn had only limited contact with her birth family when she and her sisters were growing up. She believes the conflicted relationship with her adoptive mother might have been the cause. "She may have feared that I might reach out to my [birth] family when I needed security or motherly affection, and even go back to them, but that wouldn't have happened."

Madelyn discovered her birth father's family by accident. While she was in college, she went home with a girlfriend who lived in the town where she was born. They decided to look for Madelyn's old home. Somewhat lost, they asked a lady for directions:

> It was really bizarre! That lady turned out to be one of my aunts--one of my dad's sisters. That blew my mind! She hugged and kissed me, and then went into her house and called every relative she could find. Soon, a number of aunts, uncles and cousins came over to meet me. They were really excited to get to know me and meeting them opened up a new side of my life.

> Meeting my father's family helped me to better understand who I am. However, connecting with my paternal birth family was also confusing. I don't know how to express it. I was glad to see my birth family and they were glad to see me. Yet, I didn't feel any real strong ties with them — like I'd missed anything. They have *beaucoup* [many] problems. This one's dying. This one's getting divorced. This one's got kids and is not married. I thought — this is not the kind of life or atmosphere I would have wanted to grow up in, but I'm glad we know one another as adults and can keep in touch now.

Turning to her birth mother's family, Madelyn noted that interestingly her maternal grandmother was very much the family matriarch. "She was the one person from my birth family that my adoptive mother allowed and encouraged me to keep up with." Her parents often wrote this grandmother and sent change of address information when they moved. After she became old enough, Madelyn corresponded with her regularly, and had fortunately gone to see her just before she died.

My grandmother's death really made me think about my birth mother. There's some love that I missed from not growing up with my real mother. I really wish I had known her better. My grandmother gave me a lot of photos of my mother, and that helped me get a sense of how she looked. She was about the same age I am now when she died, and some relatives say I look like her when she was a young woman. I wonder what kind of relationship I would have had with her if she were still alive. I know that I wouldn't have liked being raised in the type of atmosphere she lived in, but I just wish that I'd known her. Sometimes I think about how well I'm doing, and I wonder if my mother knows.

Then, smiling at Greg, she added:

To be honest, I'm lucky that I didn't stay in my birth family for economic reasons. Since my real family was very poor, I wouldn't have had a chance in the world to attend college. College opened up a whole new world for me, and I wouldn't be married to Greg or be an artist if I hadn't been adopted.

Discussing Her Birth Family with Her Adoptive Parents

While adoption was not a common topic of conversation in her adoptive home, Madelyn remembered vividly one evening when she mentioned that she missed not getting to know her birth mother, and was deeply hurt by her adoptive mother's response:

She reacted in a cold way, saying: "You're lucky. You don't understand what you've got. You shouldn't be trying to hatch up those things." I became upset and started crying, and she just walked into her office and shut the door. I added to the problem by rebelling and saying things like, "I'm not yours." You can't say that kind of stuff without raising tension. I'm sure I thought I was the only person in the world who experienced these things. Now, I see that it was just typical for the teenage years to be a challenging time--especially for a child like me who remembered her original family.

Madelyn has little recall of her birth mother, beyond witnessing her mother's death of a heart attack, a mental picture she believes will

86

remain with her. As noted above, she remembers more about her birth father, and is grateful that her adoptive father encouraged discussion both of her birth family and of the adoption:

> In fact, my adoptive dad is a gifted musician and composer. He wrote and recorded a song about us being adopted. Dad never made it a secret that we were his adopted children. I always felt that there was love there.

Relationships Outside Her Adoptive Family

Unlike some adopted people, Madelyn never felt "different" in school, in church, or in the community, and even remembered that being adopted could sometimes garner special attention.

> I would announce that I was adopted, and then I'd get a bunch of attention like: "Oh, you poor thing." Actually, no one knew or paid attention to my adoption unless I mentioned it.

> No one had to encourage me to go to college; it was just assumed I would. There were so many things I wanted to do and so many friends and people I wanted to meet. My mother said that you had a good time there.

"Family Secret" Revealed

Madelyn had shared many struggles but none as intense as what her birth father put her through. As she spoke about this tragic time, with Greg at her side, she seemed to feel empowered to overcome it.

> With my religious background, going to college and seeing these guys sleeping in my room with my girlfriends and drugs and everything that was going on was a real blow to me. I thought, "Oh no, I will never get through this world. I'm an outcast because I don't do this, that and the other." Then I found out that I could adapt and get through just fine.

At this point, Greg gently interjected that it was time to bring up the fact that Madelyn's birth father had sexually abused her. I could sense Madelyn's embarrassment and discomfort.

When the interview began, Madelyn had seemed relaxed, but now red patches developed on her neck. In spite of this, she bravely continued to tell her story, hoping her experience would help the public better understand the complex issues that older adopted children face. I felt a keen sense of admiration for her feelings and appreciated the support Greg provided. He said:

> I didn't find out about that until right before we were married. If she needs to talk with a professional person, it will not be about the transition of going from her birth family to her adoptive family. It will be about the child abuse she suffered from her birth father. That's the hardest thing I think she has had to deal with.

Based on her experience, Madelyn expressed a strong belief that it is important for older children to work out past issues before entering the adoption process.

> I made a direct transition from my birth father to my new adoptive family—and that was hard.

> I had to sort through my feelings on my own, but it would have helped me a whole lot to have been able to talk things out with a professional--when I was small and even as I got older. After I was adopted, I feared that I might not be able to love my adoptive father because of the abuse I suffered from my birth father. How would I relate to him? When it came to physical closeness with all men, I was really prejudiced.

> I kept the abuse a secret until I was 16, and even then it came out in a rebellious manner. When my adoptive mother said something about how much my real father loved us, I yelled, "Well, that just couldn't be true or he wouldn't have done what he did to me." Then I told her what he did.

She was encouraging and understanding. We talked about my dreams for the future and my hope of going to college to study art. My mother explained that college could open up a new life for me.

Looking Ahead — Money and Things

As far as future dreams, it depends on whether you're talking with Greg or me—we don't agree on everything. I'd be happy with a Mercedes and he'd be happy in a Chevrolet. I think I've always had this preconceived idea that I don't want to pinch pennies and have to plan where the next dollar is coming from.

At one point, Greg had this part-time job while he was in college. It was this social club kind of thing--playing golf with the guys and going to the country club--I thought maybe I would like that. Then I found out that there was a conflict for me--I really couldn't keep the religious values and lifestyle that I had been accustomed to with my adopted family and affiliate with people in that group. Now, I'm just kind of in the middle. I'm trying to find happiness again with the church people and the church activities and yet I still want nice things. So, I haven't found the balance yet.

Would They Adopt an Older Child?

Like most newlyweds, Madelyn and Greg were sorting through their ideas for the future. Their opinions on lifestyle and "how much money is enough" varied, but their discussion was open and lively. So far as children are concerned, both were eager to be parents and had definite ideas regarding not only natural children but adoption.

Madelyn saw beginning a family after, perhaps, five years:

I keep telling Greg I want a little girl, and I want her to be my friend, and feel close to me. I want her to have everything that I didn't experience with my mother. A boy, I think, would be a bit harder to raise. Either way I'd like my kids to experience things and try things for themselves. However, I'd let them know the basic standards that Greg and I have--of what is right and wrong.

Since Greg and I have just been married a month, I really haven't thought about adopting an older child. However, we might. Adopting an older child is a big challenge, but I think being adopted can give children new opportunities to grow and change. My own experience would help me to be more understanding and more helpful to an adopted daughter or son.

Greg then shared an interesting idea:

It's kind of futuristic imagining a kid who is being adopted being able to watch potential parents on closed circuit TV. If that were possible, it would help eliminate a lot of shock. It would make the kid feel like he or she had made the adoption decision. It seems like it would take a lot of the fear out of what a child was getting into. If Madelyn had been able see her adoptive parents on closed circuit TV, she wouldn't have experienced the total confusion that she did--wondering where her new home was going to be. She would have known where she was going to be living and who would be taking care of her.

Interest in the Adoption Study

As our interview drew to a close, Madelyn expressed a lively curiosity about the results of the study. She was eager to know how many others were being interviewed and to compare her experience with those of the other participants. It is her belief that regular therapy meetings with a specially trained social worker would have helped her as a child — especially with painful memories of sexual abuse and adjusting to her new adoptive family. She wondered aloud if adoption might have negative effects on some children. She was impressed that my study interviewed adults, not children: "When adults are interviewed, they have had years for wounds to heal."

SECTION II

Life About a Quarter Century Later:
Madelyn in Her 50s and 60s

Madelyn's current home is a long-day's drive from my own—even on a fast but monotonous interstate. As I turned off the multi-lane highway, the Spanish-moss-adorned live oak trees framed the roadway as my car's GPS guided a course along the banks of a coastal marshland. As I approached Madelyn and Greg's "low-country" home, memories danced through my mind of Madelyn's traumatic transfer from her birth father to her adoptive parents and the painful revelation of sexual abuse.

Tonight was different. Madelyn had become a confident, outgoing person. She warmly invited me into her beautifully decorated home that abounded with her artwork—from watercolors to oil paintings to beach objects she had carefully selected and skillfully decorated.

Greg soon arrived from a business meeting at his accounting firm. After he removed his sport coat and lowered his tie, he joined Madelyn and me for refreshments.

During our first meeting, I had sensed Madelyn's vulnerability and her desire to make something valuable of her life, but tonight she was proudly claiming victory over childhood trauma and adversity. Her husband and 10-year-old twin sons casually listened in while they attended to other matters. When she mentioned the sexual abuse, it seemed to be an issue she had defanged.

> Let's see—how have I changed in the past 25 years? I'm still doing what I set out to do career-wise. I've had years of training and practice and excellent formal instruction by outstanding college professors. All of this has helped me to develop as an artist.
>
> When we moved to this small town, I was worried about continuing

91

to grow creatively; but to my surprise, I found an informal support group of artists who asked me to join them. We encouraged and critiqued one another--that helped me to further sharpen my technique. They also helped me to get my paintings displayed locally. To my surprise, I was "discovered" by a New York City art critic who was driving through the area. The publicity didn't make me famous, but since then I have had no trouble selling my paintings.

My husband grew up here, and he wanted to move back home. Living here has been great for all of us, but I've had to make my own niche. In addition to finding time for painting, I started teaching art courses at the community college. I was also busy being a mom to our older son, Dave. I took him to ball practices and games, served as the PTA president and stayed busy 24-7.

I would say that we're well known here. I'm on the boards of the community college and the historical preservation group. Living in a smaller town is something that fits us as a family. When I was in college, I imagined myself as a New York celebrity artist. My college roommate would kid me that I wasn't going to New York, and that I was going to end up with a station wagon with the wood paneling on the sides and four kids and a dog. I'd say, "Oh no, not me!"

I became pregnant with our little surprise twin angels, Matthew and Mark, when I was around 40 years old. So, we have three children. The twins are now almost teenagers, and Dave is in his 20s. Dave is in the Navy right now, training to become a Seal.

I was 25 when I had Dave. I took good care of him, but I also put in a lot of effort to achieve success and gain recognition. It was different when I gave birth to Matthew and Mark in my 40s. I wanted to spend more time with them. At that point, I was established enough to make some major changes in my life. We built an addition on our house for my studio, and I turned the art sales over to an agent. I'm achieving my most important goal--to see that my own children won't have to go through the mess and uncertainty I went through as a child. We have three great sons. We're just "old" parents these days. We don't know any other parents as old as we are with young children.

My Sisters Continue to Have Problems —
Why Are We So Different?

Recalling having become "little mother" to her sisters after their mother died, Madelyn expressed real confusion regarding why they "have not found themselves" and what had caused such differences given the fact that all three shared both a genetic history and the same adoptive home.

> I feel like I'm constantly their caretaker. They're always calling me to get them out of jams. I tell them, "You had the same opportunities I had. Do what you want to do. Get to where you want to be. You've got to do it, I can't do it for you."

Did the divorce have a negative effect on Madelyn's younger sisters?

> It was a very difficult time for all of us. Our adopted parents filed for bankruptcy. They lost everything. I was on my own and I had to put myself through college. My sisters could have done that too, but didn't. What made us all respond so differently?

> I persevered, but that might just be something that's in me that has nothing to do with the adoption, I don't know. Even as a very young child, I could see that we were very poor. I knew I didn't want to grow up like that. I just pushed and knew I wanted things to be different. If you want it, you've got to go after it. You've got to make it happen. Nobody's going to give it to you.

When Greg pointed out that all of the sisters are self-employed, Madelyn agreed, "We're all entrepreneurs."

Why Didn't Someone in Our Birth Family Keep Us?
I'm Glad They Didn't!

Reflecting on her earlier life, Madelyn said:

> I've come to terms with most parts of my early life, but one question still nags at me: why didn't someone in our birth family keep us rather than letting us be adopted? For example, my biological father actually had 11 brothers and sisters. After he died, why couldn't

one of them have taken us?

Some years later, she asked one of those 11 siblings, her aunt, who responded: "You just wouldn't understand. At that time, we were all very young and unmarried or had just gotten married and were barely able to make it financially. Believe me, honey, you were better off."

Then Madelyn added:

> Superficially, I accepted her explanation; but if one of Greg's brothers or their wives died, we would take their kids in a heartbeat. Still, I'm glad they didn't raise us! My life would be quite different. Adoption exposed us to things that we'd never had. Before I was adopted, I'd never slept in my own room. I'd never been on a boat ride. I'd never seen or heard of pizza. After I was adopted, I was awestruck. It just delighted me every time I discovered something new. Christmas, oh, Christmas was just fabulous. We were very fortunate that all of us were adopted together. If we'd been split up, I would have definitely gone looking for my siblings.

Madelyn and Her Adoptive Parents: Changes for the Better

Remembering her relationship with her adoptive parents at the time of our first interviews as having been characterized by her " breaking away from my teenage rebellion years," Madelyn candidly described herself as headstrong, and mused that perhaps her adoptive parents were equally strong-willed.

> After becoming a parent myself, I began to realize my adoptive parents were like me — just human. That helped me take a more mature view, to move away from blaming one or the other. They began to be more my friends than my parents. I realized there really were two sides: they both had problems that just weren't going to work out.
>
> It's ironic. My adoptive father was a respected Christian singer and

94

choir director, yet he would bad-mouth my adoptive mother. She, however, would never say bad things about him. Being put in the middle was stressful. I tried to play the mediator, because I wanted to have a relationship with both of them. I was going to do what was needed to make that happen.

Extended Family Bonds Continue to Grow — Both Birth and Adoptive

Greg pointed out that from an outside perspective it would be hard to argue that Madelyn's adoptive parents treated her and her sisters any differently than if they had been birth children. Madelyn said that might be true. She added that there were times when foster children were introduced into the family, causing extra stress.

> We had one foster child my mother still mentions. She was a trouble-maker, and my sisters and I didn't like her. We used to say, "Don't bring her into the bunch. She's not real family." We felt we were like real blood-kin children, and she was a trouble-making outsider.

> Looking back now after many years, it dawned on me that it took special parents to take the three of us. It just blows my mind now to think about it. We all had some issues. It took a lot of love and patience to raise us. It helped that a lot of church people also supported us.

Reflecting even more on her birth family, Madelyn added that while some of them are "as nice as can be," others are "real rough rednecks."

> Actually, now I'm more affiliated with my adoptive family than my birth family. Still, it's interesting that some of my birth family members have artistic skills. I've heard that there were several people in our family who were good in art, and that my biological father loved animals. One of my sisters and I are really animal lovers, too. Things like that make you wonder--did I get that from my mother or my father?

Madelyn's Children

Turning her attention to her own experience as a mother, Madelyn admits to being concerned about her older son, Dave, who is in training as a Navy Seal.

> It's dangerous work and he's subject to go all over the world. It's tough on him. He said, "You don't understand, Mom, it's the hardest thing in the world to do. If I can do this, I can do anything."

Madelyn and Greg: A Full Life

Madelyn and Greg relate well and complement one another. She has transformed her life in remarkable ways to become a loving, caring wife, mother and grandmother. (Dave has married and has children.) Her primary goals are, as she explained: " I am 'hell bent' to see that my family and marriage remain stable, and I never want my sons to doubt my steadfast love for them."

While they have not chosen to adopt, and feel they are perhaps too old to make such a choice now, Madelyn admits to having wanted a daughter.

> In hindsight, we wish that we'd pursued adoption. It never seemed the time was right. Then we were blessed with Matthew and Mark.

> I've told lots of people along the way about my adoption. If people question me about problems they may face with older child adoptions, I say that there are helpful programs out there nowadays that didn't exist when I was being adopted. If families can get the right support and backup, it makes a big difference.

> They might have a success story or they might not, but that's true with your own birth children. You can't control what they do.

Greg agreed. He has a friend who is having a difficult time as the adoptive father of a teenager. I told him: "You are going to love that child just as much as if she had your blood—it's just hard not to." His opinion, he said, derives from his having seen how close Madelyn and her sisters were to their adoptive parents.

Before Madelyn and I were married I would have guessed that adopted children might not be grateful for their adoptive parents— that they might really resent them. As screwed up as her sisters are, they continue to be appreciative that they were adopted.

Recalling the grateful speeches Madelyn's sisters made at their adoptive father's funeral, Greg suggested she might want to share the videotape of the event, but Madelyn felt it would be too emotional an experience for her. She did point out, though that they stay in touch with her adoptive relatives. Since her adoptive mother's second husband has died, they often visit with her or take her for weekend trips.

Impact of Madelyn's Adoption on Her Marriage and Children

Near the end of the interview, Madelyn focused on the effects she believes her background has had on her marriage and family.

We've been through some rough times. About 15 years ago, I didn't think we were going to make it. We went to counseling and I told the therapist, "I am just the opposite from some of the others in my family: I never want to leave a marriage. I want to make it work no matter what. I came from two families that fell apart, so I am just determined to make it work."

That difficult period and the marriage therapy brought a big turn around time for us. We went forward as a couple. We revamped everything. We were married more than 30 years ago. Our children are doing well. Overall, I'm happy with my life.

I left Madelyn and Greg's home feeling upbeat—that although scars remain from early abuse, deprivation and trauma, one can overcome such misfortune and become a productive, caring, sensitive individual. More important, it was evident that Madelyn is proud of her accomplishments and appears pleased with her life and family. Despite the trauma of separation and finding a new family, she believes that older-child adoptions can be powerful!

Postscript: Madelyn in her 50s

After meeting with Madelyn, I mailed her the transcript. Once she had had the opportunity to review and make changes to her adoption story, she responded with the following email:

> I did wonder if I should have spoken any more in depth about the sexual abuse I suffered when I was young. I often hear people blame their problems on their past, and I have to sometimes tell them I have had a rough background too, but choose to not let it define me. You just make choices to overcome and move forward. . . . I don't know what others you have interviewed have shared about their past before their adoptions, so maybe just mentioning it was enough.

I replied to Madelyn assuring her that it was not necessary to go into details about the sexual abuse. The most important question for readers was how she managed to overcome her traumatic experiences and move on with her life. Professionals can learn a great deal about childhood resiliency from courageous people like Madelyn. Later we talked by telephone and she shared the following information.

> How did I deal with the sexual abuse? I guess when I was really young, I didn't know any different and that it was wrong. You are expected to love your father. Then as a teenager, I felt very uneasy around men. As I told you, I didn't tell my adoptive parents about the abuse until I was 16. I don't think they believed me at first, but then they finally came around.

> I think the sexual abuse started after my mother's death. I don't ever remember her being around. I just don't know if she was at work or if it was after she died. There was a story that my biological uncle, my mother's brother, shared with me as an adult. My father was 25 years older than my mother. When she was only 16, she would go up to the store that he managed and hang out with him. She ended up running off and getting married to him without her family's permission. Supposedly, there was a rumor going around that he went after younger girls. That caused me to wonder, did he already have that "illness"? Once mother was gone, I filled in.

Some of the memories are so painful I've tried to block them out. I told my husband before we got married, and he felt really bad for me. He said, "Do you need to get counseling?" I responded, "I don't think so, I think I'm OK." About ten years into our marriage, I thought, "I'll just go talk to somebody." Even then it was very hard to talk about the details. I worked through some of it, but I probably didn't go as deep as I should have. I just said to myself, "I'll let this go, I'm OK."

As far as its "defining me," there are plenty of others who have lived through similar or worse situations. It's so prevalent. I just hope telling my story will help people who have been sexually abused to realize that you need not let it determine who you become. Such experiences definitely impact your life in negative ways.

Now that I am in my 50s, it doesn't really bother me or interfere with my life. Occasionally, things come up, and I think if my life had been this way or that way things might be better. I think about it, but I don't dwell on it. I don't blame anything that pops up in my life on it.

In over 50 years of life, I've developed a very strong will, perseverance and self-confidence from living with my adoptive parents, being married to Greg, being a mother, having faith in God — and from many other sources. As I told you, I worry about my sisters. They have many struggles, and sometimes I think our [birth] daddy might have done something to them as well. Maybe sharing my background will help people see there's a whole lot more to adopting older children than meets the eye. That's why I wanted to fill in the gaps in my adoption story.

I don't dwell on my adoption like I did in the past. It rarely crosses my mind now unless someone mentions adoption around me. If it's appropriate I'll say, "Oh, I'm adopted." It's important that I know my bloodline and that I keep some connections with my birth relatives, and I've done that. It's also important to know about my family medical history for me and for my sons.

I now consider my adoptive family to be my family, or, more accurately, where I fit in best. I'm better off being adopted.

Postcript II: A Note from the Author

As *Transplanted into Unaccustomed Earth* was being prepared for publication, I met with each of the book's participants for final reviews of their chapters.

Madelyn shared that she and her husband of about 40 years were experiencing serious marital problems. Because of Madelyn's traumatic childhood, she told of her strong desire and attempts to hold their marrige together, especially for the sake of their children.

From more than three decades of observing and recording her life events, I feel that Madelyn will draw strength once again from her resilient spirit to "bounce back."

CHAPTER FIVE

Adopted at age 12

Birth, Adoptive and Adult Family Structures

Birth Family: Angela has good memories of her birth mother's love and concern for her, but also sadly recalls how she, her mother and numerous siblings struggled to secure adequate food, clothing and shelter. The children had several fathers; Angela does not remember hers. The initial plan was to have all the children move to the children's home and possibly later place them with adoptive families. However, the oldest child, a teenager, ran away and married, and the youngest child was reared by paternal relatives. The middle group of children, with Angela (11) being the eldest, moved to the home's campus before being adopted.

Eventually, they became productive, responsible citizens: a business executive, educators, a church missionary, a healthcare professional, an electronics expert, a scientist and a coach.

Adoptive Family: Angela was adopted at age 12 by a near-retirement-age couple with no birth children. They closely controlled her life, and would not allow her to communicate with her siblings and other birth family members. Under such conditions, she decided it would be better to grow up on the campus of the children's home, but she was "tricked" into finalizing the adoption. She lived with her adoptive parents until she entered college.

Angela's Family as an Adult: When she was 22, Angela married Frank, and they had a son and daughter. After Frank's death, she sought professional help. By hard work she sorted through unpleasant memories and gained insight for the future. As she prepared for retirement from a successful business career, Angela met Mark. They fell in love, were married, and greatly enjoyed retirement together. When Mark died, Angela grieved his loss, but made the most of her remaining years.

ANGELA

Angela was born into poverty, never knew her
birth father, was loved but unsupervised by her
birth mother, lived on the Home's campus, was
placed with a childless retirement-age couple
who "tricked" her into finalizing the adoption and
then isolated and psychologically abused her. Yet
in middle age she turned her life around. Her
counselor said, "You are a 'miracle child.'"

R eaders will enjoy Angela's life story—for what she has overcome, for what she has achieved, for what they learn from her, and for her resiliency and hope for the future. For clarity, her story is being told in two sections: (1) Angela: Childhood to Age 35, and (2) Angela: Ages 36 to Her Early 70s.

SECTION I

CHILDHOOD TO AGE 35

W hen I visited Angela for the original (1983) interview, she lived with her first husband and two children in a lovely suburban area of well-tended yards near Florida's Gulf Coast. Walking to the front door, I noticed that something was out of place. A pumpkin plant had extended a shoot across the paved sidewalk and a few immature pumpkins were beginning to grow. Carefully avoiding the vine, I rang the doorbell. Angela met me with a smile, and graciously invited me inside her carefully furnished home—a home with a comfortable live-and-let-live ambiance. She thanked me for stepping over the pumpkin plant, but she did not apologize for its placement. She simply explained that her children had taken the plants on as a homework project, and were carefully tending to and watching several pumpkins grow until they could be used for Halloween jack-o'-lanterns.

Angela was an attractive, petite woman in her mid-30s. Her husband, Frank, and their children came casually in and out of the den where she and I talked, occasionally joining in the discussion. I was warned, however, not to reveal the nature of my visit to Angela's adoptive father, an aged man who lived with them in a "father-in-law" area of their spacious home. He apparently floated back and forth unannounced between his living area and the rest of the house. Midway during the interview, one of the children, who served as a "scout," announced, "Here he comes!" As instructed, I shoved the still-recording tape recorder under the skirt of my chair. The subject matter abruptly changed, and I was introduced as a business friend. After a few minutes of surveillance, the older man retreated into his quarters, and the interview resumed without a loss of content or momentum.

Pre-adoption Years (Ages 0 - 12)

Growing up we had nothing. We lived in a converted service station with no running water or electricity. In fact, using it as our home was the third use of the building. Maybe building is too nice a word— shack is better. Before it was used as a country service station, it was a chicken coop. That's how crude it was. We hardly had enough to eat, and I did a lot of things wrong trying to get food for us. I stole vegetables out of a neighbor's garden and bread, bologna and things like that from a combination gas station/grocery store that was just up the road. People in our small community knew how poor we were. As I think back about it, I realize they let us kids get by with petty theft because they knew we were getting things to eat.

A neighbor caught me pulling tomatoes off his vines one afternoon, and I was terrified and ashamed. I broke out crying, begging him over and over, "Don't call the police. I'm sorry. I'll work for you to pay you back." My neighbor looked at me over the top of his glasses, and ordered me to "Stay right here." As he climbed the

104

steps, opened the back door and went into his house, I watched, petrified. In my mind's eye I could see the police taking me to jail with their car's siren screaming, but in a few minutes he returned with a bag and placed in it the tomatoes I stole and some other vegetables. He squatted down to my eye level, told me not to steal anymore and added, "If you're hungry I'll be glad to give you food." Of course, I was too embarrassed to ever look at him again, much less ask him for food.

As a child, I knew right from wrong and vowed to myself never to steal anything after I got old enough to take care of myself. However, times were hard and we had to survive. My (birth) mother couldn't take care of us. Even so, I always knew that she loved us. Although we were very poor, she gave me good feelings. How? She treated me like I was a person. We talked like friends, more like I was an adult than a little child. We would work together—like in tobacco fields. She was in some ways more like a child—like us.

For some reason, even as a child, I felt that wasn't the life I wanted to live. You don't think kids know that much, but they do. We were ridiculed because we were poor. I saw things that my mother was doing in that environment to survive and knew that wasn't the life that I wanted.

When we left our birth family and moved into the children's home, we were cut off from people we had been used to seeing everyday: our mother, our aunts and uncles, our grandparents and everybody we knew. It was like—boom—they were gone from our lives, and we moved into and had to adjust to a new world. A sudden change like that would be difficult for adults, but as children we were scared to death. I don't know or remember all of the details, but I believe our mother took us and left us with the promise that she would return. Immediately upon entering the children's home, we suffered another loss. We were split up by age and gender into separate dormitories, rarely seeing one another.

Angela described the adjustment from what she called a "free-to-do-what-you-want environment" to the structure of an institutional setting as very difficult, largely because of the loneliness:

> . . .the feeling that everybody had forgotten me and nobody cared. I still have a hard time talking about it, and it was years before I could. You're suddenly dumped in with a group of strange children with unfamiliar adults giving orders--some barking orders like you were in a military boot camp. As children we had to grow up fast— we had to learn to survive on our own. Of course, I soon got to know other kids at the home, and I was amazed to discover how much children learn from each other—both good and bad. Even there, some children thought they were better than others—they "came from better homes." I often laughed about that. Actually, we were all there for the same reason: our parents couldn't take care of us. So, we all had similar problems.

Being the eldest of the children to enter the home, Angela felt an increasing sense of isolation and desolation as younger siblings were adopted and moved away from the home.

> Being left alone without any family was terrible, and I was feeling desperate. My caseworker came to me and said that a couple had been coming in for three years wanting an older child. She asked if I would meet them. Reluctantly, I agreed.

Meeting Her Adoptive Parents at Age 11

At the very first meeting with her adoptive parents, Angela became acutely aware that their main interest was in having her play the piano.

> I can tell you how I felt inside, as they looked me over. I felt very helpless. I felt that I really had no control over being adopted even though I was told I did. I was told that I could make a choice, but I felt deep down I didn't have a choice. I hoped and prayed that my real mother would come and rescue me. She didn't. No one was going to defend me. As far as being prepared, I'm not sure that I was really prepared. I was told that the couple who wanted to adopt me were older, probably too old to be adopting children. It was a very brief

meeting. They were not the new parents I dreamed about, but I felt that I needed to have a new life. I had to do something with my life.

I was 11, almost 12, when I went to live there on a trial basis. We traveled to their Florida home by car, and I remember as we crossed the state line stopping to buy little souvenirs. They immediately insisted that I call them Mother and Daddy, and also that I take their last name even though the adoption had not taken place. Both things were very hard for me. I went on to school, and registered in their name. My parents and I never discussed my birth family or how I was feeling. I tried a number of times, and it caused huge problems. Even to this day, we don't discuss it. I respect their wishes, but it would have helped me a lot if I could have talked with them about my feelings. I ended up balling them up inside me for years.

Of course, the caseworker came to visit, but my parents didn't want me to be alone with anybody to answer questions. Even when the caseworker and I were alone, I was afraid to say anything, so I didn't.

Angela Decides to Return to the Children's Home

Just before Christmas, I finally got up enough nerve to tell my parents that I wanted to go back to the children's home. I felt I was being locked up: I couldn't go out, I couldn't be an individual, I had to do everything at their beck-and-call, and I couldn't have any friends. I insisted on going back! I told the school I would be leaving, and I had everything prepared. My parents told me that they had called, and the Home agreed to take me back. They were very upset. I understood why, but I felt that I had to go back. I wasn't growing with them.

When they arrived in the town where the children's home is located, Angela's parents convinced her to spend the night with them in a motel instead of going directly to the home. She was uneasy, sensing that something was going on.

The next morning, the truth came out. Mother announced that we were going to court to finalize the adoption. I was devastated. I had no control. Then my real mother called me on the phone. I just knew that she wasn't going to let this happen. We had one last discussion. She said it was in my best interest to be adopted, and she didn't try to save me or do anything. It felt like a prison sentence. I had no chance to escape, so it took place. I felt trapped.

Looking back, in some ways I dreaded returning to an institution like the children's home, but on the other hand I had seen older children grow up at the Home, get their education, and do fine. My adoptive parents were too protective--maybe possessive or controlling are better words. I don't think I rebelled. I'm not saying I was an angel. I'm sure I caused them plenty of problems, but I had been through a lot. As I said, they were closing me up, and I couldn't run.

They tried to pretend I had no past beyond the day I was adopted by them. I couldn't talk about my life before my adoption. I couldn't correspond with anybody about it. I wasn't allowed to see my brothers and sisters after I was adopted. My brother and sister who moved into the Home when I did wrote me, but my (adoptive) parents would not let me answer. That was horrid, because we would have had a lot in common. Who knows what would have happened? I can't predict what might have occurred, but it hurt that I couldn't talk to or even correspond with anyone who understood my situation. I had pictures of my birth family that were taken away while I was at school. I don't know where they went. In other words, everything was wiped clean.

Growing Up in Her Adoptive Home

Angela spent her time isolated not only from her siblings, but from anyone her age.

My summers were spent staying home, cleaning house, washing clothes, and not having any friends. I was always around old people: my father was over 60 years old. Fortunately, there were two older ladies that I was allowed to visit, and I walked their dog in the afternoons. I had an hour each day by myself with the dog; this time was very good. One of the ladies told me, "Take advantage of what you can, and do the best you can." That's

108

what I did—I just kept on living. We all have to keep on living, and I managed.

I wasn't allowed to see the kids at school except at school, so I never became a part of any group, though I wanted to be. I went to Sunday School, but I wasn't even allowed to be a part of their youth group. I can remember crying and pleading to attend. I was never allowed to talk on the phone very much either. As a result, I ended up not having any childhood relationships.

Soon after the adoption, Angela's father retired because of his health, and the three of them moved in with his mother, who "ruled the roost." When his mother's family visited on Sundays, she found them to be old-fashioned, but nice, and yet she didn't fit in with any age group. As she explained:

The younger ones were wild, but they were always good to me. I really appreciated them accepting me like they did. Again, my parents never let me talk about my pre-adoption life. Once, one of the aunts brought up the subject, and said that somebody in my past must have done something right because of my good manners. Of course, the staff at the Home taught us manners-- that's for sure. When family members or friends of my parents visited on Sundays, I never could join in discussions.

Entering College at Age 18

Although she would have preferred to work a year, having been isolated for so long, Angela went to the college her parents had chosen for her.

I was scared and nervous about college. I felt out of place, my parents had sheltered me for so many years. I barely made it the first year. I could have done better. As I got used to college, I loosened-up, and went out and had some fun. In fact, I had a good time, and I didn't come home except when necessary. My parents just felt I was awful, and they would come back on me a lot. I went to summer school, and by my second year I was doing better. I was calming down on my own.

My mother died during my second year, and my father said he would no longer help finance my college cost, so I had to come home. I was determined to get a job. I wasn't going to stay locked up there any longer. I took courses in computer programming and accounting, and then I went to work for an accounting firm during the day, and taught computer programming at a community college in the evenings. I worked at night because I didn't want to be at home.

My ultimate goal all through the years has been to take care of myself. I was anxious to grow up. My job became my life. I worked hard. Eventually, I ended up in computer sales, and I also met my (first) husband, Frank. We were attracted to each other at first sight, but it took us a while to go out, because he was one of my customers.

As a sales rep, I had to live for a while in another area of the state, so we met each other on the weekends. I was able to move back here, and we ended up getting married within the year. My career has moved along well, and now, I am a financial officer of a statewide firm.

Angela Marries at Age 22

Angela considered it "only honest and fair" that Frank know about her early life and background before they married, so they made the long trip to see not only the children's home, but the ramshackle, converted service station. Then shortly after they were married, they decided to invite her adoptive father to live with them.

Why? I'm not sure, but that's what we did. Soon, he was constantly looking over my shoulder. He's always wanted me to feel sorry for him. I try not to be bitter about it. He's always had a tendency to be ill or to pretend he's sick. I don't think he's really sick, but he has convinced himself that he is. We have managed to get along, but it's not that good an arrangement. People hurt each other and themselves when they don't mean to do so. There's no real privacy with him in our home. Not letting me go is the real problem.

We wanted children, and I felt we had to know my birth family's medical history so we would know what to expect as our children

110

grew up. When I was carrying my first child, one of the first things my doctor asked was, "What kind of diseases have you had?" Well, I didn't know. My adoptive father had a copy of all the diseases and vaccinations I've had, but to this day I haven't seen it. I didn't even know whether I'd been inoculated for German measles, so I had to have the shot again.

Reconnecting with Her Birth Family

Eager to reconnect with her birth relatives, Angela knew she had an aunt living nearby but could not remember her married name. After a chance meeting at a local shopping center, they have kept in touch and she has since seen most of her birth family.

Frank took me to see my real grandmother before she died. I have seen my real mother, and I still see her occasionally, as well as my brothers and sisters. We've all seen each other at least once since we were split-up as children. I like seeing them, but it's like living in two worlds. We're working our way to being closer. I also have an understanding with them. When we first got together, I explained that I didn't want to hurt my adoptive father's feelings because he never wanted to admit that I had other family. I told my birth family to call me if an emergency came up but not to let my adoptive father know who they are. Just keep calling until I'm home—then let me know what's going on.

When I started seeing my birth family again, I noticed that one brother and I were the only ones with blue eyes. Most of the family is heavyset. Everybody's short. I'm about the tallest one. We've all had some of the same health problems, which I thought was interesting.

Our family meetings have been hard for me. I know a lot of people go back and run into all kinds of problems. We didn't have serious problems, but my older sister and I don't see eye to eye. Even as kids, we didn't get along. We've managed to outgrow some of that, but we still have room for improvement.

Perspectives on Her Childhood
and Young Adult Years

Able to remember events that occurred when she was two or three years old, Angela is keenly attuned to the fact that children are aware at a young age, and has been careful to be open with her own children.

They are people, not babies. I want them to be children, and I want them to have friends and have a good time. I don't want them to grow up as fast as I did. I've told them the truth about my childhood experiences of poverty, neglect and about being tricked into adoption. Our daughter has a friend who was adopted when she was a baby, and every once in a while we talk about it. I know that as a child I kept a lot inside of me, and I don't want my children to do that. I want them to be able to have someone to go to. I'd rather they get their answers at home, but if they can't talk to us we certainly want them to feel free to talk to someone else they can trust. We are strict and yet we're not. I don't go around ordering them to do this or that. I want each of them to be their own person--not pretend to be somebody they're not.

Maybe my early experiences have made me more sensitive to other people. I can sense if people are phony or trustworthy. I can sense people's feelings. I can feel someone's hurt or their joy. I used to cry all the time. I got that out of my system. I guess maturity, marriage and children helped—just being happier makes a difference.

I do a lot of analyzing of myself. I don't know that anybody ever knows himself or herself. You spend your lifetime trying. I also try to be understanding of other people and want the same from them. You can't judge people by the way they look. You've got to choose them by what's in their hearts.

It may sound strange, but I don't regret any of my life. I'm thankful that I was in poverty when I was a little girl, that I had the experience of living in a children's home, the adoption experience, and now my present life experience. I feel it's unique to have lived so many

112

different lives. Living with a variety of people, you find that most people are the same no matter what they look like or how they live. The grass always looks greener on the other side of the fence, but when you get there you find it's the same. Life's been rewarding for me. I'm not saying that I haven't had depression and been down, but I don't regret my life or feel bitter about it. I think I've learned a lot from it. I am 35 now. When you're younger you have lots of ambition, but when you look back on life, you realize you take it one day at a time. I think the main thing that I want out of life is to see our children grow up, be healthy, and be prepared to live enjoyable, meaningful lives--to live out their dreams.

My faith in God helped me the most. My main prayer is that my children will know that God loves them. If they know that they will be able to make it through anything. We all have to make mistakes to grow. My goal is just to see them become happy and healthy people.

SECTION II
ANGELA: AGES 36 TO HER EARLY 70S

A quarter-of-a-century is a long period in one's life; many things had changed for Angela since 1983. I was prepared for changing events and appearances, but unprepared for the internal changes that had occurred. She had continued to live in the same Florida city and worked for the same firm until retiring with the rank of senior vice-president.

Even after 25 years, I easily recognized Angela—still petite and lively and gracious. She welcomed me into her attractive townhome, filled with furniture, photos, and other personal items she had carefully selected for both their beauty and their sentimental value. As I was to discover, she had downsized and discarded "unnecessary baggage" from her life—both tangible and intangible. Gone were the large home and unneeded "stuff" one acquires over time. Retained, in addition to items she cherishes, were her sense of optimism and infectious laughter.

As she talked about her children and grandchildren, her second husband, Mark, entered the living room and warmly greeted me. As we shook hands, he said he had read Angela's story in my 1985 book and looked forward to reading the updated one. Now retired, Mark is approximately Angela's age. Soon she hopes to join him in retirement, free to enjoy a more relaxed life. I sensed that Angela had given up the "suck it up and be a good soldier" role, and I looked forward to discovering how she had managed to change.

An Overview of Her Life Since We Last Met

Remembering my allusion to the pumpkin plant in *Whose Child Am I?*, Angela noted that her son who had planted the pumpkin seed earns his living as a civil engineer, but his hobby is gardening. In fact, he is a certified master gardener. He not only grows vegetables and flowers for his wife and children, but has organized his church's congregation to develop a large garden to help feed poor people.

> Thank you for your compliment about my determination to see that my children never experienced what I did as a child. I've tried hard to let my children know I love them and am concerned about them.

> What has happened to me since we last met 25 years ago? Let's see, I'll give you a quick summary. My first husband died about seven years ago. I have been blessed with great children and adorable grandchildren. I went back to college part-time and earned a four-year degree in business administration. That was a struggle, but it kept me up-to-date, and it helped me advance in my career. Last but not least, three years ago, I married a wonderful man.

> What else? When we first talked in 1983, my birth mother was still living, but she died about 20 years ago. I never knew my birth father. I guess I was the only one of us (my siblings) who never tried to find my birth father. As you remember, there were several different fathers. My adoptive father lived with us for many years, but I had to put him in a nursing home five years before he died.

114

Achieving Freedom from Control and Possessiveness

With the perspective of an additional quarter of a century, Angela still puzzled over why her adoptive parents treated her as they did, leaving her with an overriding feeling that she lacked control over her life.

I have thought about it, and I believe it was because they were uncomfortable with having an adopted child. Maybe part of it was family pride, I don't know. If somebody mentioned I was adopted, they would say, "Oh no!" Another part of it may have been that they did not have children of their own. Maybe they couldn't, and were embarrassed and hurt by it. I don't know for sure. It's probably a good thing they didn't have a baby. If they had started with an infant, it would have been sad. A little child would have never been let out of their sight. At least I had some different experiences before I was adopted. My real mother, for all her shortcomings, gave me some good feelings about myself. I had two mothers who were opposites. One, my birth mother, let me do anything with completely no direction, and the other wouldn't let me loose. I had to kind of go along to keep the peace.

You consider me a caring, sensitive person. How did I become like that after all I went through? In a couple of words, it was Faith in God. Faith in God!

You asked why I let my adoptive father live in my home for most of my adult life and care for him when he was old and sick. Looking back, I'm not completely sure. Many fair-minded people have said I shouldn't have. My first husband was like him—mentally abusive, too, especially as the years went by. Yet in spite of how my adoptive parents treated me, they helped me start a new life. Without them, I would not have had the opportunities I have had. I have always felt God has a purpose for all of us, and the things I went through must have been part of the purpose. I don't know if that justifies it or not.

You always want love. I thought my adoptive father would show that he loved me at some point in time, but he could not let himself go. I gave in to both him and my first husband. I later found out in counseling that all I did was give permission for people to continue to walk over me. I didn't realize I was doing that.

The stress involved in taking care of a sick father for five years and husband for ten years took a toll on Angela, and after they died she chose to go for two years of counseling.

You sense something different about me now? Well, I am more at peace with myself. When you go to counseling and make notes, it's amazing what takes place. When we try to make decisions, without resolving old issues, we tend to repeat the same old patterns. I feared that I was going to end up making the same mistakes again. I thought to myself, "I can make a new start in life. I have a home, a good job, my children and grandchildren." I didn't need any more trouble, and my counselor helped me find new ways to live.

I wasn't the mother I wanted to be until the last few years, but I have learned how to be the mother I always desired to be. I now enjoy the roles of mother and grandmother. Unfortunately, we can't go back in time, but we can talk about the past, and learn to make peace with it.

I have also gotten to know my birth family better. For example, when my birth mother died, we all got together except for one brother. Then a year later, all of us met together for a few hours, and there was a reunion two years ago. My older sister and I have had disagreements since childhood. She made sure I wasn't invited to the reunion, but an aunt called to be certain I knew about it. I then called my older sister to ask what was going on. I did attend along with my daughter. Also, my son came down later and took videos of it.

Finally, I'm all right being "me" now. When my first husband died, I took a year off to decide what I wanted to do. I bought this smaller home and downsized. I picked out the furniture I wanted in this house from the larger home I sold. I had my children get what they wanted, and I sold everything else--and started fresh. I feel good about that. I think about the past; it will always be in my mind. Relatives of my adoptive parents still call me once in a while, and I'll go and see them. I don't need to get involved with them unless I want to--it's okay to take care of myself now.

One thing I have to worry about is anger. You go through various stages when you work through unpleasant things, and I went through a stage of being really furious. I didn't realize I was so angry with my adoptive father. I learned in therapy that it is okay to be angry, and I learned that my adoptive parents and my first husband had character disorders that I couldn't do anything about. Of course, I was also worried about my kids and their emotional health. I encouraged them to get help with what they went through, and my daughter has received counseling, especially regarding feelings about her father.

I'm flattered that your graduate students read my adoption story. If you ever have a chance to talk to any of them again, tell them I'm a different person than the "victim Angela" you interviewed in 1983. It takes a lifetime to grow up, doesn't it? If another family had adopted me, things would have been different; but who knows if it would have been better. I learned from my mixed-up childhood how to survive, and I had to survive on my own. As an adult I worked hard, but my first husband didn't work half the time. I wanted to make sure my family was taken care of. I supported both of my children through college, and I am retiring at the end of the year. It has been tough, but I've gotten through it.

Angela's Epiphanies

When I asked Angela if there were any epiphany-like events at any point that helped her turn herself around, she recalled two quite distinctly.

One. I was in the hallway. Both my husband and my father were yelling, trying to get my attention. I just couldn't take it anymore, and in a fit of desperation, I told my husband to get me out of there. My father turned to me and laughed in a hateful way saying, "I had to call the police on you many times." That brought back painful memories.

Soon after I moved into their home at age 12, he had begun threatening to have me locked up in a juvenile detention home or a mental hospital when I got angry or defied either of them. He would dial the police department and then hang up. I could see clearly what I had become—his dominated daughter. I knew what to do. Anger was building up inside me, but I was in control of my emotions. I walked straight up to him, stared into his eyes, and said, "I have lost a lot in my life, but I will never, never lose my mind because of you." I was determined that I would never again give in to him, regardless of what he did or said, but at the same time it made me sad. For many years, I had hoped he and his family would really accept me as his daughter. They never did. There were a lot of hurtful incidents. I was just that adopted child!

Two. I had always handled everything myself, and never in my adult life had I asked for help from anybody. When my first husband, Frank, became seriously mentally and physically ill and threatened to kill me, I told him that we would have him committed if he continued. He kept threatening, and when I asked for help Hospice sent over a team of three people: a nurse, a social worker and their chaplain. The four of us listened, for three hours, as my husband raged at me. His true feelings spewed out. It was unbelievable. I can't really describe its impact on me. It was terrible, but also positive. It broke my heart, and it set me free. I had guessed, at times, during all those years we were married that he really didn't love me, and as I heard him rant and rage, I learned that, for him, I had been more his mother than his wife. I can't express how much it hurt, but I can tell you it set me free. I needed to know the truth. If I had not heard him say those things, I would have felt guilty and still be, as your students said, "trapped"!

Fortunately, when Frank passed away he was in the hospital. I was at home, but I had this feeling that something was happening. I called the hospital, and they told me he was dying. One of our dogs, the one he fussed at and cussed at all the time, went over and looked at his picture until about the time of his death, then moved away and laid down to rest. In a different way, I experienced the same thing: I could put Frank to rest. When he died, I thought that I was going to cry, but I didn't. You can't deny your feelings. He was better off; he's better where he is. He was sick, very sick. I never asked for him to come back. I wanted him to go into the casket. Maybe that's not right, but he was certainly not happy here. I saw the smile on his face in the casket, and I wouldn't wish for him to have to come back here.

Whether that makes sense or not, I don't know. Like Christ taught us, knowing the truth can set us free, and hearing how Frank felt was a terrible experience—but it set me free. Not that I haven't thought about him. He was part of my life for a long time. Sometimes I feel guilty because I couldn't do anything to help him, but I couldn't control that. There wasn't anything I could do. It wasn't my fault.

I think often about growing up from age 12 with my adoptive mother and father. I lived with them only six years before going away to college. From the experience of raising my own children, I realize you grow up with your children—it's a gradual thing. If you bring an older child into a family, there is an abrupt change for both the child and the parents. When I was 12, I thought I was 25. My daughter works as a guidance counselor. Like her students, I knew it all. It is a big responsibility for the adoptive parents, and it can be a traumatic experience for older adopted children.

I am getting better about not feeling guilty for things I can't control. Yes, my adopted parents made me feel guilty--all the time! I cleaned the house; I washed the clothes; I scrubbed the floors; I did everything. I never went out. I went to one football game while I was in high school. No one could come over. So I'm blessed to have made it through all of that, and to have come through it as well as I have. Now, I'm free at last.

Meeting Mark—Beginning a New Life

After long years of what she called being "very careful" around personalities like those of her adoptive father and first husband, Angela decided she would avoid being surrounded by such people. Then she met Mark.

Mark and I were married three years ago. When I met him, he was so nice and thoughtful that I didn't know how to act. I had never been around somebody who treated me like that. I didn't know how to trust somebody who is so kind. I still don't trust a lot of people. To be able to sit down and have a conversation with no one yelling is really nice. My kids, my grandkids, and his kids all love Mark.

We all get along great, and that makes a big difference in our lives.

You are right, I am happy, but it has taken a while. Since I was a child, I've always tried to put on a good front. Life is not supposed to be easy. Anytime I thought things were unbearable, I remembered that Christ died on the cross and people heckled him. Why are we any different? Nobody said we shouldn't suffer. We have to learn from it and move on.

When I was raising my kids, I told them if I had everything, I wouldn't give them all they asked for. They didn't get an allowance; they went out and worked and earned their own money. When they went to college, I paid their tuition, but they earned their spending money. My son was extremely involved with Young Life (a Christian youth organization) in college. He loved that experience, and he met wonderful people. It changed his life so much. Now he and his wife are very active in their church.

I've kind of made a life of my own. I don't have the desire to go back now, and that's okay. I don't owe anybody anything anymore— except for respect. I've tried to be respectful to people in my life, both in my birth family and in my adoptive family, and I expect the same from them. My children have the opportunity to decide if they want to interact or not with them. They have been involved with both sides to some extent. Now, I rarely see any members of my adoptive family except by chance. Even on my birth side, I don't see them often. When they all get together now, I often don't attend the gatherings— because I don't need the stress. I decided I don't have to take it.

Dreams for the Future

Angela is forthright about her hope that her firsthand account of how adoption feels will help people, especially parents who are considering adoption, to be more open.

Parents must be sensitive to listening and talking openly with their adopted children. Older adopted children often have been traumatized, neglected and abused, and their needs must be taken seriously. There are a lot of school-age children who are waiting to be adopted. People think first of adopting babies and young children, but I hope more families will consider adopting older children. Older adopted children can be wonderful additions to families, but families must be patient and let older adopted children join them at their own pace.

At the same time, she sees before her a life that is full and abundant.

What about my future? Well, retirement is interesting because I have worked all of my life. I may work some, but mostly I want to enjoy my children and grandchildren. Mark and I want to enjoy each other, and take life a day at a time. I know I can find ways to stay busy. We like crafts, working in the yard, and doing things together. He is a woodworker, and I like crocheting. We also want to do some volunteer work together.

My grandchildren are small now, but I will share my life story, including my adoption, with them. I've been honest with my children. After their father died, they told me I had not given them enough attention in the past. I can't make up for what has happened, but for the past year, I have talked with my son by phone every Thursday evening. It's been wonderful. I talk with my daughter every day. That way they know that I do care. Fortunately they are nearby, and I live halfway between them.

Was there a person who stands out as my cheerleader during my chaotic childhood? No, I just had to keep plugging along. Finally, I became "me." As a child I would wave to everyone, and I was always happy. That was okay—that was "me," but I lost "me." Now I can be "me" again, and nobody can stop me.

When my daughter was in college, she and her best friend stopped by the house after a psychology class, and asked me about my resilience, "How do you keep on going with all you have been through?" I answered, "When you have been to hell and back, nothing matters any more." It's true—you know you can survive.

Postscript I

Once Angela's adoption story was in its final stages, I revisited her as I did with the other book participants. As her story was read aloud, she made comments and corrections, and these were later incorporated into the manuscript. As our meeting was concluding, she added the following comments:

> Most of us go through life wondering if we made the right choices, but we do the best we can. I'm trying to put the events of my life in place now. I'm thankful my mind and spirit are still sound. I called my eldest sister last spring, and I said, "I'm coming to see and talk with you—just the two of us." She's the one I mentioned that I often had conflicts with as a child and as an adult. It was a good experience for both of us, and I'm glad I did it.

> You asked if there are some final thoughts that may help children and families better cope with adoptions. What does the term adoption really mean? Is it an ownership process or a loving, caring and freeing process? I have a letter my adoptive mother wrote me while I was in college that said she owned me and that she had 'paid good money' for me, meaning the adoption fees, attorney costs and expenses that were related to my adoption. She had a better heart than my adoptive father did, and I don't believe in hindsight that she meant to really hurt me so deeply, but I cried and cried after reading her letter. I later realized that she hadn't felt she owned me. She was actually hurt over something else, and that was a convenient way to vent her emotions. However, words like "ownership" can be upsetting for adopted people like me.

> It's also important for the entire adoptive family—aunts, uncles, grandparents and cousins—to accept an adopted child into the family system. For example, I was left out of an inheritance from a relative that I believed loved and accepted me. Typically, in our state, if an inheritance is to a class of people, like a group of cousins, it isn't necessary to list specific recipients. I found out, however, that this person had deliberately excluded me. I cried and cried.

> It wasn't the idea of the money—I've made sure that I'll have enough

funds to live comfortably in retirement. What hurt was that I wasn't considered part of the family. Ten dollars would have let me know I was accepted. I've had a lot of "slaps in the face," but I didn't expect this one. I have no idea why I was left out except that I'm not a blood relative.

When I asked Angela, as I have the others, to summarize their thoughts and feelings about their adoptions, she recounted what her counselor had told her:

"You are a 'miracle child,' and there is no way that you should have become the educated, responsible and caring person that you are--it's just a miracle."

Dr. Powell, I'm glad you think I have become a new person. I think so too! Now I can sit down and read a book without jumping all over the place. It's a good feeling.

Postscript II

I later learned that Angela's beloved second husband, Mark, died. As in the past, Angela relied on her lifelong resilient spirit to bounce back.

CHAPTER SIX

Ages at the time of their mother's death: Joanne, almost 8;
Maynard, 6;
and Benny, 4.

Birth, Adoptive and Adult Family Structures

Birth Family: The day the children's mother, then in her late 20s, was killed in a horrific automobile accident, their father, then in his mid-30s, was driving the car but was not at fault in the accident. Nonetheless, he blamed himself for his wife's death. His excessive self-blaming seemed to trigger a mental breakdown that led to three years of treatment in a state mental hospital. After their mother's death, the children managed to survive together in inadequate, temporary care for almost a year. Joanne then lived in the children's homefor a few months before being adopted at age 9. Maynard, considered "hard to place," lived in several foster care settings, interspersed by brief placements at the children's home before his adoption at age 9. Benny, also considered "hard to place," lived in several trial adoptive homes before being permanently adopted at age 8.

Adoptive Families: The children were not allowed to communicate with each other for 14 years. They did not reunite until they were young adults.

Adult Families: After high school, Joanne began working as a waitress, but once her daughter was born, she enrolled in a community college and earned an associate degree with honors. She was employed as an administrative assistant until the economic downturn of 2008/2009. Since that time she has struggled financially, but has been a good mother to her now-grown daughter. Maynard never married, and he lived with his adoptive parents most of his early adult life. He established and operated his own home repair business. After his adoptive father died, he helped to take care of his aging adoptive mother until her death. Since that time he has moved to be closer to his sister and brother. Benny lived out of state until recent years and now resides near Joanne and Maynard. He was married and is now divorced, but has no children. The tragedy of their mother's sudden death and other childhood difficulties continue to "haunt" the three siblings more than four decades later.

JOANNE, MAYNARD AND BENNY

The horrific automobile accident killed the children's mother and led to three years of psychiatric hospitalization for their father. Not only did this terrible tragedy impact the lives of Joanne, Maynard and Benny as children, its memories continue to "haunt" them over four decades later.

The older child adoption stories in this book were originally told by each participant individually. They were then transcribed as separate verbatim accounts. When siblings told their stories, the result was often a great deal of redundancy. In addition to being repetitious, the book to soar in length.

I therefore began to experiment. An example: by cutting and pasting Joanne's, Maynard's and Benny's memories of how they learned about their mother's tragic accidental death, I constructed an imaginary three-way conversation. It accurately related the details of the event, and at the same time provided clarity, avoided repetition and made it possible to juxtapose their different insights. And by pretending they were interviewed together, I was able to use their own words. When I shared with the three siblings their imaginary conversation, most of it verbatim clips from interviews, all three agreed it accurately expressed their thoughts.

Section I

Initial Interview: Joanne 22 and Maynard 20

Benny Interviewed Some Years Later

Painful Memories

Most of us can identify painful dates, both public and personal, that seem firmly stuck with "emotional glue" in our long-term memories. The attack on New York's World Trade Center on September 11, 2001, is such an indelible public date. For these children, May 4, the day their mother was killed, was what Maynard called "the first day to the next part of our lives." When I interviewed Joanne, Maynard and Benny, they appeared to momentarily move back in time—as the anxiety of that day surfaced. During one of her interviews, Joanne recalled:

> Today is May 4. I'll always dread that date. This is the day Mother was killed in that horrible wreck. It's doubly hard today, because it's Monday, the exact day of the week and the calendar date when she died. I get blue and depressed every May 4, but I'm handling it better. I'm making progress.

The Day of Their Mother's Death

The day had begun early. Their father hand-milked the cows and then began calling, by name, assorted farm animals and pets to feed them extra rations for a long day. Their mother shooed the hens off their nests and gathered eggs for breakfast in a fold of her apron before returning to the kitchen of their simple, orderly home, which, like many mountain farm homes of that era had electricity, but no modern appliances or running water. As she was baking biscuits, she called the children. Maynard quickly dressed, and, as part of his morning routine, went outdoors to tell his father that breakfast was ready. It was, he remembers, "a picture perfect life in some ways, but even then it was crazy in other ways. We were poor, but we ate like kings because of the farm."

128

The crazy-making part was that, although not quite six years old, Maynard felt compelled to keep his father's dark secrets. He traveled with his father almost everywhere, even on hunting trips, and despite excuses he heard, Maynard knew his father was having affairs. He realized that such activity was wrong and if his mother found out about it. . . "It would break her heart—Mother couldn't handle it."

On that fateful day, after the family had eaten and dressed, their father hustled all of them into the family car. It was a short drive from their farm to Aunt Susie's mobile home. Sleepily, Joanne, almost 8, Maynard, soon to celebrate his 6th birthday and Benny, 4, stumbled out of the backseat, each one carrying a few toys, games and books to occupy their day. Alongside Aunt Susie, they waved goodbye to their parents. Turning onto the interstate, their father headed the car toward a medical center, several hours away, where his wife had an appointment. Suddenly, tragedy struck. A speeding car plowed into them. Steel smashed against steel, creating a thunder-like sound that pierced the morning air and scattered hunks of automobile fragments along the pavement. Police and emergency personnel soon arrived. From what she learned after the accident, Joanne described the scene:

> Remember, this occurred over 40 years ago in an old car that lacked seat belts and had a wide bench seat. My mother was trapped inside it. My father watched helplessly and prayed for our mother's survival. Tragically, she died at the scene.

Their father was taken by ambulance to a hospital. He and the driver of the other vehicle miraculously suffered only minor physical injuries.

Although the accident occurred in mid-morning, the three siblings did not learn the terrible news until late afternoon. As the day progressed, Maynard grew more and more anxious. His parents had told him they would return by mid-afternoon. He knew something was wrong. Adults came to Aunt Susie's home, whispering to one another. Then someone blurted out that his father was okay, but his mother was never coming home again. He was devastated, but he kept thinking, as young children often do, that his mother would somehow magically return—that this was like a fairy tale and there would be a happy ending. Instead, he remembers, "I went from living in a farm-like paradise to living in Hell."

Benny, then 4, was playing in the yard and also sensed something was wrong when the adults went inside. Then one of his cousins ran from the house to tell him his mother was dead. Voice trembling and face full of remorse, he recalled:

> I told her, "No she isn't; you are lying!' She kept saying, "Yes she is!" I ran away and hid in the back of a junked bus for I don't know how long before they found me.

Joanne, two months from her 8th birthday, was joking with her cousin, as the two were supposedly taking a nap, when she heard voices she didn't recognize. After her aunt told the two girls to be quiet, they strained to hear what was going on, and before long her aunt returned and relayed the terrible news. She remembers:

> For a few moments, I pulled the sheet over my head, wanting to pretend I was having a bad dream. I cried and cried and prayed to God for her to return. Of course, she never did. Looking back, that's when I started to feel angry and depressed. You saw me like that at age 22 when you first interviewed me. It wasn't until years later after my daughter, Tammy, was born that I started to get over it.

Maynard was the only child to attend their mother's funeral service, tagging along after his father. His memories are stark:

> Up to that point, I couldn't accept Mother's death. I kept thinking she was going to come back. Daddy was falling apart. Before they closed her casket, Daddy held me up and told me to kiss my mother goodbye. I kissed her on the cheek. I felt the coldness. I can still feel the coldness of her skin. I knew then she was gone and was never coming back.

Joanne had a slightly different memory of their father taking them to the funeral home the night before the funeral. She says:

> He made Maynard, Benny and me look at Momma's embalmed body and then kiss her cheek. After that, I threw a fit and wouldn't go to the funeral the next day. It was a tough time to go through—learning

of Mother's death—then seeing her dead body and having to kiss her cheek. You can't get that out of your mind. Each year, when the 4th of May rolls around, I feel uneasy and depressed.

She concluded that it was perhaps her reaction that prompted the decision to keep Benny from the funeral service. "I think they saw that a 4-year-old was just too young for that."

Finding New Homes

For a short time, aunts and uncles cared for the children. Joanne and Maynard have continued to feel a sense of rejection that their birth relatives allowed them to be placed in a children's home and later adopted. Benny saw it a bit differently, assuming the cause might well have been lack of sufficient resources. As he explains:

They were just poor mountain folks. They had trouble taking care of themselves and their children. Taking on three more children was something I don't feel that they could do. I never held any anger toward them for that.

Maynard remembers the three of them being moved to an elderly woman's house:

I think Daddy paid her something to keep us. We were basically her slaves in a sense--we took care of her and we had to live there a year. I spent my first grade year there and then our aunts and uncles talked our father into taking us to an orphanage.

Maynard also recalls vividly his father's state of mind and health after the accident:

My father went kind of crazy. He turned to drinking all the time. That's one of the reasons we were taken from him. The accident wasn't his fault. The patrolman charged the other driver, but Daddy blamed himself anyway. I believe those affairs added to his guilt. My mother was not the kind of person who could have dealt with my father if she had found out. Those kinds of things come around; my father would have slipped up, and that would have been bad.

131

The weird part of it is, before the accident, I was my father's favorite child. I was with him almost everywhere he went. I knew both the good and bad sides of him. After our mother's death, I suffered some serious abuse from him. Somehow he believed his infidelity played a part in her dying. Because I knew what had gone on, I think he took it out on me. As he became crazier, the abuse got worse. He would have killed me, or I would have tried to kill him. It was good for me to get away from him, but the children's home was like a prison camp for me. It was not a fun process.

Despite his young age, Benny also has vivid memories of his father's emotional instability:

I don't remember when or how long we lived there, but Daddy had rented a trailer for us to live in. One night, the three of us kids were sitting on a couch, and he was sitting across from us. Daddy kept telling us to be quiet, but we kept talking. He must have been drunk, because he pulled a gun out and said: "You'll be old enough to have your own gun some day, and we'll just go outside and settle our differences that way." As soon as the gun was put back into the cabinet, I took off running. I hid some place, and I don't know how long it took them to find me.

More than a year after their mother's death, the three children were placed in the children's home. As was typical at that time, they were placed in different dormitories/cottages by gender and age. We now know that severing the relationships of brothers and sisters after they have lived through emotionally traumatic events is "the wrong medicine." For these children, it was devastating. In many ways, they had been relying upon each other for support and survival. Benny's simple recall is compelling: "That was the last time I saw my brother and sister until I was grown. I was so little I can't remember the exact time frame."

Joanne believes that their father was urged to "send us to the Home." She elaborated, sharing the misery she experienced:

When we were dropped off at that hellhole, we were left with the impression that we would be there only until our father got his life straightened out. I was there for about three months. Too long! All

I remember was a nightmare. I was one of the youngest ones in the home and the youngest girl in my cottage. The older girls just mercilessly picked on me. Maynard and I were there at the same time, but we rarely saw one another. I was told that Benny was not close by and I couldn't see him. Later, I found that was not true. That's wrong—you need to be truthful with children.

Maynard's memories are no better:

I didn't understand anything. It's like you take away a little animal from its momma, and it doesn't know what to do. It's just wandering around looking, just wondering where its momma is and not knowing. The day we were dropped off, I had no idea where we were or why we were there. I was told my father would be back, that he needed time off. Joanne was adopted two or three months later, after she entered the home. Benny and I were considered hard-to-place kids. During the several years before we got adopted, they moved us in and out of foster homes. Foster parents would say, in effect, "We have had enough of you; we're taking you back to the Home." It seemed they were the rulers, the controllers. It was almost like I was a volleyball or ping-pong ball. Being raised on a farm, I was familiar with the principle, you raise the cattle, and you butcher the cattle. I really felt in a sense like I was just a cow being slowly slaughtered.

The experiences of the three when they were finally adopted varied. Joanne, who was placed within months of arrival, remembers being surprised at the whole process, but grateful for the results.

We were not aware that we were to be adopted until after we moved into the children's home. What were my adoptive parents like? They had to be good people to take in somebody else's kids and raise them. I have one sister, who is also adopted, and two foster sisters from welfare. Because my adoptive parents loved us all alike, I feel like they are my sisters. Unfortunately, my adoptive parents died before they ever got to know their granddaughter, Tammy.

In Benny's case, a rocky beginning spawned a happy ending:

I was actually in the home's foster care system for three years, living

133

with several families with short stays back at the home. I was so young I really didn't understand what was going on. I don't remember much about the foster families except one that spanked my bare bottom with a leather strap when I did something they didn't like.

I was considered a brat and uncontrollable, and a social worker put me in a foster home with a lady who had a reputation for working with troubled children. I guess, she straightened me out. After those years with her I was told there was a family who might want to adopt me. They came to the foster home to spend the day with me, and we had a great time. They were real nice people. Then they came for a weekend, and again we had a great time. I definitely was ready when the time came for adoption. I still have the little tag I wore for the airplane ride to their home. It was my 8th birthday, and I remember walking into their house and finding it full of presents. It was nice; they were good people. I was the only child. My mom always wanted a child, but for some reason they couldn't have any children. They had taken in foster children in the past; and they had two foster children after I came to live with them, but they weren't free for adoption. My adoptive parents knew I was from a big family, and continued to care for foster children because they wanted me to have some children to play with. They did that for me. Other than that, I was pretty much an only child. I moved out at 21.

While Benny's introduction to his adoptive family seemed smooth, Maynard's tough transition continued as he was adopted and placed in surroundings that were unfamiliar to him. Nathaniel Hawthorne's phrase "unaccustomed earth" (that is used in this book's title) reflects Maynard's unsettled life. Before moving to the children's home, he, Joanne and Benny were frequently moved about. Then, in the Home's care, he was moved from campus to their foster care homes and then back to campus. Maynard's memories are compelling:

I was a wild kid and didn't care about anything at that point in my life. After you are at the children's home for a while, you realize no one (from your natural family) is going to come and rescue you. As I mentioned, it was like a prison camp—that's how I felt at the time and that's how I feel now.

134

To Maynard, the foster home placements seemed like a series of unsuccessful paroles. When he moved into an adoptive home near the Atlantic Ocean, everything was different: rolling mountains covered with hardwoods were replaced by flat farmlands and pine forests; the way people talked—the tone of their voices and the expressions they used—was unfamiliar; and rocky soil had become sand loam. How could he find his footing there, he wondered, both physically and emotionally? For Maynard, this was truly "unaccustomed earth."

I had never been in an adoption process, and one day I was told that there was a family that wanted to adopt me. No family before had wanted me. I went with them for a week's visit. Then "Boom,"I was living "Down East." It was like going to the other side of the world at the time—the longest trip I had ever made in my life. My adoptive mom tells how I stayed on the floorboard in the back of the car during the whole trip. I was petrified, and they knew that. They helped me settle down. After I was there a week, they decided to keep me; and after another week or so we went back to the Home to sign documents. That's how fast the process went; it was a year later, of course, before the adoption was finalized.

One of the key things I remember about that time in my life is how my last name changed every time I went into a foster home. That's how they kept up with me in school. My name changed four or five times. Teachers and other adults didn't know what to call me, and after a while, I didn't care what they called me anyway. I felt I truly lost my identity. I could relate to the title of your first book, *Whose Child Am I?* That's how I felt.

After my adoption was finalized, I used my adopted last name. I kept my original first name, "Maynard," which came from my birth grandfather, and my middle name from my birth father. Doing these things actually helped me keep my identity as much as possible.

Accepting Adoption

For these children, adjusting to and growing up in their adoptive families was akin to leaping into and becoming citizens of a new world.

Maynard: When I moved into my adoptive family, I had to totally change—not just my last name, but my behavior as well. In my last foster home before my adoption, where the neighborhood made it easy to get into trouble, I roamed the streets and did whatever I wanted to do. At my adoptive home it was almost like moving back to a farm situation--near a city but really out in the country. I was a very unruly and tough person at that point in life. I had been through too much, seen too much, and it was like, "If this is the next stage in life let's get on with it." My adoptive parents totally impressed me. If I had had to put up with some of the things they had to go through, I wouldn't have liked me. They stuck by me, which shows the type of people who adopted me. How did I make such a radical change in behavior? I willed it. Basically, I have lived with my adoptive mother and father since age 8. When they died, losing them was tough. I have lost two fathers, and then I lost another mother. My adoptive mom saved my life once upon a time, and she has done so several times since. I truly see it that way. Her husband, my adoptive father, was a perfect example of the type of man God wants fathers to be—a perfect reflection of our heavenly Father. As a Christian, I believe that we are all adopted into the Kingdom of Heaven. That was the way my adoptive father accepted and treated me—I was his own child.

My adoptive father provided me with a sense of love and caring that my natural father never seemed to have. My natural father could have cared less about what was right or wrong; it was whatever he wanted to do at the time. With my adoptive father it was: "This is wrong" and "this is right"; you are not going to do the wrong; you are going to do the right. I saw the line. It was very clear and very distinct. I still feel that my adoptive family is my family. I love them just like I always have; and I still love my real family, too.

I had bad memories of my real father. I really didn't know if I wanted to see him. I had mixed feelings about whether I should trust him or not. Then, after 14 years I met him and saw that he had changed. I realized I had some love for him too.

Benny: My adoptive father and I weren't close at first. I don't think he really wanted children. He adopted me because Mom wanted a child. He and I really argued a lot, usually about Mom and the way he made her feel. Don't get me wrong: he was a good father who took me places and did things with me. We just never really connected until toward the end of his life. He had diabetes, and because of gangrene his leg was amputated just below the knee. When the same thing began to happen to his other leg, he wouldn't let them take it off. That took a lot of courage. When he was in the hospital going through that, we became closer than we had ever been.

The relationship with my adoptive mother was clear: I was her son and she was my mother. She couldn't have loved me more if I had been biologically born to her. She took care of me that way, and I felt the same way about her.

At first, it was like: "Here are just two more people in my life. How much fun can I have? How much trouble will they let me get into?" As I grew up, I began to realize my adoptive mom did care about me. Unfortunately, as she became older, her health steadily declined and she had to start using a wheelchair. She moved to be closer to relatives. Finally, she was hospitalized because she had difficulty breathing, but they didn't think it was serious. Then I got a call that she had died unexpectedly. It was a real shocker. Before her death, we stayed in touch. We'd talk by telephone at least once a week. We were close right up to her death and her death really hurt me badly. I don't know any more to say; I felt like I was her child. Before that, I didn't know whose child I was. It was like there were a series of adults in my life--and they decided who was the boss at a particular time.

Joanne: It's kind of hard to describe the relationship I had with my adoptive parents. I always felt that maybe I was special because they picked me out--and they had a choice. They sometimes felt that I never accepted them. Of course, I was carrying around a lot of resentment—afraid of getting too close to them and of being rejected and abandoned again. They never could understand that. Maybe it came from seeing how fast my birth mother was taken from us.

When you interviewed me in 1983, I guess I hated my "birth" father because of the accident and all that had happened. I can't say that I love him now, but I can accept that he became mentally ill after my mother died. My anger toward him has softened over the years—especially after he died. He might have gotten me into this world, but my adoptive parents were the ones who stuck with me. They took me in and raised me when nobody else wanted me.

Understanding and forgiving their birth father for "giving them away" has been a difficult and lengthy process for Joanne and Maynard. Joanne believes that when he told them he intended to come back for them after he got his life straightened out he was sincere. As she says:

> He signed the adoption papers, but now that I'm older and know more, I realize he could hardly read or write. I truly believe in my heart that he did not know what he was signing. After that, he went from bad to worse when he found out his children were adopted and he couldn't get us back.

At their father's funeral, his youngest brother told the children: "You don't understand the months he cried himself to sleep once he realized what he had done."

Soon after his children were placed in the children's home and after he had signed documents freeing them for adoption, their birth father entered a psychiatric hospital for three years of treatment. With the perspective of an adult, Maynard says: "I now realize how tormented he was. He hated himself and everyone else. I can now look back and imagine what my father went through—three years of hell."

Maynard illustrates his point by showing me a painting his father made during the latter part of his hospitalization. He noted:

> This picture is powerful, because it shows the Biblical scene of the Pharaoh's daughter as she snatched Moses out of the alligator-infested water—a dangerous environment. That is how my father felt; he found healing by doing these paintings. He felt like he was casting me, my sister and my brother into the alligator-infested River Nile in a reed boat, but wonderful families found us and adopted us.

Tearing up, Joanne added her comments:

> We went to my (birth) dad's funeral. I had thought if I got a phone call that something had happened to him, it wouldn't bother me, but

when the call came it was like "Oh no!" He had health problems—sugar, heart problems and things like that. I don't think he ever took good care of himself. After our mother was killed, his life went to pieces. He said he would die alone, and he did, because his second marriage fell apart. Looking back, I could have changed that, but hindsight is 20/20. I had made contact with him before, but I didn't visit like I should have. He had pictures of my daughter, and I had taken her to see him. Maynard and I went to the memorial service. My father had pre-arranged to be cremated, and they were to bury his ashes at the foot of a nephew's grave. I said "No." If he was going to be cremated, and if it were possible, I wanted him to be buried with my mother. Relatives kept telling me it couldn't be done, but I checked and found that it could. So we made the arrangements. It brought a sense of peace and closure for Maynard and me.

Joanne and Maynard were the only two who attended the funeral. Benny was at that time living in the Midwest. Still, their attendance, in Maynard's words, "opened some doors with our birth relatives."

Reuniting as Young Adults

As Joanne, Maynard, Benny and I talked, I asked them about growing up in separate families: "How much and how often did you think about your birth siblings? Benny was the first to respond:

Benny: All the time. I didn't see them for 14 years, didn't understand why they were gone, and longed to see them again. My adoptive parents were told that I was not allowed to contact my siblings until we were all legally adults, and even then they would have to consent. That made me mad, but I gave up on it until I was 18. Since I'm the youngest, I knew we were all adults. Finally, I got us all together again, but when the three of us met as adults, it was like meeting strangers. Maynard and I had been really close as children, but I felt an awkward distance between us.

Joanne: I was 22 when all three of us got back together. It was exciting. Of course I knew better, but I was expecting them to be little bitty, and I found them to be taller than I was.

Maynard: Meeting my real brother and sister was weird. I didn't

139

know if they would accept me or if I would accept them after 14 years. It all happened real fast--in about three weeks. We had all been raised in different ways, but I could see how in some ways we were still the same. We even look alike—especially Joanne and I.

Benny: After the initial meeting, we all decided to make a trip to the mountains to see our aunts and uncles up there. It was the same thing. It was like meeting strangers.

Maynard recalled the experience with mixed emotions:

There was one thing that really bothered me. Some of the family asked, "Why did you come back?" Others, however, came up and just hugged me and hugged me and hugged me. That made me feel good, like I had missed 14 years of being a part of my real family. I felt cheated because of that. I was loved by my adoptive family, but there was something missing.

Even the connection among the three siblings frayed over time. They got together two or three times in the first six months, and tried to keep in contact, but what Maynard called "the distance and separation of life—doing different things"—broke the bonds. Maynard and Joanne stayed in touch, but Benny moved away and lost contact.

SECTION II

A QUARTER OF A CENTURY LATER
Joanne's Life from Age 24 to Mid-50s

En route to Joanne's place of employment, I drove by a wooded park in the center of town where we had first met 24 years earlier. I remembered her as an angry "victim" of the tragic death of her mother, puzzling over why her birth father "signed the papers" to give her away and why her extended birth family did not make room for her and her siblings in their homes.

Driving on, I arrived at her office building. We met in the conference room where she was employed as the administrative assistant. She anticipated my first question:

> So you want to know how I got to be an administrative assistant? I was a waitress for 25 years. Unmarried, I had a child at 36. I had been going with Tammy's father for 18 years, and when she turned 3, I said to myself, "Waiting tables isn't going to cut it." On the day I turned 40, still working as a waitress, I enrolled at the community college. Not quite a year later, I fell at work and the injury required knee surgery. I have never been able to work again in that type of position. With the aid of disability insurance, I attended college full time, and graduated in 2004 with honors. Many people told me, "You're too old to go to college. What are you thinking? You'll never finish. You'll never get the job you want." But I can think to myself now with a sense of pride, "Look at me. I've arrived."
>
> If I had attended college when I was younger, I wouldn't have fared as well. I graduated in May and located a part-time job by August. Last year my position became full-time. Tammy's 8, almost 9, and she will be a fourth grader this fall. At her age, I had to leave a known environment and move to a strange place, the children's home. Then, I was adopted, which changed my name. After my experience, I am determined that if anything happens to me, she will not go into "the system." I feel sure her daddy would raise her, but he's older. I've made provisions for my foster sister or my niece to raise her. Because of what happened to me, I think along these lines. Most people don't consider that you might be here one day but gone tomorrow. I have life insurance on myself, so she will be taken care of if I die while she's growing up. Family members— people she has known all her life, like my foster sister—will raise her. She's not going to live with strangers!

Not only has Joanne changed to meet Tammy's needs, Tammy has changed Joanne's life. An example is their church membership. Joanne's earlier lack of interest in church was perhaps related to her work schedule and her wondering how God had permitted the tragic death of her mother to occur. Although she allowed Tammy to attend church with her former foster sister, she remained adamant that she would not join a church that required baptism by immersion, declaring: "Mommy does not get her head under water." When Tammy decided to be baptized, she asked her mother to join her. They jointly prayed about this. "Two weeks later we were baptized together," Joanne smiled. Now they are active members, an experience Joanne reflected upon:.

> It's bizarre in a way, but since I have begun going to church, I can look at things in a different light. I told Maynard recently that I thank God we were adopted. My life is what it is today because of what happened. I am an achiever. When I set out to do something, I am determined to do it. If we had stayed in our hometown and not been adopted, we might be in jail by now, serving time in prison or living on the street.

After a pause to mentally sort through her thoughts, she resumed:

> I never leave Tammy without saying "I love you." I'm a firm believer that everything happens for a reason. I think that's why God brought me, Benny and Maynard together at this time in our lives. There's a reason, but I am not certain what the reason is yet. I have been very open with Tammy about my past. She really doesn't say a whole lot about it, but several times I have noticed her sitting and looking at the picture album of my early life. She'll look at an old photo, like one of my mother, and then ask questions like, "Momma, does this bother you?" She's very understanding, and she's bright. I think it's best to share my past with her, so she knows it's not some deep, dark secret that I'm embarrassed about. She's aware that she has my adopted family nearby, and she has my birth family living about an hour's drive away in the mountains. To her, they are all family, but sometimes, as a child, it's hard for her to understand the difference between birth family and adoptive family. Growing up was not a happy-go-lucky experience for me, but I want Tammy's life to be different.

Maynard's Life from Age 20 to Early 50s

Maynard and I met in the living room of his adopted mother's rural home—the same room where we met originally. His adoptive father, now deceased, had hand-built the home many years before. As Maynard greeted me, he re-introduced me to his adoptive mother. She was reclining in an easy chair with a walker nearby. On a bookcase

142

near her, she proudly displayed photos of Maynard and her biological daughter, along with several Bibles and religious books.

Hearing his mother's voice once again brought to my memory an urgent telephone call I had received from her several years before. She pleaded, "Maynard is in jail charged with possession of drugs. Will you help him?"

I contacted his attorney and probation officer, sent a letter recommending rehabilitative treatment and parole, and included a copy of Maynard's chapter from *Whose Child Am I?* Along with a testimonial from his minister, this information helped convince the judge to order Maynard to participate in a rehabilitation program rather than remanding him to prison. Now the "table has turned," Maynard as a middle-aged person is helping to take care of his adoptive mother.

In 1983, Maynard told about graduating from high school, and completing courses at a nearby technical college, but he was not sure what occupation to pursue. He was working with a carpenter. Foremost on his mind was the task of mentally sorting through the momentous events of his life: his birth mother's sudden death, several foster home placements, his adoption, and his recent reunion with his natural family. He wanted his life story to help others understand how frightening new families and new places are to children moved away from their known environments--often abruptly and without warning. "It was like 'Put your things in a paper bag, let's go!'" he remembered.

A quarter of a century later, he had his own home repair business. I was curious to learn in what other ways his life had changed since our original meeting 25 years ago. Had his difficulties with the criminal justice system changed the inner "trusting" nature of Maynard? Such questions raced through my mind as we began the interview.

> What's different now about my life and my feelings about adoption from what I told you 24 years ago? Some things are about the same and some are different. You know, of course, about my arrest, my time in jail, and later my parole. After that, things went pretty good until about 2000, when, still hanging around with some of the guys I got in trouble with the first time, I got convicted of something I didn't do. That put a stab in my heart and life. I had to shut my business down while I went into a court-ordered, year-long process

143

of treatment and rehabilitation. I was going backwards—into the mold of not trusting anybody.

The judge gave me a choice of going to a 12-month-long Christian rehab program in a group home or going to prison for 15 years; I choose the treatment program. In that year, I learned a lot about myself. I realized I had to face a lot of things I had not dealt with as a child. I have learned that forgiveness is the greatest key in life. If you don't forgive, you don't have a release in God's eyes, and it's God's eyes that really count anyway. This is the biggest part of life. I had to learn to forgive my father, and forgive even people whose names I have forgotten--I had to forgive and release. Once I had done that, there was a sense of peace and contentment with life that I had never had before. It was a spiritual and emotional experience.

On a day-to-day basis, I don't have much financial security even at this point, but it doesn't bother me. I've never had that in my life anyway. For most people, having a 401(k) is an automatic thing, but it doesn't bother me because God has taken care of me all through my life. I came back here to live and rebuild my home repair business. People were pleased with my work. I picked up the majority of my old customers again, and they recommended me to others.

If you haven't gone through being adopted as an older child, you would probably have trouble understanding the concept. You can't act as if it didn't happen. Part of me wants to shut it off, not remember it, and let it go, but I can't do that. I haven't met my expectations in life, but I don't even know what some of them are yet.

Surely children's homes, orphanages and foster homes have changed somewhat, but I experienced some mean, hateful people in those environments. Some of them were not there to help children; they were doing it just to make a living. As a child you see that and understand it. The good part is that I have developed a capability to read people. I can instantly know (*snaps his fingers*) if they have evil or good in their hearts. I have that capability. You really learn things like that from going through difficult childhood situations.

I ended up in a wonderful adoptive home, but there was always the "what if. . . what could have been." Even now, I constantly have

144

to keep in check letting my mind wonder how things could have happened. The reality of my childhood was my imaginary play world. That's how I checked out and got away, so that all the things that happened to me didn't drive me crazy. It's hard to explain how I felt and how spiritual experiences affected me. It has been an interesting walk through life.

I usually go up to Joanne's in the summer to be with her and her daughter, Tammy. That's a cool part of my life at this point. When I travel up there, Joanne, Tammy and I usually drive into the mountains to see our birth relatives. I'm always struck by how much we look and act alike, but their perspective of me is how I was back then. Also, some of them are in denial for not taking care of us after our mother was killed, and they have not forgiven themselves.

Over an early morning breakfast interview, Maynard filled in some gaps on the lifelong effects of his adoption.

Adoption changed my life, both positively and negatively. For example, I won't get any inheritance from either my natural or my adoptive family. My natural father and my grandfather owned a nice little piece of land in the mountains near my hometown. My sister, brother, and I lost all inheritance rights to it when my father signed the adoption papers. That really hurts. I would love to have some of that property. My adoptive family already had a daughter born to them. I am not at the same level of family ownership as she is. About a year before she died, Mom told me she and Dad had decided 20 years ago, when I was in jail, to take me out of their will. That's basically why I lost my inheritance, but it's also part of the adoption process—that's how it works.

In my eyes, it's not just property or money, it's a sense of belonging, of feeling included—that's the loss factor. It will always be that way.

The positive side is that I would have never become the person I am if I had not been adopted. Instead, I would likely be in prison now. There's no doubt in my mind about that.

Yes, I went through hell, but my faith in God helped me get through tough times. Oh yeah, forgiveness is the key to everything—all of

145

> this—even to the point of forgiving my father for not taking good care of me and forgiving my brother and sister for leaving me at the orphanage. Those two don't have a clue that I had to forgive them for those things. It wasn't something they consciously did and could control, but from a child's (memory) perspective, they left me at the orphanage and didn't even say bye.

As he struggles to maintain his composure, Maynard continues:

> You've asked if I have changed in the past 25 years. Yes, in that aspect, I would say, "Big Time." As a child, I blamed my natural dad for my being in the orphanage. I hated him so much that I wished he would die. I have never expressed that to anybody. The only way you can get through it and have self-confidence in life is to forgive. A lot of forgiveness is forgetting, not amnesia forgetting, but choosing to forget.

As we talked, I could tell that Maynard has achieved some inner peace and purpose through his roles as a son, brother and uncle.

Benny's Life from Age 19 to Late 40s: Rescue and Gradual Recovery

Joanne called in early January saying that she and Maynard had traveled to the Midwest over the Christmas holiday to bring Benny back to the South, where they were born. Since Benny was temporarily living with her and her daughter, Joanne wondered if I might be interested in interviewing him for another perspective on how adoption had changed their lives. As she explained:

> You could consider it 38 years since Maynard, Benny and I have lived close to one another. We are still trying to know each other— our personalities and our ways. Maynard called me earlier this evening to ask how things were going with Benny, and I told him we fight one day and the next we are the best of buddies.

A week later, on my way to interview Benny at Joanne's home, I had breakfast with Maynard to clarify information he had shared. After we had finished our discussion of his adoption story, I asked about Benny's return. Maynard said Benny had gone through a difficult divorce and had gotten involved in drugs. This news had led Maynard and Joanne to fear for his physical safety and mental health, and they had convinced him to come to live near them. Maynard added details:

> Benny cleaned himself up, and called three days after Christmas to say that he was ready to come back. Joanne telephoned me on New Year's Eve saying, "We're going to get him." Five days later we were on our way. We took him out of hell, and brought him home. What do I mean by hell? Have you ever been in somebody's home in the daytime, and it crawls? That's where Benny was living. I'm talking about mice, rodents, snakes, and God only knows what else. It crawled! We loaded a 14-foot trailer, and drove back. That was a three-day adventure. We got him back where he will have a chance to start all over again. He began a construction job yesterday. He'll have to save some money and get his driver's license and things like that before he can get out on his own. He's been through a lot. He also lost his adoptive mother in the last year. Once she died, he didn't have anybody in life. That's one of the reasons we needed to get him back home. Here he will have us.

When I arrived at Joanne's home for my appointment with Benny, Joanne and her daughter, Tammy, welcomed me and introduced us. Picking up a copy of my 1985 book, *Whose Child Am I?*, Joanne confessed to Benny, "I had a hard time getting through Maynard's story. I was a basket case for two days. If anyone looked at me, I just cried." With her car keys in one hand and Bible in the other, she declared, "We'll be gone for a little over an hour." Noticing that Benny looked a bit uptight, she added, "I got emotional when I did my interviews, too—especially the last one."

As she opened the front door to leave with Tammy for a Wednesday night prayer service, she joked, "We'll leave now, and give you two some privacy," then added, "Don't let him bad-mouth me, John."

Like Joanne and Maynard, Benny was likeable, candid, insightful and thoughtful as he carefully answered questions.

> What is my relationship like now with my sister and brother? After we initially met as adults, we couldn't see each other often because we lived a pretty good distance apart. Then I moved to the Midwest, and

we were even further away from each other. Now that I'm back here, I can see us making up for lost time. This is something we probably should have been doing since I was 18, but it didn't seem to work out.

I don't know what would have happened if the two of them had not come to rescue me. They knew what was going on in my life, and that's why they kept trying to find me. They wanted to get me out of that situation, but I was too stubborn and hardheaded to listen. It was like, "If I'm going down, I'm going to go down by myself and not take anybody with me." It goes back, I guess, to being in and out of a lot of foster homes. It was no big deal to be pulled out of the ones I didn't like, but I liked some foster parents and didn't want to leave their care. In one instance, I was so attached to a foster family I had to be dragged down the steps into the social worker's car. Those foster people were nice to me; they cared about me; and when the social worker said I couldn't stay there, I lost it.

Why couldn't I stay there? I was so young that I can't remember all the reasons, but I felt for the first time, since my real mother's death, that I was really cared about, and for the first time I began to care about somebody else. One night, these foster parents went out to dinner, and got a babysitter. I was probably 6 or 7, and I literally cried; I bawled. I was so afraid they would not come back, I would not go to bed. The babysitter finally had to call and get the foster parents to come home early. It seemed to me that anytime I let myself care about someone, they would die or go away. I got to the point where I wouldn't let that happen. I would not let myself care about anybody.

I felt a lot of love and security from my adoptive parents, but it took me three years before I fully let down my fear of being hurt and let myself truly care about them. That fear of close relationships carried over to my adult life. I was 32 before I let anybody else come into my life. I'm not making excuses, but that's why it hit me when my ex-wife did what she did. She took off and left me.

What are my dreams for the rest of my life? I'm in my 40s. I'm looking forward to watching Tammy grow up. That's something I missed being halfway across the country. I am just getting back to where I like myself again. A couple of times, I've given up. I didn't care if there was a future or not. The fact that Joanne and Maynard care about me encourages me to care about myself. For now, I want to get back on my feet. I've got a job, and maybe I can again start working as a mechanic—a field I was trained in. I want to get my own place and live a simple life. I've always dreamed of marrying and having a child of my own. I'm not giving up on that dream, but I'm not putting it in my scheduled plans either.

Conclusion

All three agree that their adoptions had changed their lives in positive ways. Calling herself a "hellion" and a "heathen," Joanne reiterated her adoptive parents were "good people," who also adopted and fostered other children. Benny said his adoption was "the best thing for me," and characterized his relationship with his adoptive mother as: "I was her son. She was my mother." Maynard agreed that his adoption was also an important part of his life. He added: "My sister, my brother, and I also had to heal from the difficult times in our childhood. It's taken us years to do so."

Maynard offered a perspective on how families in crisis, such as his was after the sudden death of his mother, might have opportunities to stay together for intensive counseling and decision-making before children were placed out of their natural family systems. His idea is similar to the "family clarification" process developed by the late Dr. Alan Keith-Lucas, Alumni Distinguished Professor Emeritus and his colleagues at the University of North Carolina at Chapel Hill (UNC-CH). The central idea is that in situations like theirs, consideration should be given to placing entire family units together in well-supervised and supported residential environments, where. intensive, time-limited, "family-clarification" work can help families understand and decide what is in the best long-term interest of their children. The optimum result is that families positively change and resume full care for their children. Failing that, families might decide, or the courts might decide for them, to release the children for adoption so that other families could take on this responsibility. Maynard elaborates:

Note: As indicated in the beginning of this chapter, Benny was not initially interviewed until 25 years after Joanne and Maynard were first interviewed. The information he shared, however, adds important perspectives to their family story.

At the children's home, I was in an institution with over a hundred kids who were also emotionally messed up. We hated where we were, and I even hated myself. That way of treating children can be changed; that way of approaching adoption can be changed. It took 20 years, but my natural father was finally healed, restored and forgiven. He forgave himself, and he became a totally different person—more like the man that I knew before the accident. He had to go through his three years in a mental institution. Looking back to the time before his mental health deteriorated, what would have happened if Joanne, Benny and I could have stayed together—with him—in a safe, supervised and protected place that provided healing for all of us? I'm not arguing against adoption; my adoption was one of the best things that happened in my life. However, if our birth family had gone through that kind of healing, and then we children had been put into adoptive homes, it would have been better for our birth father and for us, and easier on our adoptive families.

Supporting One Another as Mature Adults

Clearly, Maynard and his siblings are keenly aware that their commitment to supporting each other is central to their present and future lives. They have reunited and without hesitation support and sustain one another. After Maynard's adoptive mother died, there was a question about where he might live. Joanne instinctively said, "He can come up here so that the three of us can look after one another."

Postscript I
Lunch with Joanne, Tammy, Maynard and Benny

The process of contacting participants, conducting and transcribing interviews, analyzing data, and writing this manuscript took several years. During the final stages of completing this book, I traveled several times to meet with most of the participants to go over their adoption stories.

On one occasion, when I met with Joanne, Tammy accompanied her. I was struck by the young woman's politeness and poise when she excitedly talked about her acting, dancing and singing training and her

150

participation in an upcoming production of "The Sound of Music." Joanne beamed, and I thought to myself: "Joanne has accomplished her major goal, raising her daughter in a stable, loving and supportive environment—and being sure that Tammy does not have to endure a traumatic, uncertain childhood."

Soon Benny and Maynard arrived and joined us for lunch and conversation. Joanne spoke first:

> With the economic recession, I've been unemployed for almost two years, and I've had to pick up whatever work I can. Right now, I take care of a little 85-year-old lady in the mornings. I've been sitting with her since the end of June, and now she has a special place in my heart. I'm not sure if I've told you before, but I've been chronically depressed for years. Recently, I have seen a counselor who believes this goes back to my mother's sudden and tragic death and all the "mess" that followed. Don't get me wrong. God has blessed me with many good things—like Tammy, my friends, my brothers and other family. Still, what I went through as a child continues to haunt me.

Joanne took a carefully wrapped package from her purse and continued.

> I have some photos from past years that we might enjoy looking at and talking about. Here's a picture of my adopted parents and here's one of all of us when we were kids and living with our (birth) parents. Everybody says my (birth) mom and I favor each other.

Looking at another photo, Benny grinned at Maynard:

> That's your convertible. You loved that car. After we got back together [as young adults], you would come and visit me, and we'd cruise in that car. That was fun!

It was obvious that they were enjoying themselves--reminiscing about earlier times, and joking with one another.

Benny brought the conversation back to my adoption book.

> I'm very interested in your book. I'm hoping it's going to do some good things to help people know how the adoption system works, and how it's not always right. As I told you when you first interviewed

me, the three of us were not even allowed to communicate with one another for 14 years. For me, that was from age 4 to 18. We weren't allowed the opportunity to grow up knowing one another. That's just not right. It made it hard for us as adults to have close relationships, because we had to learn each other's ways again. We had to learn to trust and to look after each other. I drifted away from Joanne and Maynard, and I was sinking further and further into trouble. There's no telling where I would be if they hadn't rescued me. When they came to get me we weren't that close. Now I've got my sister and brother close by if I need somebody to talk to. We now live in the same town, so we see each other more often and we talk more.

They were joking with each other as we ended the conversation. Smiling and teasing her brothers Joanne said, "Now they aggravate me to death!"

More quietly, but enthusiastically, Maynard offered these comments.

After my adopted mother's death a couple of years ago, I began to realize how crazy the adoption system is for older children. When we are no longer children and grow older, who is our family? My brother, sister and I were cut out of any inheritance on the birth side of our family when our father signed those adoption papers. It's not just about property--it's about belonging and really feeling a part of our birth family. We can go and visit our birth aunts, uncles and cousins, but we didn't grow up with them--we're like guests that come to visit. Now that both of the people who adopted me (my adopted mother and father) have passed away, where do I fit in with my adoptive family? Thank goodness Joanne, Benny and I have each other now, and we can all enjoy watching Tammy grow up.

Postscript II
A Christmas Telephone Call

About mid-morning the day after Christmas. I was surprised and pleased to receive a telephone call from Joanne, Maynard and Benny. Joanne began the conversation by wishing me and my family a Merry

Christmas. Then she added:

> For Maynard, Benny and me, this is the first Christmas that we have been together since we were children. We need each other now, and it's wonderful that we live close enough to celebrate Christmas and other special days together—and that we can help each other all year long.

Joanne handed the telephone to Benny, who said:

> Thanks again for doing another adoption book and telling my story in it. Please emphasize that older adopted brothers and sisters should not be separated at adoption without making sure that they can stay in touch with one another as they grow up.

Maynard was then given the phone and after a Christmas greeting, he remarked:

> We've known each other for a long time now. Thanks for your interest over the years in older-child adoptions. Please share my idea of having supervised and protected places where whole families can live together after they go through a tragedy like we did--when our mother was suddenly killed. Such places can be places of healing and forgiveness when they have good counselors and staff to help every member of the family—both adults and children.
>
> I'm glad I decided to move close to Joanne, Tammy and Benny. Now we can look after each other. I need to make a new start in life, and being near them and having their support, I believe I can.

CHAPTER SEVEN

Adopted at age 7

Birth, Adoptive and Adult Family Structures

Birth Family: Lee was the youngest of a large family of children whose father drank heavily and abused their mother. Although she died before he was 6 years old, Lee has very loving memories of their mother. After her death, he and his siblings were moved about in the public foster care system.

The sisters were the first to be returned to the birth family. The boys were first placed in a community group home. Lee was adopted when he was 7 ½, and the other brothers eventually returned to their birth family.

Adoptive Family: The couple who adopted Lee had a biological son, and the two boys developed a close relationship that continues into their adult years. Lee was also quite attached to his adoptive father.

Adult Family: Lee and his wife Betty have one son, a daughter-in-law. and several grandchildren.

LEE

Lee is a man of few words, but his thoughts and advice can guide readers to a more thoughtful understanding of older child adoptions. For example, he believes that such adoptions are like marriages in that both children and adoptive parents must be free to choose one another.

L ee is a philosopher. He neither looks nor speaks like some more stereotypical philosophers I knew in my college-going or college-teaching days. With his long hair pulled back into a rubber band and a baseball cap covering his head, he looks like a man most comfortable in the mountains. Still, he is a "wisdom thinker," who gets to the heart of the matter. What he has to say about older-child adoptions is profound.

When I first met him, Lee had lost his job in a mountain industry during an economic recession and moved his family to another town hoping to find employment. He and his wife, Betty, had already sold many of their furnishings, and were invited by friends to move into the unfinished basement of their home. Betty had used colorful bed sheets to tastefully partition the space into rooms, and also "spruced up" used furniture with attractive pillows and throws. With her creativity, this space became a home that radiated warmth and comfort. As we talked, she served iced tea and cookies, and I felt comfortable and welcomed.

During the interview, I asked Lee how satisfying his life was. With no hesitation he reached over, patted Betty's arm and said, "Couldn't be better."

When their son came and sat comfortably on his father's lap, Lee tenderly held the boy in his arms. He wants to be sure that his son never doubts the love and concern that his parents have for him. The boy is a responsive, intelligent fifth grader, who the year before had attended a special summer program for gifted children in their community. I could sense the love these three people share. When I called him for an appointment, Lee had told me he would be glad to see me, but warned they "didn't have much." I left their home feeling they had a great deal.

Lee remembered that after his mother's death early in his life, he had longed for her love and care as he was moved from place to place prior to adoption. He was reared for a period of time in the children's home, then adopted at age 7 as part of the agency's older-child adoption project.

Like the others in this book, Lee is devoted to his family, and has a honed sensitivity for understanding other people's feelings and motivations. He experienced violence and chaos in childhood, but he is neither cynical nor bitter. He fervently maintains that older adopted children are far more capable of choosing adoptive families than social workers or prospective parents believe. Lee is an excellent guide to help the uninitiated understand what being adopted as an older child entails.

SECTION I

INITIAL INTERVIEW: LEE AGE 28

Childhood and Early Adulthood

Adopted when he was 7, Lee remembers little of his life with his birth family, other than the fact that he has brothers and sisters. "Our mother died when I was about 4 or 5," he recalls, "and we were all shipped out [placed together in a small group home for children]."

Betty explained that the group home was near the children's hometown. Soon after Lee and his siblings were placed in the group home, his sister returned to their (birth) family. As he put it: "Our kinfolks didn't want us boys—they wanted the girls."

Lee and his brothers then moved to the children's home, where Lee became part of the older child adoption project. He was adopted, but for some unknown reasons, his brothers returned to the birth family.

When Lee left the Home to go with his adoptive family, his brothers were there for him to tell good-bye, but his sisters were already gone.

In response to Betty's comment that such a leave-taking must have been difficult for all the brothers, who were not yet teenagers, Lee was philosophical: "You don't have a choice. You do the best you can."

Betty agreed:

> Look at the changes an older adopted child goes through. When they are old enough to know what's going on, they lose their blood parents. Lee's adoption was good because he got a great family, but he had to leave his brothers and sisters behind and didn't know what had really happened to his blood parents.

Turning to her husband, she continued:

> Lee, in your mind, you're wanting to be happy, but how can a little boy be happy with such changes going on? It's hard to keep a large number of children together, but they could have let you visit and stay in touch with one another. You came out really well.

Now focused on his early life with his birth parents, Lee mused:

> We got broke up because my daddy was sort of a drunk.

> When he would come in drunk, Momma would hide us. She was always the one that took care of us, and she did the best she could. I know she gave me good love and attention, because of that I didn't want to forget her. I carried her picture around in my wallet. She was a very, very good person. It seemed like every night, my father would come walking through the door, put his foot through the black and white TV, and grab Momma and throw her around like a rag doll. We all sat there watching, scared. More than once, things got so bad that my oldest sister would grab me and throw me out of a bedroom

window. Then everybody climbed out. Finally, my mom died. Then, my daddy went to jail, and he died, I believe, shortly after that.

Betty pointed out that Lee was lucky that his adoptive mother was not threatened by his love and admiration for his birth mother. Lee looked lovingly at Betty and their son, sleeping in his arms and said:

I love Betty to death. I love that boy to death, too. Ain't no doubt about that. I never had that kind of love and caring when I was a child. When you don't have it, the loving and caring, it takes awhile to "put it back."

Turning his attention to the time he spent at the children's home before his adoption, he noted:

Living in a children's home as a little boy is not a good thing. Trust me it is not a good thing. I didn't know much about adoptions. I just stayed in a room there with a half dozen others, and everybody just talked back and forth, feeling scared and wondering who was going to go next. They tried me in two or three [prospective adoptive] homes to see if I'd like them. I stayed in each place for two or three weeks—maybe a month. It's just hard to describe how a little kid feels, going from one place to another. Every family seemed to want you to live with them, but I wanted to wait until the right family came along. Do I remember any of those places? Just one, where their birth son gave me an old black Bible. I was so close to staying there, because I liked him a lot. The daddy was a policeman, who kept his gun on the table next to his bed, and somehow that didn't click quite right for me.

Pointing out that Lee owns guns now and loves to hunt, Betty suggested that his memories of the violence in his birth home most probably were the source of his fear of guns as a little boy.

Lee continued:

How did I know when the right family came along? When I first met my adoptive parents, I remember they picked me up and took me to the amusement park. I guess I just fell right in with them, for no reason, I don't reckon. I used to joke and tell everybody that Momma threatened to whip me if I wouldn't stay. She still tells everybody that.

How long did it take before I felt kind of at home there? For years I had a problem calling my adoptive mother "Momma." I don't know why, but I just didn't feel like she was. I just figured I was staying there because they wanted me to. It wasn't too long ago that I first called her Momma—not long before I got married.

From the beginning, I called Daddy "Daddy." I guess it was because my real Daddy didn't mean a whole lot to me, but the new one did.

Betty noted that Lee had mentioned that he could not "just drop" memories of his birth mother, but his adoptive family became "just like they're blood kin. It just took awhile for him. . . ." As Lee put it, "I fell right into my adoptive home."

The family's acceptance of Lee included his adoptive brother, a "birth child" two years older and the extended family. He therefore had no problem changing his last name, and felt completely accepted, "even a little more than some of them who are blood kin."

According to Betty, Lee is naturally a shy individual, a point that Lee affirmed when he discussed reconnecting with his birth siblings. "Momma said that if I ever wanted to find any of my real brothers or sisters, all I had to do was ask," he remembered, "but I never have. I'm planning on looking them up as soon as . . . it takes money to do anything. I'm going to have to get the money to go to the children's home and find out exactly where they are, how old they were when they left, and get their names and everything."

Despite his diffidence, Lee had no problem fitting in at school. Indeed he found that being adopted was a plus in some instances. "One boy I ran around with in high school told everybody that he was adopted because I was," he said. "He thought it made him some kind of hero."

Reiterating that the closeness with his adoptive family continues, Lee pointed out that two weeks before he had gone to visit his adoptive family, taking pictures and spending the night. Lee, in fact, is eager to return to the mountains to live, but faces difficulty finding employment. "All I would need to return is just to get us a place to live and go back to work there. I'd be set for life."

The same strong feelings apply to his son, whom Betty smilingly insists he "spoils rotten." Lee is open and enthusiastic about his feelings: "You can't find a better one. I feel a lot closer to him than most parents do to their kids. You see people who just don't watch after their kids or do anything for them. They just let them run wild."

In trying to explain Lee's closeness to their son and willingness to help "especially at night," Betty suggested her husband is "more loving than most men," whom she saw as "hiding their feelings."

Maybe it's because he's adopted," she reflected, "but he is more gentle and caring. He's a good husband and a good father, and I wouldn't trade him for anyone."

Again, Lee was adamant in his opinion that "there's nothing like a momma and daddy," and described successful adoptions of older children as like a marriage:

> That's about as close as I can get. You just got to pick them out. Both parties have got to have the freedom to choose and to feel good about their choice for it to work. I'm not much on advice; but I knew when I met my adopted family that we clicked. I knew that it would work out okay.

When Betty characterized her husband as "being able to understand people before he really gets to know them," she noted his sensitivity might well have been developed when he was a child as a means of self-protection.

Lee was quick to point out that his positive assessments of personalities included the Director of Social Work of the children's home (Cliff Sanford, Chapter 3), whom he characterized as "like a daddy, really— for a long time." He then explained:

> Every month or so—something like that—he'd come by 'cause

Momma would send him my schoolwork for him to see how I was doing. He'd also check to see if I still wanted to be adopted before the official thing went through. You always knew that he was going to come. If something did happen, he was going to take you away. We got Christmas cards from him, and we wrote back and forth for years.

I visited again with Lee, Betty, and their son some months after the initial interview. They had moved from the basement apartment into a small house. Betty had decorated their home beautifully for Christmas, and Lee had hung trophies of mounted deer heads from his hunting trips—one with a bright red bow around the antlers. As we talked, Lee combined sensitivity about the feelings of other people with the physical toughness of an outdoors man who can hike and hunt all day over rugged mountain terrain. He pulled a Bible from a bookshelf. Years ago, when he was visiting prospective adoptive families, a policeman's son had given it to him. Holding the Bible in his hands, Lee reiterated with great emphasis his opinion: "Don't make a child go live with a family unless the child fits right in with them. When things fit, it can be wonderful, but when they don't, it can be a living hell."

SECTION II

LEE'S STORY AT AGE 57: ABOUT 50 YEARS AFTER HIS ADOPTION

I visited Lee and Betty the week before their 33rd wedding anniversary. Lee was still working at the same plant and hunting deer. He pointed out he had "been adopted for about 50 years now," and noted he and Betty had an 8-year-old grandson and that his adoptive father had died. The couple spoke animatedly about how much they enjoyed camping with their son and his family, and Lee added emphatically, "I also love working." Then he switched gears to discuss the reason for the interview.

I feel the same way about my adoption experience as I did when I interviewed with you for your first book. Nothing I will share has changed.

163

Like I said, I was blessed with great adoptive parents. Since my adoptive daddy has died, I try to see my adoptive mother as often as I can. The way the gas prices are now, I can't afford to go there and back as often as I want, but I call her every weekend. We see my adoptive aunts and uncles about every time we go up there. I think we see the family more as we've gotten older. I call them a lot. I don't know any of my birth family aunts and uncles, and I believe my (birth) grandparents are dead.

Recalling how deeply he was affected by his adoptive father's death, Lee explained that his adoptive mother was in failing health, and that his adoptive brother (their birth son) lived with her to be of assistance. The victim of three heart attacks himself, Lee had undergone quadruple bypass surgery, but proudly pointed out he had been back at work for four years and was "doing fine."

Then the couple turned the conversation to their son, Lee proudly showing a framed photograph. Taking turns, they described him as easily fitting in with the adoptive family, and a hard worker, who, in Lee's words. "gets along well with people, and can do or fix almost anything. . . .There ain't nothing that boy can't do. He works hard like I do, and he works for the same company I do."

Years previously, the couple had contacted the children's home to get information that might allow them to contact Lee's birth siblings, and were given the names and all available information. Lee and Betty's attempts have been unsuccessful. Even notes they left in the siblings' files elicited no response.

The lack of connection clearly haunted Lee:

My adoption comes up to my mind every day. I think and dream about people that I may never see again—especially my sisters and brothers. I would definitely suggest brothers and sisters stay in contact with each other. I tried, but they are lost to me. I carried that picture of my real momma forever—until it was about gone, but I never had a picture of my brothers and sisters. It's hard to stay in touch with them without pictures--or names and addresses.

164

Betty pointed out that in addition to the emotional issues that arise, health information also is affected. Never a smoker and a man who lived a healthy lifestyle including walking regularly, Lee was surprised by the heart attacks. Betty believes the condition might have been hereditary. As she explained:

> It would definitely be helpful to know Lee's inherited health risks. I can see why a child's privacy might need to be protected, but when you're a grown man or woman, why would they not allow you to have information about your birth family? It doesn't make any sense. The only thing that might happen is that you might go to see your family and they may not want to see you. That's fine—you just have to learn to live with it. If they do want to see you, that's getting a family back together. With all he's been through as a child, Lee could've gone either way. He could've been like his real daddy or his real mom. But he chose to be like his real mom and his adoptive parents. Lee's a good man.

Lee was quick to place credit where he felt it was due:

> I think I turned out as well as I did because of one person: my adoptive daddy. He put the wheels on me, and made me work hard. By the way he lived, he put a heart in me. Just thinking about that man passing away, brings tears to my eyes. He was the person I wanted to be my daddy. Even though he's dead, I still love him. We got along great, and that's it. I can tell who's phony and who's real. I picked the right adoptive family. And I picked the right wife too, no doubt about that.

Betty grinned, "Oh, I like that. It's not blood that counts. Your adoptive daddy was your father."

Agreeing, Lee again reiterated his points about the importance of letting children choose their adoptive families. Then he and his wife turned their attention to their current lives. Lee described his three major goals as: "keeping her—my wife, loving my family, and working as long as I can."

When Betty reminded him they also hoped for more grandchildren, they warmly described their love for their daughter-in-law and their eager anticipation of the imminent birth of a granddaughter. Betty concluded: "Our son and his wife know if they need anything, no matter what it is, they can holler at us and we're there."

When Lee added, "Whatever he needs, he can call me. There's nothing I wouldn't do for that boy," Betty pointed out that it was his custom to never leave a member of the family without saying "I love you." And, with obvious pride she added: "He's always done that. Our son is the same way. Even though they are men, they are not ashamed to say they love each other."

Their exchange continued as our meeting drew to a close.

> **Lee**: I want him to know he has a daddy.

> **Betty**: You want him to know there's always someone there for him.

> **Lee**: I always will be. Always have been.

As I was leaving, Betty came over to Lee's chair, and gave him a hug. Joking with Betty, Lee looked up at her and said, "I am just a lonely child." Betty joked back at Lee, "You're spoiled rotten. I know that."

Walking to my car I thought to myself, many things have changed for Lee and Betty during the past 25 years since I last visited them, but I could still sense the love that Lee and his wife have for one another. They are both tender, caring, loving people. I felt honored to spend time with them again.

CHAPTER EIGHT

Ages at adoption: Dana, 7; and Jason, 8

Birth and Adoptive Family Structures

Birth Family: A full-time homemaker facing terminal cancer, Dana and Jason's mother was deeply concerned about what the future held for her six sons and one daughter. Before she died in her early 30s, she arranged for her youngest child, only a year old, to be given to a family she knew and trusted so that he would not be adopted. Her oldest child, 16 when his mother died, stayed at home with their father, a low-wage worker in a manufacturing plant. The next two sons were placed in the children's home, but never adopted. Two of her other children, Jason, 7, and Dana, 5, also went to the children's home, and they were adopted by "strangers" and moved into "unaccustomed earth" environments.

Adoptive Families: The Clarks, who adopted Jason, had no other children. The Bartons had two older biological daughters, who were in college when Dana moved into their home. The next-to-the-youngest child, age four when his mother died, was placed in a foster home, but declined to be adopted by his foster parents when they expressed interest.

DANA AND JASON

Dana and Jason struggled with the following
questions: Who is my real family? Is it my
adoptive family, my birth family or a mix of both?

SECTION I

INITIAL INTERVIEW: DANA 25 AND JASON 27

Reflections from Childhood to Early Adulthood

When their mother died, Dana's and Jason's family dissolved. Their memories of their birth family were quite similar, but I heard from them markedly different stories about their adoption experiences. As Jason explained:

> My adoption went smoothly. I was adopted by the Clarks at age 8 and became their son. Dana, however, had a stormy adoption experience. She was placed for adoption at age 6, but her adoptive parents took her back to live on the children's home campus when she was 12.

To make Dana and Jason's adoption stories easier to read and to avoid repetition, I pretended that they were initially interviewed together in 1983. At the end of the chapter, I also pretended they met with me at Dana's farm. In fact, they were interviewed separately, and their verbatim responses were spliced together, using additional words and sentences only for transition and clarity. Jason and Dana read the revised manuscript and agreed that it maintained the accuracy of their individual statements.

On the afternoon of our meeting, I drove slowly along a street of attractive but modest homes. I spotted the house matching Dana's description and noticed a slender, attractive young woman sitting on the front porch waiting for me. Her 5-year-old daughter was playing nearby. As I started to park on the street, Dana waved and motioned for me to park in her driveway. Her welcoming words and cheerful smile surprised me. I had been initially unprepared for her--expecting someone with an angry "chip-on-her shoulder" type of personality. Instead, I found her to be an open, humble person with insightful observations. As we sat on the porch waiting for Jason, Dana spoke quite sincerely.

> I'm glad it worked out that you are interviewing me. I feel the experience I went through should be told. I believe it will help somebody else in the same situation. Although my [birth] family all lived together in a very small, run-down, three-room house, I can remember some happy times. Then, things just fell apart.

When a car drove up and parked behind mine, I knew this had to be Jason. He had an "All-American" appearance. He greeted me with a firm handshake, pulled up a chair and began talking with us. I found him to be a responsible adult: a proud husband and father, a college graduate, a guidance counselor and coach in a private, church-sponsored high school, and a person who is actively involved in his church and community.

As brother and sister, Dana and Jason appeared to enjoy bragging about each other. They also discussed the irony that our interview was on Dana's front porch, where they had reconciled, after 14 years of separation. Dana told about Jason's athletic accomplishments as an outstanding high school and college baseball catcher and noted how he had become a successful coach and teacher. Jason seemed to appreciate her comments, but he did not come across as a boastful, "look how great I am" kind of person. In fact, I discovered him to be the opposite—a person who thinks of the needs of others and who is grateful for the opportunities life has afforded him.

As we talked about Jason's background, he shared a photo-scrapbook of

170

his life. It was obvious that he had invested lots of time and energy in this project, and I complimented him on how comprehensive and well organized it was. He said it meant a great deal to him because it "tied all his life together," from his birth to his current life with his wife and young child. As he turned the pages of his scrapbook, he began to fill in the details of his early life.

> With nine people living in just three rooms, all of us brothers slept in one bed. As an adult, I appreciate the comforts of a middle-class lifestyle more than most, and I also appreciate the struggle our [birth] parents had just to keep us going. Our mother didn't work outside the home, and our father worked as a laborer. He didn't make much money, but he did make enough to provide food for the family.

Leaning forward slightly, and dropping his voice, he continued:

> It's kind of scary looking back at what we went through. I was only 7 when our mother died—so I remember very few details. Since we had no plumbing, we used an outhouse and took baths in a big, tin tub. At Christmas, the Salvation Army would come around. We'd get to select a gift or two for our mother and father and our parents would pick out toys for us. In short, we were poor, but it's not some-thing I'm ashamed of—I'm kind of glad I experienced it. In some ways it helped us to be creative. For example, we didn't have a sled when it snowed, but we would find an old car hood or something like that and go sleigh-riding. We learned to be self-reliant.

A Tragic Year—Their Mother Dies

At once nostalgic and honest, Dana agreed:

> Yes, we were a poor but close-knit family. All that changed after mother got sick. I was only 5 years old during the last six months of her life, but I can remember the pain she suffered and hearing her cry out in agony. As long as she could, she took good care of us. Being so young, I didn't know what it was all about when she died. I just knew my mother wasn't there anymore. It was very hard on my daddy.

Eyes glistening, she described the drama that resulted.

> The night she died we were separated. Our lives changed completely. I went with my grandma for a short time and stayed in her log cabin home. Then several of us stayed with an aunt, and my older brother went somewhere else. We were all scared, upset and not sure what was going to happen to us. My daddy knew he couldn't keep all of us by himself.

Life at the Children's Home

While they agreed their father was overwhelmed (he never shared his feelings), neither Dana nor Jason was sure precisely what role their dying mother had played in arranging for them to be placed at the children's home. Dana remembered their mother was involved in the initial planning, aware that she was dying, but has always wondered whether she would have agreed to having unknown families adopt her children. Ruefully, she admitted, "I don't know the real story. I have always wanted to ask, but then I just thought I'd leave well enough alone."

She expressed similar limited understanding of her father's feelings, because he has never explained why he signed the papers. As she matured, though, she began to put herself in his place.

> All of a sudden, his wife was gone, and he had to give up his children. Explaining it would have been hard on him, but I think it would have helped all of us in the long run. We were each caught in the same bind, and neither Daddy nor us kids knew how to get out of it.

For his part, Jason recalled:

> I just cried my eyes out because my daddy was not with us. At least, I had a brother and my sister, Dana, in the cottage with me--even though my brother and I didn't get to see Dana all the time. The cottage was divided—one section for girls and one for boys. Of course, Dana was in the girls' section. I vaguely knew what was going on—basically that I'd have to stay there. Another brother, who was four years older than me, lived in the older boy's dormitory, and he knew more about

172

our father and our future than any of us. When we could, we huddled around him to find out what was going on. That helped a whole lot.

Jason excelled in sports activities at the Home. His success as an athlete, especially as a baseball player, helped him to feel accepted and comfortable on campus.

Dana, however, had a different perspective. As a young girl, between six and seven, she was bullied by older girls and did not receive the individual protection, attention and affection she needed from her "matrons." She spares no emotion in her description:

> In some ways, it was like a prison. The older, meaner ones would bully the little ones, and then tell lies to get the younger girls in trouble. In that big an institution, with about 16 kids in my cottage, the staff couldn't control it. It wasn't family-like. You didn't have somebody to hold you if you cried. It was no life for young children.

Jason was quick to agree, noting that two sisters, then called matrons, "ruled with an iron hand," and that he was very much in need of support from his siblings.

According to Dana, the "iron hand" all too often held an implement: "You even looked at them wrong, you got a whipping. That paddle came out quick. Back then you could do that. Can you imagine bringing a paddle out now? It would be abuse. I remember bending over, taking my whacking and going to bed."

She admitted to having learned a valuable lesson from the rough experience —"It taught me I could survive and it made me promise myself that I would never treat kids of my own that way." Still, she argued vehemently against the institutionalization of young children.

> Even though Jason and another brother were living in the boys' wing of our co-ed cottage, I felt terribly alone and scared to death. At a young age, you're growing; you're starting to set your ways and your mind. I haven't seen an institution yet that was good in giving tender love and care. It's just a place to put a child because they have no

mother or father. It can be good for children of 13 or so, but for a young girl like me, it was traumatizing. All of a sudden I lost my real family and had to live on a big campus. I didn't feel at peace with all the changes. It was scary.

I did have a caseworker, but how does a caseworker relate to a frightened six-year-old who is scared for her life because older girls severely beat and bully her? Although we arrange for relatives to care for her, my own five-year-old daughter is depressed and scared even if I'm gone only for a weekend. You need a lot of love at that time in your life. I have nightmares when I remember the bullies picking on me and other new little girls in the cottage. I try to block out those memories.

Jason remembered a more comfortable experience during the year he was at the Home before being adopted, noting that despite the terror dealt out by the matron sisters his avid participation in all kinds of athletics gave him some relief.

Finding Their Adoptive Families

Dana and Jason were legally adopted by different families, but always wanted to remain in contact with each other. Jason's adopted parents reluctantly consented to a few meetings during the year before his adoption was finalized, but once the adoption was official, his adopted parents stopped all contact between him and his birth relatives. Dana and Jason did not see, talk by phone or communicate in any way with each other again for over a dozen years. Both still recall quite vividly their separation from their birth family, their moves from the children's home, their placements with their adopted families, and their long separation from one another and their other brothers.

Dana explained she had found the year before her adoption terrifying:

It was a combination of things. First, I was so young that my mother's death just confused me. Then the bullying by the older girls and harsh treatment by the matrons scared me to death, and kind of shell-shocked me. I've got to be honest, I don't remember what people, like the social workers, said to me about adoption, but in my mind I wasn't really prepared. It was probably mentioned, but I must have blocked it out.

My first clear memory about being adopted is of an incident that happened early one morning. I heard my dormitory matron say, "Dana, you have to get cleaned up and put on a pretty little dress."

I said, "Well, why?"

She answered, "There are some people who are going to come talk to you. If it works out you're going to be living with them from now on."

There was another little girl who was up for adoption at the same time. We sat side-by-side looking out of a living room window waiting until our prospective parents arrived.

It's funny. I remember seeing my adoptive parents walk up the hill to my cottage, but I don't remember meeting them. They were just strangers, nicely dressed, very well groomed, and a lot different from what I was used to seeing. Even as a small child, I realized they looked very wealthy and acted like important people.

At Christmas, I had been sent to one of the Home's "visiting families" where I stayed for several days, and then came back to the campus. A lot of people took in children for the holidays, and it was nice. I thought maybe what my matron was talking about was the same kind of thing. But it wasn't--it was like moving into a different world--and staying there.

Jason, two years older, had even clearer memories of his young childhood experiences and they triggered a range of emotions for him.

My experience of meeting my adopted parents was quite a bit different from Dana's. I visited with several different families for holidays. When my social worker told me one couple I had visited during Christmas wanted me to visit with them again, I agreed. After that, my caseworker didn't actually mention the word "adoption."

She just talked to me about how I liked the family, and asked if I were interested in living with them. I can remember saying, "No." I didn't want to be separated from my brothers and sister, and I also felt they were too old (mid-60s) and set in their ways. They just didn't feel like the right family for me.

Later, my caseworker described another couple and mentioned adoption, and I agreed to visit them over a holiday weekend. About two weeks later, she told me that these people wanted to adopt me and asked how I felt about it. Since I really enjoyed being with them and felt at home there, I told her it would be fine. To ease my anxiety, my caseworker said, "Once you adjust, it will be all right." I give her a lot of credit for making my adoption such a smooth process. There were only two challenges—adjusting to my parents because of our age differences (Mom was in her late 40s and Dad was in his early 50s), and not being able to talk freely about my adoption and birth family with them. They didn't have any children of their own.

Taking her turn, Dana remembered her adoption:

I know it had to take longer, but in my memory everything happened fast—like all in one day. Suddenly, it was "Boom!" I was in a strange city, and didn't see my brothers again for years.

Recently, my (adoptive) dad remembered how when we were about to drive away, one of my older brothers looked at him and said, "Mister, you'd better take good care of my little sister." My brothers cried and I cried. They didn't want their sister to go, and I didn't want to be separated from them. My dad said that really bothered him. As he put it: "The look in his face could have killed; and that hurt me." It took all day to drive from the campus to my new home south of the Atlanta airport. I was frightened, but as the miles went by, I thought about how rich they were, and I said to myself, "Boy, I'll get new clothes and lots of toys." We drove up to this big house—I didn't believe people lived that way except in the movies—and they took me up to my own room. Remember, after the first part of my life in a run-down, three-room house with my (original) parents and six brothers, I lived in a campus cottage. The contrast was like night and day. It was unbelievable! It was like a fairy-tale story!

176

They had beautiful dresses and toys laid out in my room. The bed had a frilly bedspread. All the colors matched. I had never seen anything like it. It was magical! Months later, the magic was beginning to wear off, and I got to thinking I wanted to be back with my real brothers, maybe go back and visit or have them come see me. I wanted to see them a lot!

Jason described his adoption experience as "pretty easy overall," noting that since he was only 8, he didn't understand all that was happening, but enjoyed living in his adoptive parents' home.

My new parents were caring and cared about me. At first I hesitated about changing my last name, but then I agreed to it because the longer I lived with my adopted parents, the more I enjoyed and identified with them. They are super nice people, who encouraged me to do my best in school and helped me believe that I could have a successful life. Without them, I definitely wouldn't have attended and graduated from college.

My adoptive parents didn't encourage me to stay in contact with my brothers and sister, but they did let me visit with my real dad right before I was adopted. He came to the children's home a couple of times. I assume it was to sign adoption papers, but he never mentioned what was happening to me. I wonder how much he really understood. Fortunately, my caseworker did a good job of preparing me—-explaining that I wouldn't be around my brothers or sister each day, and probably wouldn't see my real father for long periods of time. The first time I visited my real dad it was okay, but when I visited him again, I think my adoptive parents were afraid I might want to stay with him, so they stopped the visits.

After I was adopted, I didn't see my brothers, sister or other (birth) relatives until I graduated from college at 21. My adoptive parents wanted me to be a Clark and forget that I was first a Boone. I think they hoped I would stop thinking about my past. We very seldom, if ever, talked about my adoption. Even now that I'm an adult, I don't bring it up, because it makes them feel uncomfortable.

For the first couple of years, if I had made contact, heard from or written to my brothers and sister, I might have run away from my adoptive home, but to have been separated from them for over a dozen years was wrong.

Living Separately in their Adoptive Homes

As we talked, I learned that Dana and Jason continued to have different experiences after their adoptions were finalized—a year after placement. Dana described a hot-and-cold, roller coaster type relationship with her adopted parents, Jason had peaceful experiences and overall felt a strong sense of belonging.

Dana's adoptive parents had two (birth) daughters who were in college when she became part of the family. Her role was distinctively different, as she remembers it:

My adoptive sisters were really well-behaved girls. I was the "meanie," who did naughty little sister things, but they accepted me—as did my other adoptive relatives. My adoptive parents did not say so directly, but they wanted me to call them Mom and Dad. I called them Mom and Dad when I talked to others about them, but I never called them that directly until I was grown. Mom said that just tore her up.

In contrast, Jason readily accepted the love, support and permanency his adoptive family provided. He described his transition into his adopted home a bit differently:

It took almost two years before I started feeling like a Clark. When you're not with your birth relatives for a long time, you don't forget about them, but you have to move on with your life. I made new friends at school and at church. Maybe the most important person who helped me make the transition was my daddy. I became really close to him. He took me places in his truck, with me riding shotgun. We enjoyed doing many things together like fishing, and he cheered for me at my ballgames. In short, he treated me like his son—just like I had been born to him.

Dana's adopted family was very comfortable financially, and she realized that their lifestyle opened up a world of opportunities she wouldn't have had with her birth family. Still, their conservative religious beliefs frustrated her.

> Dad had a good-paying job as an airplane captain, and it took him all over the world. He loved Mom and pampered her with gifts from everywhere. They were well-to-do people, and I got just about anything I wanted. We even traveled to Paris for a vacation. Can you imagine celebrating your ninth birthday at the Eiffel Tower?
>
> A sore point for us was religion. They had very strong religious beliefs, and took us to church on Wednesday night, Sunday morning, Sunday night, and often on Saturday and Saturday night. I just felt like I was pushed and pushed into religion. Everything we went to was religious. It just didn't go down with me.
>
> My adoptive parents were pretty strict. In some ways, they were stricter than the children's home. The funny part is that I now find myself being strict with my own daughter. I thought I'd never do that with my child. All their friends and everybody at church knew I was adopted. I'll be honest with you—I would play the poor little adopted girl role to make friends, to get more attention, and to manipulate my adoptive parents.

Jason listened thoughtfully as Dana told about the turmoil in her childhood. At this point, he joined in to explain how much he loved his parents, but continued to be frustrated that he couldn't talk openly about being adopted. It's interesting that the adoption was more of an issue for Dana than for Jason. He explained:

> No one brought up my adoption in school, in church or anywhere else, and I didn't feel any different from other kids. I felt accepted in my extended adoptive family too. My parents wanted children, and my mother had experienced two miscarriages. I was really their first child. Even at 8 years old, I was still like a brand new baby to them. Everyone thought of me as just part of the family, including my grandmothers, aunts and uncles. The cousins who were my age were very accepting. I had fun playing with them, and I often stayed

overnight with them and their families. They didn't say or act like "You're my adopted cousin." I felt like I was their blood-kin cousin.

My adoptive daddy had a good job. He worked for our local power company and was licensed to work on high-power lines. On Saturdays when he was off-duty, he made extra money wiring people's homes. He took me with him, and I enjoyed that. We got along well. Mom had a small florist business next to our home. I'd help her out, too. When I got old enough to drive, I made deliveries for her.

There was still that little nagging discomfort. I felt like a Clark, but I wasn't allowed to talk about my roots as a Boone. My adoptive parents couldn't bring themselves to accept or talk about the fact that I had a birth family. They didn't want to be reminded that I wasn't their own flesh and blood. Maybe if we could have talked openly about my adoption, they would've known that I loved them, and wanted to live with them, and be their son. My (adoptive) mother still wants to hold onto me . . . even now that I'm married. That's made it tough for my wife. My mother just doesn't want to lose me, and she's afraid she might. My dad has the same fear, too, but that's not going to happen.

As she listened, Dana realized that she, too, felt her adoptive father was more a real father to her than their birth father had been, even when they lived with him.

Our [birth] daddy was a poor man who just worked all the time. How could he give any of us individual attention with seven kids? My adoptive father' enjoyed children, and at first we got along fine. I can remember some good times with him. We'd go swimming in the summer and do fun things together all year long. Our relationship was great initially, although several years after my adoption we were at each other's throats.

Continuing with her story, Dana added details about the tension she felt with her parents.

Once things starting getting bad, the friction between us just seemed to escalate, and I was ultimately returned to the children's home. Remembering the events that led to my being sent back there just blows me away. I was just bad. When I was about 12, I got this urge to see my real family. I had not seen them for maybe four or five years. My adoptive parents agreed to make all the arrangements. After everything was worked out, Dad flew me in a private plane to an airport near the Home. One of the caseworkers met us, and drove me to the campus. My brothers who were still there and I spent the whole day on the campus together. It was great!

The next day the caseworker drove me up into the mountains to the village where I was born. Remember I was accustomed to a nice home and neighborhood with my adoptive family. My real father's yard was cluttered with old cars and parts, and the house was really small and in need of painting and repairs. A strange man came out of the house, banged on the window and told me to get out of the car. He asked, "Don't you know who I am?" I said, "No!" Then it hit me—I was shocked—it was my birth father. I had thought I would recognize him any day, any time, but I was wrong. You forget! You've got an image in your mind, but it's not the face, the voice or the mannerisms you remember. You want your real father to be a certain type of person, and he's not. He looked completely different. His life had changed since my mother's death. I don't even talk to him now except on the phone. I call or send him birthday cards, and then he'll talk to me a little bit. He's just in his own little world. I remember seeing him go through my mother's death. When she died, it just tore him up. He cried and did things that were unusual. He's now remarried, and he's happy. I'm glad for that, but I leave him alone. I don't tell him how to live, and I accept the way he is.

After a day with my real dad and extended relatives, I returned to the children's home. Even after my short visit with my brothers there, it was an emotional experience to go our separate ways. We all cried when it was time for me to leave.

Returning to my adoptive parents' home was a terrible time for me and for them. I deliberately said mean, hurtful things to them like, "You're not my real family." I was so unsettled. I felt pulled in two directions: first, I felt disloyal not living with my birth family, the Boones; yet second, I realized I didn't have it so bad living with the Bartons, my adoptive family. Maybe it was part of my teenage rebellion kicking in,

181

but I got to thinking to myself, "Why can't I live with my real family? I'd rather be with them than with this adoptive family, even though I've been getting everything I want." I had always compared the two families, but this urge to live with my real family started getting bigger each day. I just rebelled at everything. It just got awful. I cussed at my adopted family. I ran away. I did all the things that a rebelling child could do, just for revenge. I acted up for about a year.

In sharing about this time of her life, Dana described herself as a "demon," recognizing she did everything in her power to sabotage the placement. She changed a few letters in the adoptive family's name then combined profane words with it, scrawling offensive phrases with lipstick on the bathroom mirrors at home and in the family's church. By contrast, she wrote slogans extolling the merits of her birth family. Then she met Calvin.

I was still 12, he was 19 and we were going to run off and get married. I was in love, but he was bad news—a drinker and just a no-good person. My adoptive father had him arrested and put in jail. That got to me. I thought, "What kind of person is he to do this to Calvin?"

Now as an adult and parent, I can better understand their frustrations and actions, but it got to where I got whippings almost every day. My adoptive father and mother originally didn't believe in spanking. It was a religious belief. They never spanked their birth daughters, and I wasn't spanked until I started getting into serious trouble. My dad whipped me—hard—and it hurt! Looking back, I really can't blame him. What else was he going to do? Here's this girl who just won't behave. She won't mind! She's sassy! She cusses at us! She's dating this no-good guy who is seven years older than she is. What are we going to do with her?

My adoptive parents took me to these religious groups, and I would just sit there and huff and puff. That didn't work. You just can't push something on a person who's got a strong will and a strong mind. They're not going to do what you want them to do. It's what the person can do for himself. At that time, I couldn't have cared less if my adoptive parents lived or died. It was awful!

It got so bad that to keep me from running away, my adoptive parents hired workmen to install special tamper-proof screws on my windows and had a lock installed on the outside of my bedroom door. At night when they locked my door I felt like a caged animal, and all of this made me angrier and angrier. Maybe that's all they could think of doing to keep me safe and out of trouble, but the tension in our home felt like a ticking time bomb that was about to explode. It was like we were at war with each other.

Dana Is Returned to the Children's Home

Dana's memories of moving from her adoptive home were stark:

One morning, all of a sudden, my adoptive parents announced they were taking me back to the children's home. Terror flooded my whole body. Memories of living there as a little girl flashed through my mind—the bullying, the cruelty of the matrons who ran our cottage, the lack of love and care—but there was nothing I could do. I couldn't stop shaking and crying and thinking, "How can they do this?" It was like the death penalty. I begged, but they wouldn't discuss it with me—their minds were made up. Mom started packing my clothes, and Dad was putting my things in the car. As we traveled, they said I was not told about my move until that morning, because they feared I would run away or maybe try to hurt myself.

Late that afternoon, I saw the children's home campus come into view. In my mind, I could see and hear one of my brothers—many years before—slowly reading out loud the "Children's Home" sign as our birth daddy drove through the main entrance. Years before, I had been in my birth father's worn-out pickup, and now I was in my adoptive father's luxury car. Yes, I was back at the children's home— once again trembling, filled with fear and uncertainty.

After that, there were times when I wanted to go back to live with my adoptive family. My father later told me it wasn't a month before they received a letter from me begging them, "I'll be good! I'll behave! I won't be the way I was anymore!" They didn't write or call. I felt like they didn't love me anymore.

At the children's home, you had to talk with your caseworker once a week about how you were feeling and doing. The caseworkers were nice. They understood and tried to help, but it was a difficult time of my life.

Once I was back at the Home, I was blessed with good house parents, a young couple not at all like the matrons I had had during my first stay. The new house parents were extremely good with kids—you knew where you stood with them. When I moved in they laid it on the line: "Here's your room, Dana. We'll do anything we can for you. If you need us, we're here. This is a list of the cottage rules. If you don't think you can comply with them, then we'll think of somewhere else we can put you." End of conversation! Maybe because the two older birth children in my adoptive family were away in college, my adoptive mother took care of the inside household duties herself. I never learned to cook, sew or do the other things that a mother usually teaches her daughter. Living at the Home as a teenager was a different story. I had to mature quickly and learn to do my part of the cooking, washing clothes, and cleaning. I grew up pretty fast.

My first stay at the Home as a little girl was terrible, but my second time as a teenager was good for me. In my adoptive home, it felt like I was at war with my adopted parents. At the children's home it was not just me—alone—battling adult authority. I was part of a group of kids, many of them just as angry and rebellious as I was. Somehow it didn't seem as strict.

My adoptive parents and I had struggled because they wanted me to change from a Boone to a Barton—to accept their lifestyle, their strict religion and all that went with it. Yet I didn't completely accept my birth family's lifestyle either. It's funny, now that I think about it, but in some ways the children's home was a neutral place to grow up as a teenager. There was family pride there. We'd go to school, and say in words or by the way we acted, "We're the Home Kids; don't mess with us."

That was kind of fun, but at the same time I felt "labeled," as if I were wearing a tee shirt that said "Property of the Children's Home." Even now, many people in this town know that I used to live at the

Home. Like yesterday, at a birthday party for one of my daughter's friends, I was introduced as: "This is Dana, she grew up not far from here—at the children's home." The introduction wasn't intended to be a put-down, but you do really get labeled. It's not fair because I think I grew up, matured and improved at the Home.

Unfortunately, Calvin, the older boyfriend Dana intended to marry followed her to the Home. A moment of reckoning came one day when Dana was faced with deciding whether to "escape" the Home with Calvin or to follow her house father's guidance and stay.

Being sent back to the Home was a wake-up call, and I thought I'd better start behaving. However, after several months, Calvin called to say he was coming to get me. I sat on a high spot and watched him circle around the campus. Even when he wasn't in sight, I could hear the loud roar of his jalopy's muffler.

My house father had been informed of everything I had done up to that point and warned that Calvin might try to come after me. I pointed for Calvin to go up to the backside, and my house father, tipped off by some other kids blocked the drive between me and Calvin. In a soft, but firm, voice he said, "I don't think you want to do that." When I asked why not, his response was clear: "You're not my child, and I'm just trying to do my job. Either you come back to the cottage with me and do what you're supposed to do, or if you run off with him (pointing at Calvin), I'll call the police. They will pick you up as a runaway and arrest him for contributing to the delinquency of a minor. You won't be coming back here. You'll be going somewhere worse, so I think you had better go on back to the cottage."

His straightforward words sent a message zinging through my brain. To be honest, I don't know if God intervened or it was my house father. I couldn't tell you . . . but the message sure got through to me—loud and clear!

It was one of those life-changing moments. I had to decide! Was I going to continue to rebel or was I going to start growing up? I muttered some profanity under my breath, opened the pickup door,

185

and slid into the passenger seat as low and as far away from my house father as possible. As the truck bounced along the gravel drive to my cottage, I remember feeling like a prisoner who wanted to be captured. At the same time a flood of different feelings rushed through my mind—anger, relief, embarrassment, and defeat. My housefather didn't say a word until we arrived at the cottage. Then he said, "You need some time for yourself," and told the other kids and staff to leave me alone. I first sat alone under a tree crying. When it became really dark, my house father came out to get me, and I kept on sobbing. Altogether, I cried for about four or five hours. Most people try to talk to you, but my house father just left me alone. He didn't make me go to meals or to school the next day. Some weeks later, he said, "I just let you get it out of your system." Boy, going with Calvin would have been a mistake—he ended up in prison.

Although still legally adopted by them, I never visited my adoptive parents the whole time I lived at the Home as a teenager. At first, they thought that I would put them through all those problems again, and didn't want me to come. After a while, they changed their minds and almost begged me to visit them—especially on holidays like Christmas. By then I just didn't want to go, and I also didn't have contact with my real family, whom I had put on a pedestal in the past. My birth kinfolks never came to visit me or even called! Even my real father didn't visit.

Choosing to remain at the children's home was a milestone decision for Dana. The months after her return weren't easy at first, but meeting another girl who had also been returned from an unsuccessful adoptive placement boosted her confidence. Dana began to realize she wasn't the only person who had trouble adapting to an adoptive family. As time progressed, she reached another personal milestone by becoming a mentor to other girls.

During my teenage years, the Home, in many ways, became my family. When some of the younger girls started to act out—big time—I'd say, "Look, you're not going to get anywhere being like that." They'd look at me like, "Who are you?" Somehow, I have a knack for helping others calm down and think about what they are doing to themselves. So, I'd begin with something like, "You have experienced nothing compared to what I've been through."

Dana's Quest to Unite with Her Brothers

When she was about 16, Dana decided to look for her brothers. When she asked a caseworker for information on Jason, her request was denied because his adoptive parents had placed a notice in his records prohibiting the provision of any information on his whereabouts or current life situation. She did, however, have some information on others, as she explained:

> I knew where three of our brothers were. The oldest was living on his own in our hometown, the youngest was growing up with the family Mother had chosen for him, and the third was serving in the Air Force. The others were living with one of the Home's foster families.

> With the foster parents' agreement, my caseworker drove me to see them, and we spent the day together. It wasn't a week later that these boys also moved back to the children's home campus. I asked them why they wanted to return to the Home and they said, "When we found out that you were living here, we wanted to be with you!" Even though the three of us had been separated for years, we all still felt the same way: we wanted to be together. We all live in different places now, but we're very family-oriented. We feel strong ties with each other. Even as adults, we are still learning new things about each other, because we didn't grow up together. Jason, you were the hard one to locate, but I was determined to find you.

Dana Locates Jason

With a smile on her face, Dana looked at Jason and talked about finding him and the peace that it brought her that they were again a part of each other's lives.

> I had reconnected with all my brothers except you. After graduating from high school, leaving the children's home and getting married,

187

I had this strong urge to find out if you were alive or just what was going on with you. I was free to do what I wanted. I asked the director of the children's home for help, he said, "Dana, you know I can't do that." When I said I might try to get some kind of court order, he insisted it wouldn't work. After that, I sort of gave up on seeing your record, but it upset me, Jason. I thought since we were both adults, they should give me your last name and your current address. Such rules don't make any sense, but it seemed pointless to fight them.

A couple of years later, I was completely surprised when the same person (the director of the home) called to say, "Mr. and Mrs. Clark, Jason's adoptive mother and father, have invited you to attend his college graduation."

I thought it was a miracle. I was thrilled and excited, but to this day, I sense your mother was unhappy we found each other. She probably wanted you to know your real family, but also feared you might drift away from them and she would lose her only child. Jason, I know she dearly loves you. Sending the invitation was, I believe, her way of telling me, "Try to look him up."

The director of the children's home told me over the phone what you looked like, gave me your address and telephone number and said the Clarks had sent pictures as well.

I remember my heart started beating faster. I didn't know what to do except to call you right away. You answered the phone, and in my nervousness, I stupidly said, "Can I speak to Mrs. Clark?"

You said, "Yes, just a minute."

I thought, "I have talked to him!"

Then your mother got on the phone and rudely told me you didn't want to see me or have anything to do with me and to leave you alone! I was devastated. My emotions were all over the place: sadness and crying, rage at your mom, being puzzled and wondering why you didn't want to talk to me. All the while I was praying that I would meet you face-to-face.

After a sleepless night, an amazing thing happened! I noticed a

188

pickup truck pulling into my driveway. As I peeked out of a window, a neatly dressed, strange man walked up on the porch and knocked on the door. When I carefully opened the door, he said, "I'm Mr. Clark, Jason's father." I invited him in and gave him a cup of coffee. He had trouble getting his words out, and suddenly he just broke out in tears. Amid his tears he said that a brother should know his sister and a sister should know her brother, "By gosh, if somebody wouldn't tell me where my sister was, I would think that's the worst thing a person could do to a family. You write Jason and see what goes from there."

I believe the reluctance was mostly on your mom's part, but being a mother myself, I really can't blame her. She finally had a child; and after raising you for over a dozen years, she was afraid she would lose you.

When I wrote you, you wrote back right away and said your parents had told you as you were growing up that we didn't want to see you. They made up lies like: "They don't care if you exist. They don't want anything to do with you. They don't consider you part of their family." Your parents felt frightened and desperate about the possibility of your meeting us, but they were wrong to feel that way.

I quickly answered your letter saying, "I do want to see you. I want to know who you are! How can I meet you? I'd like to take you up in the mountains to our home place and introduce you to our family. I've already met some of them." Receiving my letter just seemed to tickle you to death! As I remember, you and I first sent letters and exchanged photos.

Jason added his perspective on how he had felt as he met Dana and his other siblings.

I chose to attend a small but excellent college near my adoptive parents' home. I was a day student but was actively involved in the college's programs, especially the athletics. Just before earning my degree, I moved out on my own. Dana, that's when I started to search for you and our brothers. I don't know if I was being macho or heroic or whatever, but I wanted to find you all by myself—to do it like an explorer. When I found out that my adoptive parents had contacted you and our brothers without telling or involving me, I felt resentful.

Yes, after we made contact, I remember we stayed in touch mostly by letters, along with some telephone conversations. You gave me the inside scoop on everyone: their ages, where they lived, if they were married and if they had children . . . that sort of thing. In one letter, you invited me to go with you to the high school graduation ceremony for one of our brothers in our old hometown. Even though I was grown and thought of my self as a "tough guy" athlete, I was scared to death to meet you, my brothers, my real daddy and our other relatives.

Jason and Dana Meet Again After 14 Years Apart

After many years without seeing each other, Dana and Jason finally established contact again and arranged to meet at Dana's home. While as children and teenagers they had lived separately for many years, they remembered having a strong sibling bond in the years before their adoption. Dana remembered how she felt preparing for the meeting:

I carefully fixed my hair and went out on the porch to wait for you, Jason. I waited and waited. Finally, you arrived. You must have been scared because you brought a friend with you, just like I asked a girlfriend to wait on the front porch with me because I was so nervous.

I saw this car slow down with two guys in it, but you drove on by. I knew it was you driving. The car stopped at the corner, hesitated, turned around and drove up my driveway. I thought to myself, "This is it!"

You jumped out of the car and exclaimed, "Well, get up from there and give your brother a hug!"

I shot back, "I haven't seen you in over a dozen years and you want me to hug you?" But we did hug. It was real warming; it just lifted me up! I really can't explain how satisfying it was. Since Mother died, I had felt this nesting urge to get us all together, and it was happening.

190

Jason's memory was quite similar. He admitted to driving by and explained:

> I was so scared I didn't want to stop. I didn't know what to do or say. It was an emotional situation. I felt my heart beating fast. Stopping at the corner stop sign I wondered what to do. I said to my friend, "That could be my sister." He laughed, and said he felt sure it was you. So I turned the car around and drove up to your house. Sure enough, it was you.

Dana then recalled the conversation the two had had about the Clarks, whom Jason insisted he considered his mother and father:

> You said you knew we had a real mother but you didn't remember much about her. It was a crazy reunion with you, but it turned out all right.

Unsure what to expect, Jason remembered feeling as if he were meeting a good friend whom he hadn't seen for a long time. Instead, he was reuniting with his biological sister, and they had been separated from each other for 14 years..

> You were happy, and I was happy but there were no tears or anything like that—no crying. After being apart for so long it felt strange because . . . blood-wise you're my sister, but my memories were still of you as a little girl.

Jason and Dana Visit Their Birth Family

We had been talking for a long time, and Dana recognized that we might be thirsty. As she got up to get us drinks, she said, "Jason, why don't you tell about meeting our birth family when we attended our cousin's high school graduation."

Jason remembered driving Dana to the village in the mountains where they were born.

> Everybody kin to us, it seemed—our father, our brothers, aunts and uncles, and cousins—was at the graduation, and they warmly wel-

comed us. It felt like I was being inspected, like they were looking me over, kind of judging me and trying to figure what type of person I was. Of course, I was doing the same thing with them. After a couple of days of being there, the reality of the situation set in. It was like we were seeing good friends after being apart for a long, long time.

Dana returned to the porch with a tray of refreshing drinks and settled back into her chair. Jason continued his description.

When I saw our birth father, it was not as emotional as it was with my brothers and Dana. It's not easy to explain, but seeing the way he lives . . . his lifestyle . . . didn't bring any family feelings, any closeness or special emotions. We sat down and had a little talk. I told him that the family I'm with now is the family who raised me, and I see them as the family I identify with. I don't know if that hurt or upset him. We talked, I'm still his son, but that's about it.

I couldn't tell if he feels any pride in me—in what I'm doing and what I've accomplished—because he really doesn't talk with me. He's closer to Dana and vice versa. He's all right health-wise. After our mother died, he remarried twice, the last time was about a year and a half ago. He's still living in the same house where all of us were raised as little children.

Dana pointed out that since their mother's death, it had been hard to communicate with their father.

Dad had this big home life and then nothing. Before Mother died, he had people who loved him and cared about him, and then "BOOM!"—they're gone. I used to blame him for letting our family fall apart. I thought, "How could he give my brothers and me up to other families? How could he do that?" As I've grown up, I've looked at the situation from a different perspective and have concluded, "What else could he have done?"

Dana and Jason Describe Their Lives as Young Adults

As young adults, Dana and Jason had gained perspective on their life experiences. Dana had worked to emotionally settle many issues and to grow in her coping skills with her adoptive family, birth family and in other areas of her life. Her confidence had also steadily improved. She reflected on these issues as we talked and shared her adult view of her marriage, motherhood and her adoptive parents.

> Don and I have had a good marriage. He played for the home's basketball team, although he lived with his family, just a couple of blocks from the campus. We started going together in high school and got married right after we graduated. Gosh, time moves on—that was eight years ago. Now we have our daughter and someday hope to have more children. Things are going well for me personally.

> My husband and I feel like we're one person. We're really in love, and I love being a mother too. I've always tried to be sensitive to my daughter's needs. I don't want to grow up being a mother who is just an old fuddy-duddy. I want to grow as a person who can help my daughter. It scares me sometimes. When we get angry at each other, I get frustrated with her. I don't want her to grow up and hate me. I want her to love her mother.

Remembering the contrasting feelings she felt toward her adoptive parents, Dana elaborated:

> What kills me is, I used to say, "I'm a Boone." I would go around writing that on everything and make sure my adoptive family would see it. I just wanted to hurt them. Since I've grown up and married, I've wondered about my anger toward my adoptive mom and dad. They're just people!

> I really do love them now, but it's been a struggle.

> Although he was justified, I never disliked anybody as much in my life as I did my adoptive father when he brought me back to the children's home. Overall, they've been good to me. We could have grown closer years ago, but we're doing it now. A positive turning point for us was when Mom came up here to help when my baby was born. She cleaned the house, prepared meals, and helped take care of my baby. She didn't have to do that. It made a difference in the way I feel about her. It honored and celebrated the birth of her granddaughter. My mother and I are getting closer now and talking.

193

Maybe that was our problem. We didn't talk.

Another improvement Dana has recognized and welcomed is in her own self-confidence.

> I've always felt kind of dumb, but Don encourages me. When I get down, he'll say: "You're not stupid!--I wouldn't marry a stupid person." He's real good for me. For a long time I depended on him for everything—for my thinking, for just walking down the street—but I've learned to be more independent, and I want to be a good wife and mother.

> We are making a new start; we're moving to another city soon. My husband has done really well as a salesman and designer for a high-end ceramic tile company. This move is a promotion. He started at the bottom as an installer and is now being trained to become a branch manager. I'm ready to go with Don and help him.

> Am I satisfied with my life? I'd say it's great! But I want to go further. I used to work as a bank teller, and I also worked in auditing jobs. I worked at a little hamburger joint when I was in school just to have some money and so I could buy furniture when I got married. Now I just want to be a good wife and a good mother. You know, just be happy. I enjoy being happy. I've been through rough times, and I want to stay happy—and I think I will.

> How have I put all of this together? I think and talk to myself a lot. The other night I thought I should try to do something to help girls and boys who are going through the same adoption struggles I experienced. I feel for them. You get confused and hurt in the process, and you don't know what to do. It really hurts. Don says I could never be a counselor because I'd get upset over everything. I am more sensitive and bothered than most people by certain things—like seeing a mother smacking and screaming at her child. It just goes all through me. I almost cry when I see things like that.

Dana has learned to forgive and let go of many past hurts. She has come to believe that her traumatic "growing up" experiences have helped her to become stronger, more confident and mature. Hearing her story brings to mind the words of Ernest Hemingway and I shared his thought with her: "The world breaks everyone, and afterward, some are strong at the broken places."[1] She agreed:

> Yes, I feel stronger. When I'm facing some rough spots, I'll say to myself, "Well, as a child, I went through rough times, and I can face this stuff. I can get through this. This is nothing compared to things I've dealt with before.

Jason's life has continued to be positive into adulthood. He's a dedicated guidance counselor and athletic coach, and he recently won the "Teacher of the Year" award at the private, church-related high school that employs him. While he loves sports, his marriage and his 2-month-old child have now become his top priorities.

> My wife and I were married about two years ago. I really love being married. We just had a baby two months ago. I'm just getting used to being a father. It's great, but it changes your life.

> I'm the first person in my (birth) family to graduate from college, and I'm really proud of that. I played sports in high school and college. My best sport was baseball. I was a catcher, a position that means you sort of manage the game on the field. Now that college is behind me, I get a special pleasure out of coaching, officiating and counseling. That is a way I can thank people who helped me—by helping children and youth.

> I must confess I'm a sports fanatic, and my sports involvement has helped me adjust to new situations, like living at the children's home and moving into my adoptive home, new school and community.

> I appreciate the many opportunities that have been given to me. If I hadn't been placed with my adoptive parents, there's no telling where I'd be. I know I wouldn't have gone to college, and I probably wouldn't have finished high school. I do regret, however, that I didn't have my brothers or sister to talk to while I was growing up. Since my adoptive parents were older, they were more like grandparents than parents.

> I'm definitely satisfied with my life. Beyond my family there is another person I want to mention. My high school coach really

helped me. He encouraged me to go to college and influenced the career I chose. I decided I wanted to do something in sports, and at first I was interested in sports rehabilitation. Then, I started thinking about getting involved with teenage kids, hoping I could help them make something positive out of their lives. That's why I went to college. I don't know where I'd be right now if I hadn't had sports in my life.

As far as my future dreams for my son, my wife and myself, I just want so much for all of us. I really haven't gotten involved with my 2-month-old boy. Because fatherhood is so new to me, I'm getting to know him more each day, and the more I know him, of course, the more I love him. I want to share my life with others and not just be self-centered.

Jason's Suggestions for the Adoption Process

Jason was quick to say that he appreciated the opportunity to talk about his adoption experience, because he hoped his story would help other people.

If adoptive parents received some help in communicating with and preparing for their adopted child, it would make a big difference in the whole adoption experience. When I was young, I really enjoyed the things my parents did for me so I wanted to be around them. However, as I grew older, there was just such a communication gap that we really didn't understand each other.

It would have helped my adoption process if the Home had provided a social worker to come and talk with my parents and me on a regular basis. However, once the adoption was official, I never heard from anyone at the Home. This may have been because of my parents. A lot of things have been kept secret by my (adoptive) parents, and there are probably still secrets that my parents know and I don't. They have their reasons why they have acted this way, but it would have been nice if we could have talked openly together about my adoption.

More visits to my adoptive home prior to my living there would have helped me adjust. Thankfully, I had a good caseworker, but it was difficult to take everything in with one or two visits. I had to give up living with my brothers and Dana, and at the same time I had to adjust in my new life. My adoptive parents, like many couples who adopt children, almost viewed me as a baby, although I was about 7 years old at the time of my placement. An adopted baby or younger child doesn't have any conscious memories of their lives the way I did as a 7-year-old.

I had no problem calling my adopted parents my mom and daddy. We got along really well. Daddy and I were especially close. I had no problems with them except when it came to talking about my former life with my birth family.

SECTION II

DANA (MID-50S) AND JASON (LATE 50S) REFLECT ON THEIR ADULT LIVES

Dana's Husband Dies and She Rears Her Children

In 2007, I located Dana's lovely home only a short way, as a crow flies, from the children's home. Now in her 50s, Dana lives in a vastly different world. She resides in a prestigious subdivision, and drives a sports car, but that is only part of her story.

A "For Sale" sign is staked in Dana's front yard.

Dana's late husband, Don, had developed a special artistic talent for creating and constructing elaborate tile designs for floors, walls, swimming pools and murals. In fact, he won numerous awards as an artist, creating unique designs using pieces of tile, stones, stained glass, etc. A few years into his career, he established his own firm, and developed it into a highly successful business with branch offices scattered over several states. The couple moved up the "social ladder" into an upper-middle class lifestyle. In his mid-40s, Don sold the business and retired from the custom tile industry. As he and Dana began to think about new career adventures such as raising and boarding horses, tragedy returned to Dana's life. An athlete all his life, Don died of a heart attack after an early morning run, only a few months after the sale of his business was finalized. Dana, once again, had to rely upon her resilient spirit for her own and her children's welfare.

For three years after Don's death, Dana continued to live in the comfortable home that she and Don had purchased. She wanted her children's lives to remain as stable as possible. A few months before our 2007 interview occurred, she had decided it was time to make major changes in her life.

Thank you for commenting that my home is beautiful. I like it, too, but I've decided to sell it because so much has gone on here. Maybe we can make a fresh start by moving. I've purchased a farm that, years ago, belonged to my birth grandmother. It's about a two-hour drive from here in a beautiful valley with mountains all around it. It will put me closer to several of my brothers and other birth relatives.

The biggest change in my life has been the death of my husband. Other than that, how am I different now than I was 25 years ago? I'm now in my 50s, and I'm involved with all my family--my birth family and my adopted family. After our birth mother died of cancer, our birth daddy continued to live in our hometown. Since that time, he has passed on, as has my adoptive mother, and my husband—all about four years ago within five months of each other. That was hard on all of us. My adoptive dad had a hard time with Mom's death. They loved each other dearly. Dad retired as an airline pilot and moved to Florida. We keep in touch by email and phone calls.

I've managed to turn out all right. A number of factors have made that possible. It was with God's help, mainly. I really believe in God, but I don't go to church. My adoptive parents tried to force their strict religious beliefs on me and that turned me off from church. Their views of God just didn't go down well with me, but with God's help I've managed to get through a lot.

My husband and my children also got me through tough times. Don helped me to believe in myself. Then we enjoyed raising our children together. Two are grown: one is in college and the other is married with a little girl a year old. My other children are in middle or high school. Raising my children has helped me to mature and become more confident--especially after Don's death, when I became a single parent. My kids have relied on me, and in different ways, I've relied on them too.

We still have some struggles, but, all-in-all, things are going pretty well now. One of my children had an especially tight bond with his dad. The year after Don passed away, he had a hard time. Thankfully, professional counseling helped him. You can never quit being a parent, can you? I told my daughter, "Now that you have a child, she is yours for a lifetime."

It's not easy to lose someone you love. Don's death was a shock, but life had to go on. I am a little bit different than I was when your first book was published in 1985. My bond strengthened with my adoptive parents over the years. As I mentioned, my adoptive mom died. I told my adoptive dad how much I appreciated all he and Mom had done. We opened up and talked a lot about my adoption. I told Dad that I understood why they sent me back to the children's home. It bothered both of them, but I don't know where I would be today if they hadn't stepped in and stopped my running away and acting out. As a parent, when your child does something wrong, you feel like it's your failure. I understand that completely now that I'm a mother of several children.

I let Mom and Dad read your first book. They enjoyed it, but didn't understand why you changed the names. I explained that you changed all the names and other information to keep from embarrassing anyone. They were good about it after my explanation; however, when I told Dad you were coming, it made him nervous.

I get support from both sides of my family now. For example, Mom was here the day I learned about Don's death and she was a great comfort. Also, when Don died, all six of my birth brothers came. All of my adoptive family members came here, too, some from great distances. They were supportive as well. Mom said, "Let's get a camera to make a picture." It was funny that the photo showed that we had lined up in order of our ages — and we didn't plan it.

199

Since you interviewed me 25 years ago, I've become even more involved with my birth family. Maybe it's because I'm the only sister, but my brothers and I stay in close contact with one another. Usually we talk with each other once or twice per week. Jason and I are probably the only ones who don't talk as much. He is so busy, but when he comes in town or when I go down there, we always stop to see one another.

I've gotten to know quite a few of our birth uncles and aunts too. Usually things go pretty well with them, but right after I bought the mountain property, two of my uncles came to visit me and to look over Grandma's old farm. One of them commented, "It was a sad day when you left for the children's home. We all tried to do something."

I looked at him, and said, "What did you try to do?" The fact that no one in my birth family offered to keep us has always bothered me. If anything had happened to one of my brothers when their children were small, I would have done everything in my power to take them into my family. Why didn't they keep us? Of course, we were so poor and there were seven of us, but you would think that relatives would do anything to keep siblings in the family together.

That, of course, is an emotional reaction. I know that in the long run, adoption was the best thing that could have happened to me. I'm blessed—very blessed. I've had great adoptive parents, and I often respond to the needs of my own kids in ways that I learned from them.

They were financially able to take me places and expose me to things I had never heard of or thought about. In lots of ways, I'm just very lucky they adopted me, but I gave them a lot of grief.

You think children who are willful, like I was, tend to be more resilient? I agree with that. When my husband passed away, people said, "You are sure being strong about this."

I thought to myself, "Gosh, it happened to me when I was little, and now it's happening again. This is enough, Lord!"

Jason Reflects on His Adult Life

Jason was a young man in his mid-20s when I first interviewed him. Over a quarter of a century later when he was in his 50s, I re-interviewed him several more times. With these longitudinal perspectives, I was able to observe how Jason had become an even more dedicated father, grandfather, brother, coach and guidance counselor.

During a follow-up meeting, I immediately sensed that a major event had occurred in Jason's life. With difficulty, he shared that he and his wife had separated.

> It's ironic how our lives twist and change. You had sent me transcripts of my 1983 and recent interviews, and I read them again last night. Reading the parts about how much my wife and I had cared for each other in the past brought tears to my eyes, but time moves on! I'm thankful to say my wife and I are acting like responsible adults for the sake of our children and grandchildren. There's no screaming, cursing, or anything like that.
>
> How does the pain associated with my marriage breakup compare to the pain I suffered after my mother's death? I was 7 years old when Momma died. I didn't really understand what was happening. With my wife and me, it felt like something we had created together had crumbled after more than 25 years. When it ended, I was devastated. The pain that I felt when my mother died wasn't even close.
>
> How am I coping with this? A lot of people are supporting and helping me, but one person stands out. Bill, a long-time friend, is the one who rode with me when I was frightened about reconnecting with Dana. Before getting married, he and I roomed together for a while. Now he's a preacher living in another state. He often calls me and our talks really help. One of his remarks really sticks in my mind: "Always remember this (and I've lived by it since)—God won't put you through what he won't get you through." God has been an important part of my life. I believe He is helping me to be stronger in my Christian faith and in my life as I have gone through these troubling times. All of my children are coping with the breakup in different ways as best they can. I try to be honest and open with

them. In a way, we're all in the same boat--just trying to cope and get on with our lives.

Some months later, I met again with Jason and noted that both he and Dana had experienced marital trauma as adults, she with the death of her husband and he with the break-up of his marriage. His response was forthright:

All of us Boone children (his birth siblings) are tough. Just look at how Dana has rebounded. I'm turning my life around. When we last met, I was really feeling down, but I worked to get myself in better shape—in a better place emotionally. My children and I have a closer bond. I spend more time with them, their spouses and my grandchildren. Now I am a better daddy and granddaddy. The bonds that my children and I have created between each other have grown much stronger. We communicate more often and on a deeper level. I think my children and grandchildren have benefitted by my giving them more attention, and I know I have. I get a kick out of playing with my grandchildren. I'm enjoying my family, my church and my friends—my life is full. I also continue to love sports. I play golf, coach and officiate. I have a good time, but I'm trying to keep my life balanced.

I also have more time for myself now. I often sit down and talk to myself personally. I don't know if that's being crazy or not. I pray and have a relationship with God, and God has helped me get through this mess.

As long as my health is still good and I still have the desire, I will continue as a guidance counselor and coach. I love it and I enjoy helping people, especially children. My daughter and sons want me to date, but I haven't yet. Of course, I've met some fine ladies, but I just don't have the desire. I think if the good Lord wants me to have somebody He will help me find the right woman.

A Meeting at Dana's Mountain Farm in 2012

As I was completing this book, Dana, Jason and I met at Dana's new mountain home. It was a sunny day, and as my car gained altitude and entered "high country," I began to wonder what Dana's home would be like. I imagined an old-fashioned, strung-together, added-onto farm homestead, one part of which was her grandmother's original cabin.

What I found was more—much more—than I could have imagined. As I crested a hill, before me was a greeting-card-worthy scene. Dana had transformed what had been a hardscrabble, mountain farm and modest cabin into, what she called, "My paradise—I hate to leave it even to go to town for groceries." On the left, I saw a grassy pasture with several grazing, well-groomed horses. On the right was a nicely designed garage/barn beside a modern dog kennel to house the beloved, friendly Golden Retrievers she raises and trains. Straight ahead, I spotted her home—not pretentious, but was truly picturesque, charming and warm, reflecting Dana's personality.

As I viewed Dana's farm, I thought, "Dana has demonstrated the power of adoption to change lives." Although she lived in her adoptive home only from age 6 to age 12 and spent her teen years at the Home, these changes in her life—along with the inspiration and support of her late husband—had likely helped her see the world from different vantage points. By mixing her original birth family's culture with new knowledge and experiences, she had produced a personal lifestyle that was unique and hopeful—one that would likely enrich the lives of her children, grandchildren and future descendants.

Dana had cleverly designed and carefully used as much of the old cabin as possible to build a modern, attractive and functional home for herself. What's more, she has, to me, symbolically developed a new family identity for herself—taking aspects of her birth family, her adopted family and her married family and uniting them into a unique and positive lifestyle.

After a house tour, Dana and I walked around a lake she had created in the valley on the lower portion of her property, complete with rope swings, a floating swim platform, and a dock for canoes and fishing. About that time, we met one of her sons and some friends as they were returning, empty-handed, from hunting on the forested portion of the farm. She commented: "My children, grandchildren, brothers and the rest of the family love to come here. It's kind of a gathering spot we can use year-round." When I remembered and told Dana that during our first meeting in 1983 she said that she had a "nesting instinct," she laughed and said, "I guess this is my nest."

By then, Jason had arrived and the three of us sat down for the interview. When I asked if there were any important details that had been left out in telling their stories, they began with their birth father's funeral. Looking at her brother, Dana said:

> I remember seeing his new family sitting up front, and we were all in the back. I looked at you, and our other brothers, and noticed that there were no expressions. We were just sitting quietly. After the funeral, I whispered to the six of you, "I'm just not upset by this. As his daughter, I should have cried, and I feel embarrassed that I haven't."

After Jason strongly echoed those feelings, Dana continued:

> Beyond the surface, our birth dad and I just really didn't connect. We lived in different worlds. There was a genetic tie, but not an emotional one.

> Our oldest brother and I have had a close bond for years, and I often stop by to visit him. He lived next door to our birth daddy, but neither of us visited our daddy very much. My oldest brother commented: "Our father remarried several times, and he kind of moved on to his new families." I had similar feelings about our birth daddy. Nothing clicked with him, but with my six brothers there is heavy contact. We are all big buddies.

> Time changes things! As a young teenager, I had this strong urge to see my birth father, but it was disappointing. Right after my (birth) mother died, he would say things like, "You're my little girl--I can't get along without you." But after I grew up and was around him and tried to talk with him, there was no emotion.

> Talking about our birth dad's funeral reminds me of when my adoptive mom died. I attended her funeral, too, but I felt sad and cried. In the last few years of her life, we had gotten to where we talked on the phone quite a bit. We had good conversations, and she gave good advice. Her dry sense of humor made me laugh. She was a good person. Isn't it interesting that death can, at times, bring us closer to

other people? For example, I had two adoptive sisters, and when one died, it intensified my relationship with the surviving one.

Time Provides Healing

Continuing with that train of thought, Dana pointed out that when my original book was written, the word "adopted" had made her feel strange or different, but now it doesn't. Today, she feels part of both her adoptive and her natural family. Jason added:

> I credit Dana for connecting me with my brothers. I'm indebted to her. I see how strong she is mentally and emotionally, and I think our mother was a lot like that. I see a lot of my mother in her.
>
> Dr. Powell, let me ask you a question--you've met with Dana and me a number of times. What similarities do you see in us?

I responded that I saw them both as very intelligent, sensitive and caring people. They both are extremely committed to their children and they are determined to see that their children do not go through what they experienced. I added that they are also concerned about other people and making their communities better places to live. Jason replied:

> I understand what you've said about giving to other people and looking out for their needs. I see a lot of that in Dana and I think I share some of those same characteristics. I'm glad to say that I don't see any anger or hatred in either of us. I think we're very easy-going, yet we don't let others run over us. If we need to stand up for what we believe in, we will.
>
> I was separated from Dana and my brothers for many years, and we're now trying to establish a stronger bond. That's something we had kind of lost. I know I have a sister and brothers, but I don't have brothers and a sister that I grew up with. I've missed some of those growing-up-together memories more than anything else. Now we're filling in the gaps.
>
> You asked, who is my real family--my birth family, my adoptive family or a mix of both? I think I would have to say my adoptive family comes first, although I'm growing closer to my sister and

brothers as I grow older. My adoptive mom and dad wouldn't let me talk about my birth family, yet they sacrificed to put me through public school and college, housed me, clothed me and took me to baseball practice and games. I could go on and on describing little ways that they took care of me and loved me.

Listening carefully, Dana responded:

Jason, hearing you talk about the love and care you received from the Clarks helps me to understand why you identify yourself first as a Clark, but I'm glad we're all in touch with each other now as brothers and sister. What helped me to get closer to my adoptive family? What helped me fit in? I think it was just time. Twenty-five years ago, my thinking was a lot different. Back then, I was angry; I had this chip on my shoulder. Now, when I hear my kids tell someone, "Mom was adopted," it feels like they are talking about someone else.

Yes, adoption is a lifetime thing. I have tried to stay in contact with various members of both birth and adoptive families, and both sides stay in touch with me. When a family adopts an older child, they have to be willing to take in whatever past experiences the child brings with him or her. A lot of families don't do that. They want it all to be fresh. Parents need to understand that older adopted kids come in with a background, and they need to respect that.

Jason agreed:

That's the one thing that has bothered me. Dana, my [adoptive] Mom and Dad would never let me see you and my brothers or even let me talk about you. I don't mean they would punish me if I mentioned anything about my birth family, but I knew this was an uncomfortable subject. So for the most part I never brought it up.

Are Older Child Adoptions Risky?

During our first meeting together in 1983, both Dana and Jason expressed an interest in adopting older children, but for various reasons that never occurred. I was curious about their current views on adoption now that they're 50-plus years old. Jason's response was that his dream of adopting a child about the same age that he was when he was adopted based on his desire to do "the same favor for someone else," but added that:

> We had children of our own, however, and I got so busy with them and making a living for our family that adopting an older child never happened.

Reflecting on the rough times she had had with her adoption, Dana admitted:

> Realizing how upsetting older-child adoptions can be for children when they are placed with strangers, it's hard for me to imagine releasing one of my own children for adoption. Maybe new ways of adopting children, like "open-adoptions," can make it easier for children. I hope so.

> My being adopted benefitted me, but I don't think a lot of older child adoptions have worked out as well as mine. In all honesty, I don't think some older children should be adopted. They just have too much emotional baggage. Parents of older adopted kids have to deal with a lot of emotions, a lot of feelings, and I'm impressed and admire people who can do that. To be honest, I wouldn't do it. Babies or kids up to 2-year-olds would be fine, but when you have a child with seven or eight years of memories, I think you are asking for trouble. Some have worked out, but I suspect with careful research, you will find it has been a struggle for most people involved.

Jason reiterated that he is more positive about the adoption of older children, and asked his sister what she thought would be best for children in situations like the one they and their siblings had been in. Dana could find no solution she felt totally comfortable with. Indeed, she had had misgivings regarding her own children:

> When I had all my kids, it scared me. I wondered if something happened to Don and me, who would take them? We did find a family who agreed, but my kids were small then. Now they are older, and that's not a concern. Going back to what to do for older

kids with troubled backgrounds, there is no good answer. It just depends on the kid and the people. Everybody's different. As far as training for parents who are taking a child with a prior history, they've got to accept that reality. Talking openly and honestly is the key. If the birth father is an alcoholic or whatever, get it out in the open and help the whole family to talk about it with the child. In my adoption, Mom, Dad and I tried to talk about our dilemma before they sent me back to the children's home, but I don't think they really wanted to hear my perspective.

I'm almost in agreement with open adoptions. I know an adopted kid who is growing up with that arrangement, and it's working. They want the little boy to know his mother. I know it scared Mom because I wanted to go back and be with my biological family. Once I had been around them for umpteen years as a teenager, I thought, "What was I so upset about? Gee, they are just ordinary people." However as a younger adopted kid, I had built my birth father and his brothers and sisters up in my mind in unrealistic ways. Seeing them helped me in the long run. Adopted kids can learn from reality.

Older adopted children should be allowed to see their birth parents if they make that choice. If a child's decision doesn't work out, it doesn't work out. Do what you have to do! You've just got to get that out of your system. If you don't, it will haunt you.

I love and care very deeply for my biological brothers. Contrary to what I expected when we first got back together, there wasn't that immediate gut connection you think will be there.

Turning to look directly at Jason, she added earnestly:

When I am around you guys and hang out with you for a while, I realize that while we have a bond, some of the connection is missing—like there are gaps. It's been an interesting struggle growing up in two different families. The biggest thing for me is if a family has an adopted child with a yearning to see his biological family, let it happen. Let the child talk about it. Then if they still want to see their birth family, call them and say something like:"We adopted 'Sally' and she would really like to see you and be more involved." Temporarily it may hurt or upset the adoptive parents, but in the long run, it's going to help the relationship. I wasn't allowed to see all my brothers. It took me forever to find you, Jason.

Eagerly, Jason responded: "Dana, I'm glad you found me. You're right! We're now filling in the gaps we missed."

Saying goodbye, I retraced my drive through the mountains and into a valley. In the heart of the valley was the small town where Dana and Jason were born and lived as young children with their birth family. Some of their brothers continue to live there. It once was a regional center with thriving businesses, but unfortunately much of the town now looks deserted. Many downtown stores have closed, and large complexes of buildings that once housed bustling industrial plants have been abandoned.

It was late afternoon, and I stopped at a restaurant on the outskirts of the town for dinner. The food was very tasty, but the ambiance of the restaurant seemed depressed. There were few customers, and I took advantage of the restaurant's inactivity to ask my attentive waitress about the economy of the town.

"Everything has gone overseas. There ain't much going on around here anymore, and I guess I'm stuck here," she sighed. She asked where I was from and what I did for a living and I replied, "I'm a retired professor who is writing a book." She responded, "I've taken a couple of courses at the local community college, but gave that up." Although we talked only briefly, she seemed hopeless and "stuck" in an environment that appeared to offer few opportunities.

Headed for home, I thought of Dana and Jason and wondered what their lives might be like if they had not been placed at the children's home and had not become part of its older-child adoption program. If they had been taken in by aunts and uncles and had grown up in the town of their birth, would their lives be similar to that of the waitress I encountered—somewhat hopeless and bleak?

As I pondered such questions, I concluded that older child adoptions, with all their challenges—good and bad—have the potential to help change the course of people's lives (and their hopes and aspirations as well) in remarkable ways.

Postscript

A few months after the joint meeting with Dana and Jason, I received an email from Dana:

> Dr. Powell--Hope all is well with you. I wanted to give you an update. I am still at the farm, and things are working out okay for me. One of my daughters tells me that I have The Holy Spirit on my shoulder. I know you have made a lot of progress on the book. How exciting! I also wanted to tell you that I have been thinking a lot about older child adoptions. Recently, I talked to another person who was adopted as a school-age child. He shares my same emotions and feelings: "You always feel like you are running." Just wanted to keep giving you thoughts. Look forward to seeing you again. Dana.

Several weeks later, we sat down at her dining table for coffee and conversation. I gave her a copy of the email to refresh her memory. She read it and responded.

> I can identify with those words: "We always feel like we're running." It's like some of us are never sure how solid the ground is under our feet. We fear that somehow our adoptive relationships may fall apart. A lot of this fear may be in our heads, but it can keep us from completely relaxing and being ourselves when we are with--or even thinking about--our adoptive family. We're running through mine fields fearing that suddenly something will blow up.

Dana then focused upon her daughter's comment that "the Holy Spirit must be on your shoulder."

> She and I have talked a lot over the years about my past and my belief that God has protected me and helped me through difficult times.

My daughter is more religious than I am, and she truly believes that the Holy Spirit is always right here with us. I guess I do, too, but she is more in touch with things like that. Over the years, though, I feel God has stepped in to guide and protect me at critical times.

All of my children look out for me in their own ways, and I try to look out for them. For example, one of my sons is a good businessman. He has kind of become my business manager. I don't make any financial decisions without talking with him. In spite of this need to "keep on running," my adoption was the best thing that could have happened to me after my birth mother died and my family fell apart. With almost 50 years of experience, I can honestly say that adoption has changed my life for the better.

CHAPTER NINE

Adopted at age 14

Birth, Adoptive and Adult Family Structures

Birth Family: Marshall and a sister were born overseas to a military father and foreign mother. After the family returned to the US, another sister was born. Not long thereafter, the father abandoned his family. Although not confirmed, it's believed he was killed in an automobile accident.

Hampered by a language barrier and lacking the training for higher income positions, the birth mother worked long hours as a waitress in an attempt to keep her family together. Her efforts, however, were not sufficient, and the Department of Social Services placed the children in care of the children's home. Marshall, 9 and the middle child, a sister who was a few years younger, lived for several years on the campus. The youngest child, then a toddler, was first placed with a retired couple, who wanted to adopt her but were denied due to their ages. Later, she was adopted by another couple in their early 20s and childless. Her adoptive home was near the children's home, and her siblings visited frequently. The adoptive parents eventually adopted Marshall and the middle child also.

Adoptive Family: In addition to adopting Marshall and his sisters, the adoptive parents later had several children born to them.

Adult Family: Marshall and his wife, Alice, have several children and more than a half-dozen grandchildren.

MARSHALL

"The only advice I would give to
somebody that I was counseling about
adoption is this: Don't give up on an
older child with a difficult past—like Marshall
(who was adopted at age 14). He (or she) can
turn out just as great as Marshall has!"

(Marshall's wife)

SECTION I

INITIAL INTERVIEW: AGE 37

I found Marshall's well-maintained home near an Air Force Base. His wife, Alice, joined us for the interview and added interesting details to Marshall's remarkable life and adoption story.

Their attractive home was child-friendly and welcoming, a reflection of their personal values. Alice pointed out toys and furniture that Marshall had made for their children—a doll cradle for the daughters and bookcases for the boys—plus sturdy outdoor play equipment. In turn, Marshall noted that Alice used many of her handmade sewing and craft projects to create the beautiful decor. I also sampled Alice's homemade peach cobbler (her mother's recipe); it was outstanding.

Instinctively, I felt comfortable with this young couple, and it seemed evident that they loved and admired one another. Alice described Marshall as a reserved person who guarded his personal feelings. As the three of us talked, I marveled at his resilience and accomplishments. He had survived a chaotic childhood, had become a loving, strong father and husband, and was a committed church and community leader—volunteering to serve others in roles such as a little league coach and Sunday School teacher. It was hard to believe this was a person who had been ordered to move out of his adopted mother's home at 16.

Now, as a mature adult, he has a committed, close relationship with his adoptive family. Certainly, he must have carried unpleasant memories from the past into the present, but he had not become bitter. Like others in my study, he had developed the ability to determine whom he could trust. I felt honored that he chose to share his adoption story with me, believing his story could make the lives of future older adopted children easier.

In answer to my question of how adoption had affected his life, he insisted he could see no link one way or the other with a life that he described as "ordinary," elaborating:

> My wife and I are getting ready to celebrate our 14th wedding anniversary. I've got a great wife—she's a great woman. We have wonderful children. We're actively involved in church, and I've been employed at the Air Force Base for 12 years now. In my leisure time, I like to go fishing and play golf. I used to bowl and play basketball with some buddies, but I don't do all of that now since the kids have come along. I've told Alice many times that I can't wait 'til I start to take my children fishing with me. I took them to see a softball game last night, so they could cheer for their mother who plays on a team.
>
> I don't think I treat my own children any differently than a typical father might. I've never really sat down and analyzed anything about it. I want them to have things a little easier than I did. I do the best for them that I can. I guess if anything ever happens to us, my adoptive parents are my beneficiaries right now after Alice. We've been thinking about getting that changed. They're not really old yet—both are in their 40s—but if anything ever happened to Alice and me, I think it would be too much for them to try to raise our kids.

Eager to explain more, Alice bragged on Marshall as she spoke about his parenting and adoption.

216

He's the best daddy. He's not perfect. But of all the daddies I can look around and see, there's none that I would replace him with. He's great in a lot of ways. He takes care of them as well as I can. Not too many daddies are like that. I can go off at night and know that they will be okay. The house may be destroyed when I come home, but I know that they'll be taken care of. He took them two nights this week to pools to practice their swimming lessons when he would have preferred to go play golf. I play softball and he watches the children while I play. He just gives them himself—his full attention.

To me, what probably affected him more than the children's home and the adoption was that he remembers his mother giving him up in the first place. There is a sense of rejection—maybe a lot of other older adopted children feel it, too. Nonetheless, he's very responsible. He doesn't sit back and wait for somebody to give him something. Nobody has given us anything. What little bit we have, he's worked for it. It's ours.

He's built a wall around his emotions to protect himself. If you're not vulnerable, you can't get hurt. He won't talk about his past, his adoption or his childhood. Every once in a while—maybe once a year—he'll come up with something that happened in his childhood.

Turning to the topic of his successful adjustment to life, Marshall describes his achievement as "pretty fair," insisting there is always room for improvement. After high school, as a civilian, he completed a four-year training program in electronics at the Air Base, then earned a two-year degree and a certificate in electronics from the State Department of Education. He noted:

It's been hard to attend college at nights and on weekends while continuing to meet my family and work responsibilities. I've been thinking about re-enrolling in college this fall to finish a four-year degree. At work, we do a lot of complicated things to maintain military aircraft. There's a lot involved, and you've got to always do a first-class job. As a matter of fact, that's the reason I went back to the base for a couple of hours very early this morning—even though it's Saturday. Later, I went fishing at a lake, the first time I've been fishing this summer. I usually start in May and go at least two or three times a month.

I work a lot of overtime and a lot of long hours, seven days a week. I want every airplane I work on to remain in top-flight condition. We can't afford to risk any lives.

Then, clearly eager to be as responsible as a research subject as he is in his profession, he turned to the subject of his childhood.

I was so young when my dad left us, I don't really remember him. I just have a picture of him. I do know he served in the Army. My [birth] mom was foreign born. She doesn't speak English well, and wasn't trained for good-paying jobs, so she gave up her three children. At that time, I guess I was about age 7; the second oldest, a sister, was about 6; and my youngest sister was less than a year old.

Alice pointed out the need for "special people" to work with children, especially older adopted children who can remember their birth parents. She added:

Nobody likes to be rejected. If that could be overcome, I think a lot of the issues of older child adoptions would be solved. But I don't know how, because rejection is a fact. Adopted children want to know, "Why didn't my mother want me? Why didn't my father want me? Why didn't my mother want me enough to do things to keep me?" Marshall experienced severe trauma in his early life with his birth parents. He watched his mother be chased with an axe by his father. He suppresses things like that.

Marshall pointed out that he and his siblings would go for years without hearing from their birth mom, who had a drinking problem and "other issues." Then Alice quietly added:

Marshall has something he won't say. As the Department of Social Services was taking him and his sisters away from their [birth] mother, she whispered to them, "I'm coming back to get you. Don't let the three of you get separated." She left the impression with Marshall that as the oldest child he was the one to look after his sisters,

218

and stay in contact with them. While they were growing up, he honored her request by looking after them as best he could.

Marshall remembered that when he and his sisters were first taken from her, their mother visited occasionally—not often—and even brought bikes one year for Christmas, explaining that she was working in a restaurant across the street from a large manufacturing plant south of Atlanta. Then he described a poignant experience that occurred after he moved out of his adoptive home:

> When I was about 20 years old and had my own car and some money, I would drive around looking for her. It wasn't that hard to find my mother. I started hitting restaurants around the area. As I peeked in a front window of one of them, I spotted her. I went in and sat at a bar stool. She started walking toward me, and I knew she was my mom. She walked by me, stopped, looked me over, and said, "Marshall?" We hugged and she cried. The children's home had told us they couldn't find her. Maybe they tried, and couldn't do it. It all depends on what you put into it. One phone call doesn't do it.
>
> For a long time my birth mom was pretty hard on me for changing my last name to the name of my adoptive parents. She didn't like that. I decided there was no need to try to get my two moms together. If my real mom saw how young my adoptive mom was, it would cause friction.

Turning his attention to the actual sequence of events that led to his and his sisters' adoption, Marshall explained that he and his older sister went directly into the dormitories on the Home's campus, while his younger sister was placed with a foster family, an elderly, "country-type" couple who understood the children wanted to stay close and often invited the two older ones to spend part of the summer, holidays and weekends with them.

> They had their own milk cows and their own chickens and made their own butter. We loved to go there, and we kind of informally adopted them as grandparents. Her foster family tried to adopt my baby sister, but they were too old. It really broke her heart to leave

219

them. She had bonded with them. Losing them has affected her to this day. She still finds it hard to trust people.

Marshall then pointed out that being in the children's home "really wasn't that bad," explaining that he had a chance to work on the farm and also in the print shop during his eight years there. Because the second foster home into which his baby sister was placed was close by, he and his other sister were able to visit often. About a year after she moved in, the foster parents decided to adopt all three of the siblings. He offered a detailed description of how their lives changed:

My adopted dad loved nature, and since we lived close to the mountains, we got to do outside things with him. We went fishing, hiking, camping and really learned a lot. He was also an expert automotive mechanic, and he built his own camping trailer and his own airplane. It was a different kind of life for us. I got out more, saw new things, and got to meet different people. Since we lived near the campus we went to the same school as the kids from the children's home. However, not long after my older sister and I moved in, my (adoptive) dad was transferred to Atlanta where I now live. That move occurred in the '60s. I finished school here, and then went into the military service. After I was discharged, Alice and I met and got married.

As far as fitting into our adoptive family, I had a problem. My adoptive mom is less than seven years older than I am. I was adopted at age 14, and by the time I reached age 15, I really resented being told what to do by a 22-year-old. We had lots of conflicts and arguments. First, she lied to me about her age—telling me she was 35 or so. I knew she wasn't that old. I got a peek at her driver's license, and that told the tale. Finally, I left them and got out on my own.

What happened is that things just built-up, and it all exploded over going to church. They were really heavy into church, and, of course, they wanted us to go to church on Sunday mornings and Sunday evenings. I went to the movies on a Sunday afternoon, and I didn't make it to church that night. My [adoptive] mom really gave me a hard time, things escalated and I picked up something and threw it at her. She told me to get out of her home, and I left.

Later, she asked me to come back, but instead I went downtown, lived at the YMCA, and worked at a supermarket. We had a real nice minister at our church. I even lived with him and his family for a while before I went into service.

To be truthful, I've had some problems to work through, but I've had good people who have kept tabs on me. They were interested, cared for me, and encouraged me. After I moved out, I stayed in touch with my sisters through my adopted dad. I didn't know Alice when this was going on. I met her after I was discharged from the service. During my military time, things kind of calmed down with my adopted family . . . the family wrote me and I wrote them back . . . and I matured . . . these things helped all of us get back together.

With my adopted parents, I think the biggest problem was our ages. They were too young to adopt me—with me being 14. But I don't hold anything against them. In fact, I now consider them my folks. It is a day's drive to their home, and we go visit them at least once a year and sometimes twice.

SECTION II

MARSHALL: AGES 37 TO EARLY 70S

Interviews and Communication

A quarter of a century after the initial interview, I found Marshall and his wife living in the same home where I had first interviewed him. A skilled craftsman, Marshall had expanded and remodeled it. Alice was busy home-schooling their grandsons.

Marshall remained what Alice had called him, a quarter-of-a-century earlier: " the best daddy. . . great in a lot of ways." Asked what had changed since our 1983 meeting, he responded with trademark honesty:

Alice and I are fine, except for getting older. Altogether everything is okay. Our kids are grown, and doing well, and we have grandchildren.

I've grown closer to my adoptive family. After my wife and I married, they moved out of state to work in a Christian school for several years. Then they moved again, and my dad opened up an automotive repair business, which was going pretty well. One day, he was helping one of his brothers move, riding in the back of a truck holding down some things. Evidently, the load shifted and he was thrown off. He lived a couple of weeks in a coma before he died. I was about 38 or 39 at that time, and his death hit me hard. I miss him very much.

My adoptive parents had several [birth] kids together. Over the years we've grown closer. Mom has become like an older sister. Somehow, we've managed to work through things from the past. I love them, they're my family. She's my mom, she calls regularly, and we keep in touch. She still sends birthday and Christmas cards and notes. In fact, our children have thought of my adopted parents as their grandparents. Alice and I now probably know more about what's going on with my adopted family and their children than with my own blood sisters. As a matter of fact, we're going to go see my adoptive mom sometime this fall. On the way we'll also stop by to visit one of her daughters, my adopted sister.

Another adopted sister died from cancer. As tragic as her death was, it brought the family closer "through all that sadness." Before her death, she home-schooled her kids, and she became an expert in that field. She was in charge of testing for the home schooling group in the state where she lived and also served as a consultant, providing information and that sort of thing. As a result, Alice, is now home schooling our grandsons, and she is doing an outstanding job.

Marshall noted that two of their four children live close by, and they visit back and forth two to three times a week. The family, he reported, is close-knit:

We do a lot of things together. In November all of us are going to Walt Disney World. We went two years ago. It was great fun.

Regarding his birth family, Marshall explains:

Years ago my maternal grandmother, visited us a couple of times from overseas. She wanted Alice and me to come and visit her. She's passed away now, but when she offered to buy us tickets, the big thing was plane hi-jackings so that scared us from going and we never took the opportunity. It would have been neat to go over there. So, I really haven't connected with my kinfolks on my birth mom's side, and I don't know hardly anything about my kinfolks on my birth father's side.

Marshall sees himself as responsible for "two moms":

My real mom is part of our family too. In fact, her grandchildren, my kids, grew up calling my birth mother, "Mam-maw." I do what I can to look after both. I've gotten my real mom to move a few miles away. She's in her 80s now, so I take her to the doctor and take her to shop for groceries, and things like that.

My adoptive mom is like a combination of a mom and an older sister, and I feel like her daughters are truly like younger sisters.

How is it to have two moms? I don't say anything in front of my real mom about my adoptive parents. If she doesn't ask, I don't volunteer any information. I try to keep it low key. Occasionally, my adoptive mom will say, "How's your mom doing?" but that's it. I just keep them separated.

Having retired from 37 years with the Air Force, Marshall took a part-time job at a hardware store, relieved to be out of a position requiring that he manage other people. He was considering accepting another part-time position with his former Air Force boss for the extra income, but stressed that he wanted to "still have time to play golf with my sons."

With the perspective of added years, he was forthcoming with advice regarding older child adoptions.

If the children's home had provided us with a home-like co-ed cottage we would have been better off. Maybe there should be a maximum of only six to eight children living together in a cottage. Also, I would suggest that the Home have a therapist come regularly to check on the children. Having somebody in a children's home that kids could really talk with about whatever is important to them would help a lot. It would help clear up things about their family and their future.

I ran away a couple of times, but I can't remember now why I did it. One time, my buddy said, "Let's go." When we got back, we got our bottoms torn up a little bit. As I look back on it now, living in the children's home didn't bother me that much. I'll always remember the recreation director. I could relate and talk openly with him. There were too many kids—20 or 30 per dorm—and not enough staff like the recreation director.

Is 14 or 15 is too old to be adopted? In a way, I think it is. Teenagers, they're hard children to deal with. I can't really say that they're not fit for adoption because I'm proud I was adopted. I've had no regrets. My adoption experience and being in the children's home did make me stronger, but I don't want our kids or grandkids to witness or go through what I did. I want them to have a better home life than I had. I'm not saying that I had a bad home life. Now that I'm older and look back . . . I learned a lot.

Postscript: 2020 "It Ain't Over Till It's Over"

Prior to publication of this book, Yogi Berra, baseball's legendary hero and "accidental philosopher," died (September 22, 2015). Many press obituaries included Yogi's famous "street-wisdom" saying: "It ain't over till it's over." [1]

Too often, adoptions are considered failures if children leave their adoptive families amid anger and conflict. However, being adopted is a lifelong process. Time and other factors can provide healing. Now, about a half-century after he stormed out of his adoptive home, Marshall said, "I'm glad I was adopted." I, therefore, believe that Yogi Berra's words apply to older child adoptions: "It ain't over till it's over."

PART THREE

CONCLUSIONS

Concluding Perspectives

In the years since the original 1983 research was conducted, the landscape of adoptions has been revolutionized. A few examples:

(1) Fewer infant and young child adoptions are occurring, and conversely far more adoptions are taking place with older and special-needs children.

(2) Secrecy issues are giving way to "open adoptions."

(3) More adoptive and birth parents are choosing to remain single parents.

(4) The propective adoptive parent approval process is changing from a few social workers and/or other professionals making decisions to more group-training and self-selection models.

(5) Families who adopt older and special-needs children are being provided with non-blaming, long-term support and therapeutic coaching, plus some financial assistance.

The chapters that follow offer not only my thoughts and experiences, but the thoughts and ideas of others. Chapter 10 features Sandy Cook who has 45 years of experience in the field of child adoptions. Chapter 11 offers advice from the nine older child veterans/participants. They bring new approaches and fresh thinking to the complex task of helping children and their families (both adoptive and birth) successfully negotiate the process of "transplanting older children into unaccustomed earth."

CHAPTER TEN

Sandy Cook, MSW, Retired Executive Director,
NC Children's Home Society
and
John Powell, Ph.D., Author

OBSERVATIONS

"Adopting older children is not easy. It's challenging, but it can also be joyful and one of the most
meaningful experiences one can have in life."
Sandy Cook, MSW

Given the dramatic changes in adoption practice and policy that have occurred since my 1985 adoption book was published, I asked Sandy Cook, MSW, ACSW, LCSW, if she would join me in writing this chapter. For more than 45 years, Sandy has experienced the adoption revolution on three levels: (1) as an adoption worker, (2) as an adoption supervisor, and (3) as the retired Executive Director of the Children's Home Society of NC (the oldest and largest private adoption agency in that state). We decided to share her extensive experience and her keen insights by using a dialogue format.

Dialogue

Sandy Cook and I met several times to discuss the adoption stories in this volume. A summary of our conversation is given in this chapter. My questions and comments are in italics.

Sandy, do you believe a "revolution" has occurred in the adoption of older children in the past 50 years?

Yes, I do! Parents, professionals and many interested people are now more realistic about adopting older children. When I started in social work in the 1960s, adoption agencies focused primarily, but not exclusively, on white, middle-class Americans. Most applicants wanted young children to fill empty spots in their hearts because they couldn't have children—and they became good parents for their adopted children. In about 1960, when the supply of infants and young children began a steady decline, the number of older and special-needs adoptable children simultaneously expanded, prompting new thinking about placing school-aged children into adoptive homes.

We've witnessed many successful older child adoptions, but have some ingrained concepts from the earlier emphasis on placing infants and young children made the transition more difficult?

Yes, and I expect that in some limited ways they still influence practice today. The people in this book were adopted between 1958 and 1970, which was the beginning of the modern older child adoption movement. Some families who adopted school-aged children during that time acted as if the children were infants with no memories of their birth families. Frequently, they insisted the adoption details, especially the identities of the birth families, be kept secret. That perpetuated the secrecy notions common in the infant adoptions era. These parents hoped the children would quickly forget about their original families, but forgetting about one's origins is just not possible. Lee [Chapter 7] carried around his birth mother's photograph during his childhood and would not call his adoptive mother "Momma" until he was a grown man. Wisely, his adoptive parents understood that he could love them and at the same time love his deceased birth mother.

In what other ways have adoption practices and policies changed?

Fortunately, there has been a shift in thinking. As older child adoptions became more common and socially accepted, we began to receive applications from people motivated to adopt for a wide variety of reasons, such as: (1) feeling as if they had room for another child; (2) the desire to continue their relationship with a child who had been in their foster care; or (3) a special calling to parent an older child—perhaps a child with a different racial identity or with special needs. These people certainly weren't trying to pretend their adopted child was their birth child. When I started working in this field, adoptive families wanted older children they adopted to look like them, act like them, and accept their values. Today's adoptive parents want to improve the lives of their older adopted children, and are also more willing to accept children

230

who may not be at the top of the class. They just want their children to be the best they can be. They have more information and a greater understanding about the traumas, losses and chaos these children have faced, but that doesn't mean the adoptions are not still challenging.

Have attitudes about separating adopted children from birth family members, including birth siblings, changed as well?

Some of the persons featured in this book rightly complain that separating them from their siblings is "wrong." I strongly agree, and I'm thankful such practices are declining. Our agency stresses strengthening sibling relationships, especially for those who have lost connections with their birth parents. Only if there are compelling reasons should a particular sibling group not be placed together. For example, when children have been perpetrators of sexual abuse, and there is fear it may occur again. But even in such unfortunate situations, it may be best to maintain contact in safe ways. I've heard some colleagues say, "We could place the little ones in an adoptive family, but the bigger, older ones keep that from happening." Even then, I urge that we do everything possible to avoid splitting them up. If separations do occur, the children need regular, frequent contacts with one another, not just a Christmas visit. As the people in your book have demonstrated, sibling ties or relationships can become more meaningful as we grow older.

Joanne, Maynard and Benny's adoption stories (Chapter 6) are painful but compelling examples. Adopted separately, they were kept apart for about a dozen years. When I interviewed Joanne and Maynard in 1983 they were in their 20s and just getting to know one another again. As they've grown older, they've realized they need one another more than ever before. For example, they worked together to "save" Benny from a drug culture, and moved him near their homes. Now, the three are providing important mutual support —especially since all six of their adoptive parents have died.

Stories like theirs reinforce my belief that we should keep the bonds of brothers and sisters as strong as possible. It's appalling to remember that in years past, some adoptive parents and many professionals thought allowing contacts with birth family members would "contaminate" what they considered to be a preferred controlled environment.

Perhaps some adoptive parents, like Jason's [Chapter 8], who have had difficulty accepting their inability to have biological children send their adopted children conflicting messages.

At our agency, we talk about the idea that adoptions are frequently associated with losses on the part of the adopting parents, especially those without birth children. Childless couples experience the loss of a fantasy child they were going to create. Jason's adoptive parents (Chapter 8) changed his life in many positive ways, and Jason loves and respects them for what they have done for him. Yet even now that Jason is in his 60s and his widowed adoptive mother is in her 90s, there's an emotional place where they can't go—mentioning or discussing Jason's birth family. That, to me, is sad.

Older adopted children have many losses to contend with, such as the partial loss of their original identity, and the lack of daily contact with their birth family members. I could go on and on listing others, but the most serious one is a sense of rejection. They are able to remember that their birth family gave them up for adoption, and no one in their birth families stepped forward to take them in. Alice, Marshall's wife (Chapter 9), expressed this well when she said he was most affected by the memory that his mother gave him up, and yet that hasn't kept him from being a good husband and father himself.

How can we help those struggling to deal with loss issues?

Experiencing the ups and downs of life helps make us who we are. For older and special-needs children, our agency seeks adoptive parents who can talk about their feelings and experiences, especially times when they've successfully coped with difficult situations. How else are they going to understand and help children who have had to cope with serious issues? I've always kind of chuckled at the word "resolve," because how much do we really "resolve" anything? You don't, but you can learn to cope, find new ways to accommodate and move on.

Maybe it's a way to express inner feelings, but don't some children and prospective adoptive parents have unreasonable fantasies about their future parent or child?

Older children often fantasize that their new adoptive family members will be super-human people—sports or rock stars, rich and famous—and some parents who hope to adopt also have unreasonable expectations. Those of us working in this field are committed to helping all parties—children, adoptive families, and birth families—deal with both their losses and fantasies.

We both know the importance of post-adoption support. What types of support services does your agency provide?

When trauma, neglect and abuse have occurred during critical developmental stages, the effects just don't go away. Because adoptive families know their children best and are with them 24/7, they can play crucial roles in helping to heal the hurt. Professionals need to empower and support adoptive families, letting them know they don't have to be perfect or know all the answers. They need to be partners with adoption agencies. When social workers work as partners with the families, they can give them tips on ways to cope with difficult situations and, maybe most of all, give them hope.

The saying "It takes a village to raise a child" applies here.

These families need to be part of bigger communities. We can often help parents link-up with supportive people who can offer the kind of support grandmothers and granddaddies often provide. When families adopt cross-culturally, it's especially important to help children appreciate and be proud of their unique cultural identities. In past years, we often put adoptive families through investigation-like procedures when things weren't going well, but we've tried to get away from that. Parents need to feel free to touch base for motivation and support without feeling condemned or being afraid of being labeled as "failures." Adoptive parent support groups seem to work best when people can come and leave as needed. You want to be around people that can help you. An organized buddy system can also help. Sometimes two families are assigned to support one another, or families may informally find "buddies" during pre-adoption training groups and stay in touch.

What do you do when parents need to learn to accept adopted children for who they are, and not as the parents might have imagined them to be?

Because older adopted children have developed their own personalities and style of living, their nurturing needs, while still quite important, are different from those of infants. Researchers continue to argue about nurture versus nature, but I believe a significant part of an older adopted child's disposition and temperament derives from a mix of early experiences and genetics. Therefore, adoptive families need to acknowledge and accept that their child may not look like them, like the same things they do, or act like them. Maybe Lee's (Chapter 7) comparison of adoptions of older children to marriages is appropriate. Successful marriages and adoptions require accommodations from all involved parties. Some of the people featured in these stories suffered from severe nurturing deficits early in their lives, but somehow they have managed to become healthy, productive and successful people.

Angela (Chapter 5) is a good example of someone who, despite very challenging situations both before and after her adoption, became a successful businesswoman, and a kind, caring and loving person.

We all have something I call "God's little piece" inside us that makes us different. It can be freeing to adoptive families to see that and not try to make their adopted children like themselves. I think we've come a long way in that regard. By effectively using psychotherapy, Angela became what her therapist described as a "miracle child." She turned her life around, and ended her story by saying she rediscovered the "little child" inside her. I think of that as "God's little piece."

What changes do you think we may see in older-child adoptions?

Eliminating poverty would remove a lot of the issues we have discussed. Neglect often comes from poverty. I do think innovative programs are needed. I am also concerned about children living in foster care. It can be confusing and frightening for children to move somewhere that is temporary and wrenching to leave those they may have grown to love and depend upon. The stories of Maynard and Benny (Chapter 6) are both revealing and painful to read. Sometimes for safety reasons a child needs to be in foster care, but it should be for as short a time as possible.

Another obstacle to making older child adoptions more meaningful is related to money. As part of what I would term "inheritance inequality," several participants in this study felt they had been treated unfairly—sometimes doubly so. Children who are legally freed for adoption may lose all statutory inheritance rights from the birth family if there is no will (depending upon state laws), and also might not be included or treated fairly in wills and inheritance by the adopted family, perhaps because they are not "blood kin."

Angela (Chapter 5) again is a good example. Since she became a successful person in many areas including her business career, she did not need a portion of her adoptive relative's inheritance to enjoy a comfortable retirement. Still, being deliberately left out of the will was a blow to her sense of adoptive family kinship. The bar for inclusion in inheritances, unfortunately, seems to be higher for adopted children than birth children.

Is that changing?

Today, most parents want their adopted children to receive a fair share of the family's inheritance, but there are a few family members who subscribe (consciously and unconsciously) to the "blood is thicker than water" concept. However, such notions are becoming less prevalent. I believe one reason such bias is no longer so pervasive is that in the 60s and 70s, many people owned farms and "land" and inheritance rights were very important to them. Mountain people moved into a mobile home next to Momma or Daddy—or maybe built a house down the road. Now, in our transient society, there is not as much concern about keeping "family farms" in perpetuity. Sometimes a family heirloom is a source of contention, but such issues aren't as important today.

I can remember a couple thinking out loud: "We won't have this child but three or four years. We've been raising our other children since birth. Should we leave more to our birth children than to an adopted child?" Prospective parents need to consider these issues before they decide to adopt older children. Because childless couples seem to want someone to carry on their name, they usually leave shares of the inheritance to any children they adopt.

Many religious groups have special rituals for affirming that adopted children of any age are fully a part of their new adopted families and also of their church communities.

I agree such rituals can help. Also, some adoptive parents have "welcome" parties to honor and introduce their new child or children to family, friends and neighbors.

You mentioned that today's prospective adoptive parents are more open and flexible regarding the needs of adopted children. How does your agency take advantage of this openness?

Social workers have developed various curricula to train adoptive families, such as MAPP (Model Approach to Partnerships in Parenting) and PRIDE (Parent Resources for Information, Development and Education).[1] North Carolina requires MAPP training for all adoptive parent applicants, which certainly has improved the process for both children and parents. We have discussions led by veteran adoptive parents and also hear from older adopted children. The underlying philosophy is that we're all in this together—as partners. The agency is not telling people what to do, but helping them assess themselves. A vast majority of adoptive parents learn a great deal and use the concepts to make good beginnings with their new children. Yet, they continue to need on-going support and assistance—perhaps throughout their children's lives.

Post-adoption services are critical and should be funded and readily available to parents. We look for new service models—models that allow troubled children to remain with adoptive families in safe environments. Sometimes these are called "least restrictive environment" programs. This is an exciting concept that brings together a lot of talented individuals to assist challenging children. For it to work effectively, adoptive parents must be open, flexible and willing to share, as well as to receive assistance and support in parenting.

Well-planned and carried-out adoptions are our goals--to give the child the best possible start with his or her new family. There are horror stories about how children meet and move in with their adoptive families in just one weekend. That's not the way to do it.

In recent years, we have learned that foster parents seem to do well as adoptive parents. One residential agency that serves older troubled adoptable children first places them with foster parents. If all goes well, the agency encourages the foster families to consider adoption. This allows both children and prospective adoptive parents to keep their options open until they feel comfortable that they are a good fit.

Foster families are the perfect ones to adopt the children they've cared for and have grown to love, and many are eager to do so. Still, some foster parents only want to provide temporary care, and some with limited financial resources are reluctant to adopt because they cannot afford to clothe, feed and provide medical care for their children without supplemental financial support. Now we've moved beyond this barrier by providing limited financial support to adoptive families.

In a New York Times *article, Adam Pertman, who heads the Donaldson Adoption Institute, described the increasing number of retirees who are adopting older children as "competent vetted people."* [2]

It is exciting that we are exploring all options for our children. We know the need is so great. There are wise and experienced parents who may be "older" chronologically yet have energy and willingness to open their hearts and homes to children, ironically usually "older" children. Certainly all the usual factors of health, energy and ability to provide a safe and loving home must be considered, yet retired people offer a viable resource.

Using a wide variety of adults to adopt older children brings to mind the powerful thoughts Lee (in Chapter 7) expressed, when he said, "You got to pick them out!" Meaning that both children and the adoptive parents need to be able to choose.

I congratulate Lee for having the courage to turn down several families until the right one came along. I also congratulate his social worker and the administration of the children's home for supporting that process. It appears to me that the adopted adults in your study who were respected, listened to, and participated in selection of their adoptive parents had better feelings about their adoptions than did those who felt that they were just "placed."

"Choice" is an important word when thinking about older child adoptions. Even when children have been removed from their birth parents for neglect or abuse and

the courts have freed them for adoption, should birth parents have some part in helping select an adoptive parent or parents for their children?

We're learning a lot about open adoptions. An older adopted child usually knows the names of his or her birth family members and the places where they lived together. These children need information about their birth families, and so long as it's safe, they also need to maintain some contact with them.

We don't have many infant adoptions anymore, but of those we do have, the vast majority have a certain level of openness because birth parents are involved in the process. They often choose the adoptive families and they want to stay in touch, often sending pictures back and forth as "their child" grows and develops. Co-parenting issues can be really tough to work through, but in most cases relationships between the families are amicable. The children grow up knowing their birth parent(s), which can raise some thorny issues. Still it seems to be much better than the secretiveness that prompted many adopted adults to search for their birth families. Indeed, an open exchange was one of the goals for my professional career. I'm delighted the North Carolina Legislature has changed the law to allow it, when all parties agree.

When I was in the United Kingdom some years ago, a social worker showed a group of us how she used "homemade videos" to help children choose their adoptive families. She selected several families that she thought might "fit" a particular child's person- ality, then showed him or her videos of families that featured family pets, play areas, schools the child would attend, neighborhood children, and things the family did for fun. When a child's reaction was positive, she scheduled a face-to-face meeting. If it went well, the adoption process continued. If not, she honored the child's instincts. Madelyn's husband, Greg (Chapter 4), suggested a similar plan, and he believes that had it been used, Madelyn's move into her adoptive family would have been much easier.

We've been using such innovative ideas here in America, too. The more we can have children participate in their adoptions in meaningful-ways, the better. We just need to be careful that we don't overwhelm them or expect them to make adult-like decisions by themselves. "Lee" and "Jason" (Chapters 7 and 8) were given choices, but they made them with guidance and support from their social workers.

A number of the people in my book, even as mature adults, continue to think: "Why didn't someone in my birth family take care of me and my sisters and brothers rather than letting me be adopted?" Yet they often follow that question with a remark like, "But I'm glad they didn't. I am better off having been adopted."

If I were a child whose parents were unable to care for me, how would I feel if they placed me in a children's home rather than trying to keep me in the family system, say with an aunt or uncle? It would certainly upset me. Perhaps the "hurt" would fade over time, but for the rest of my life, some sense of rejection would be there.

A lot of kids do not really understand why their birth families don't try to keep them, and they often blame themselves. They may ask themselves, "What did I do? Was I a bad kid? Why didn't my parents get to keep me? Was it my fault?" Or, alternatively, they blame the Department of Social Services (DSS).

When it becomes dangerous to leave children with their birth parents, removing them may be the only resort available. How can it be made less anger provoking?

Child protection investigations must be very thorough, and those involved need to ask, "Have all possible support services been made available to these families?" Too often, decisions must be made quickly. While there is now more training for DSS workers in how to protect children, it remains confusing. In a model used in Florida, sheriffs and specially trained deputies investigate child abuse and neglect.[3] If children need to be removed, they use private agencies to place children in temporary, emergency foster care homes. That gets the "DSS welfare mentality" out of it and allows social workers and other helpers to deal with the feelings and emotions of involved children and adults. This is a new process, and it will be interesting to read the research data regarding its effectiveness.

Thinking about new approaches, let's discuss how "family finding" works.

It's a common human failing to find scapegoats. Departments of Social Services are often unfairly blamed for either removing children too quickly or leaving them too long in potentially dangerous homes. Kevin Campbell and his colleagues at Catholic Social Services in Tacoma,

WA, believe they have discovered a way out of this dilemma. They call it "family finding," operating under the belief that every child has about 40 or more birth family connections if you work hard enough to locate them. The idea is to locate numerous family members and then empower families to work jointly with DSS and the court system, and to decide what they think is best for their children.[4]

DSS may say there is no birth family resource person for the child in his or her record, but a family finder will find biological connections. Not all of them are going to be appropriate caretakers, but if you can call together a family meeting, somebody may rise up and take responsibility. Even if no one in a child's birth family can care for him or her, it's amazing what such meetings can do for a child's morale. Just knowing that a family meeting was held to discuss his or her future can be reassuring to a child. If an adoption occurs, a child will feel a sense of belonging to birth relatives.

The peace that can come from family finding is similar to the resolve some of the older adopted children in your book have found. They have found significant peace with the reality that both their adopted and their birth families have flaws. Yet both are part of their lives. Madelyn (Chapter 4) suffered sexual abuse from her birth father and had bitter memories from those experiences, yet while she was in college she easily found other birth relatives, saw that they were different from her father, invited them to her wedding, and asked some of them to take active roles in the ceremony.

Some of the people in your book say they have to live in two worlds, yet many have made it work for them. Marshall (Chapter 9), for example, thoughtfully looked after three families—(1) his wife, children and grandchildren, (2) his aging birth mom (now deceased), and (3) his adoptive mom (who is only six and a half years older than he is). Even though it required a great deal of time, he reached out to all of them.

He and others in the book have the benefit of long-term reflections and can now recognize positive things they have done for themselves. We expect kids to make responsible decisions too, but they're not always ready to do so, especially older kids who are being considered for adoption. They have been badly hurt and often don't have good decision-making abilities. For example, Dana (Chapter 8) was lucky she didn't get in too much trouble or get killed because of some unwise decisions she made as a teenager. Still, she ultimately became a wise and responsible adult.

Unfortunately, today's kids often get involved with dangerous drugs, and don't have as much support from society as children did when I first became a social worker. I do think past generations had more opportunities to act out their troubles without ruining their chances for becoming successful adults. Kids now often go right back into the drug scene; it's so hard for them to break free.

Could you speak about some promising forms of treatment approaches that are used to help older adopted children move on emotionally and accept their adoptions?

The agency I directed uses pieces of attachment therapy in moderate ways, such as focusing on communication and teaching eye contact. There are, however, valid concerns about some extreme applications of the model, such as intensive holding techniques--which can be dangerous. Sadly, in one case it even resulted in a child's death.

Some children have experienced severe trauma and are quite disturbed. We've had 4-year-olds who couldn't be left alone without an adult present, because of what they'd do to themselves, to nearby animals, or to other children. What is the best placement for such children? Are there home environments that can provide the safety and therapeutic help they need and deserve? Can they adapt to adoption, or will they be better off growing up in some type of group care? There are some children who are just not able to allow attachments to occur, because they have been so hurt and emotionally wounded by adults in the past and as a result are angry at the world. They might function in a group home, but to me living in a foster or group home is not ideal.

Cognitive Behavior Therapy (CBT) is another useful treatment modality, and it has evidence-based reliability. Children need permanence, a family, but I guess there will be some children we cannot easily fit into family life. My concern for such children is that they don't know how to form relationships, period. Yet many of the people you interviewed have learned to relate to others and have become good parents to their children. In spite of childhood trauma, somehow they have been able to establish and participate in close relationships.

Thinking about therapy, I believe we're all "wired" differently, and in some instances medications can help. Unfortunately, some children are overmedicated and that has more to do with control issues than therapy. Medications need to be administered with diligence and competence.

I'm all in favor of adoption for older children provided they truly wish to be adopted and are prepared and supported during the entire process—including post-adoption services. When adoptions aren't successful for children and youth, life isn't all over for them. Let's think of Dana's return to the children's home as an adolescent (Chapter 8). Her second placement there as a teenager helped her to turn her life around and become the responsible, caring person she is now. I was amazed at her resilience when I first interviewed her more than 30 years ago, and I'm even more impressed now. How can we account for the ability of some to bounce back? Dana continues to progress over her lifespan as a stable, mature adult, and many of the others in my study have done so as well.

Angela (Chapter 5) is another excellent example. Even after her adoptive parents tricked her and finalized the adoption against her will, then kept her isolated from other children and many adults, she became resilient--earning a college degree from a prestigious university, becoming a vice president of an important organization, and most important, becoming a loving, caring person. She has raised fine children, and enjoyed a great second marriage and a well-deserved retirement. Like me, she loves being a grandparent.

Over the years, I've heard other amazing adoption stories like hers. These individuals have that human spirit of resilience that allows them to ultimately prevail. Maybe people on the periphery of their lives, like the neighbors who would walk with Angela in the afternoons, made a real impact by being empathetic and encouraging.

Unfortunately, there are also some who have ended up living on the margins of society, and others have even spent time in prison. Are survival and resilience skills acquired genetically, environmentally or are they a mix of many factors? Researchers and academics can argue about that one. There are no simple answers, but we need to wisely apply what has already been learned and continue to conduct research about this important subject.

Nathaniel Hawthorne was quoted in the first chapter. His thoughts, contrary to logic, caused me to think that there may be something about "transplanting" or moving children from one environment to another (in spite of the traumatic effects) that stimulates resilience. In some adoptions this can be true even when the "earth" they were transplanted (adopted) into is far from ideal.

It is interesting that when asked how they survived amid the dangers and chaos of their childhoods, most of the participants said, in various ways, that God protected them.

Many of the adults whose stories appear in your book believed that God (or some higher power) sustained them when they were vulnerable children. God bless them for having such strong faith! I've found that children who believe there's a purpose for their lives draw security from that belief and somehow develop an ability to move on to more satisfying lives. It's wonderful that the people in your book have been able to do that.

Before we end our discussion, are there some final thoughts you would like to share with readers?

I grew up in a poor family—yet a peaceful home. We had plenty of food, warmth and love, but we had a limited amount of money. My parents were married for 10 years before my brother was born, and then I was born just 14 months later. Mother and Daddy both told us growing up how happy they were when we were finally born. It just made all the difference in my life knowing I was wanted. I knew it. Daddy said very little, but Mother told us how he would just sit and rock us as babies because he was so happy that we had been born. You know, there's something about what that does for you. They didn't physically discipline me either . . . and I was a very compliant child. Nobody beat me. What a difference that makes in somebody's life. I've felt that nurturing, and that's why I want it for everyone--especially adopted children.

Older-adopted children can also feel special, cherished and wanted like I did, but in different ways. John, earlier you said, "If both adoptive parents and their adopted children could come to believe that they are gifts to one another, enriching each others lives, most of the difficult issues of older child adoptions would be solved."

I agree with that. Adopting older children is not easy. It's challenging, but it can also be joyful and one of the most meaningful experiences one can have in life.

CHAPTER ELEVEN

THE GIFT OF
ROOTS AND WINGS:
CONCLUSIONS

"The greatest gift a parent can give a child is roots and wings."
Dean Faulkner Wells[1]

Dean Faulkner Wells' life, like the lives of several participants of this study, was dramatically changed by the death of a parent. Her father, the brother of the famous author, William Faulkner, was killed in an airplane crash a few months before her birth. Her Uncle William, who she called "Pappy," and his family raised her. At age 75, Dean used this quotation to describe her gratitude: "The greatest gift a parent can give a child is roots and wings." She added: "And the Faulkners gave me that." [2]

All children need "roots and wings." Older children who have been "transplanted" by adoption into unaccustomed earth have roots in two or more family systems—and sometimes in several cultures. As older adopted children grow up, helping them develop sturdy roots and strong wings should be essential goals for adoptive families.

"Roots" can be thought of as a metaphor for one's heritage. Children need solid roots to form a foundation for their lives. Referring to his Filipino roots, the Rev. Benoni R. Silva-Netto wrote, "Heritage is of utmost importance in our pilgrimage. The gift of roots is as important as the gift of wings."[3]

A challenge for adoptive families is to honor the positive aspects of their older-adopted children's "transplanted roots" while at the same time introducing those adopted children to their own values and beliefs. Yet while doing so, adoptive parents need to keep in mind that their older transplanted/adopted children came into their lives from earlier (and often far different) settings. Although the task may often be difficult to carry out, adoptive parents have unique opportunities to enhance, expand and stabilize their adopted children's heritages. They need to be cautious, however, to avoid "putting down" or ignoring their children's original genetic, cultural and kinship roots.

It has been difficult for some of the participants to integrate their birth and adoptive family heritages ("roots"). In many cases, the environment they were born into and the environment into which they were adopted were extremely dissimilar—in terms of income, social status, and expectations of children (i.e., educational attainment, preparation for jobs and professions, and one's dreams for the future).

Madelyn's wedding (Chapter 4) is especially interesting, because she invited relatives from both her adoptive and birth families to participate in the ceremony. As Madelyn has grown older, she has emulated her adoptive family's middle-class lifestyle (graduating from college, becoming a respected professional artist, etc.). While she, now in her 60s, has more in common with her adoptive family than her birth family, she nonetheless appreciates aspects of her birth family heritage.

Jason (Chapter 6) acknowledges that both his birth family and his adoptive family heritages are valuable components of his life. He is not ashamed that he experienced poverty and upheaval in his childhood, and he believes those experiences helped him to be resourceful and self-reliant. He also gives credit to his adoptive parents for their love, encouragement and belief in him. "I would never have gone to college, become a professional educator, or enjoyed a middle-class lifestyle had it not been for them." Although separated from his siblings for 14 years, he is also thankful, as an adult, to be connected to his birth family.

"Wings" can represent a metaphor for moving into adulthood—for setting children free. Khalil Gibran astutely noted in his classic book,

The Prophet, that parents and families need to come to terms with the reality that they do not own children: "They are sons and daughters of Life's longing for itself."

Gibran's observations refer to all children, and his thoughts may be especially helpful and of comfort to adoptive parents. He goes on to say that parents "are the bows" that can launch their children "as living arrows" into new worlds that parents cannot inhabit. Gibran's beautiful language reinforces the concept that young adults need strong "wings" to lift them up and allow them to soar. [4]

Transplanting Older Children into Stable Families Can Be Life-changing

Fresh Starts: Transplanting/adopting older children into "unaccustomed earth" environments can offer fresh starts for them and their new families. Still, difficulties abound. During this unique, complex and often challenging transfer process (varying in length from months to years), both children and their adoptive families need confidence-building support, encouragement and coaching from a wide array of sources: friends, extended family members, professionals, and formal and informal groups.

Resilience: As the stories in this book illustrate, adopted children's resilience can be remarkable. For example, Angela's (Chapter 5) story demonstrates that even when children are adopted into abusive, toxic environments, they may "bounce back." Angela's "bouncing back" process, however, was gradual—culminating in her seeking professional counseling as a middle-aged adult. Her therapeutic progress was extraordinary. Her therapist told her: "You are a 'miracle child.' There is no way you should have become the educated, responsible and caring person you are—it's just a miracle."

Families who adopt older children have only limited time spans to help their children acquire gifts of "roots and wings." The positive growth and development of people who were adopted as older children may not, however, be immediately noticed or appreciated by themselves or others for years or decades. Dana (Chapter 8) was returned at age 12 to the children's home that placed her for adoption at age 7. Although she lived with her adoptive family for only five years and much of that time was tumultuous, Dana acquired positive values and knowledge from them. She now recognizes how the experiences with her adoptive family positively changed her life, but she did not consciously realize this until she had children of her own. She explains it well:

> I am a little bit different than I was when your first book was published in 1985. My bond strengthened with my adoptive parents over the years. Before she died, I told my adoptive mom how much I appreciated all she had done. We opened up and talked a lot about my adoption. I told Mom and Dad that I understood why they sent me back to the children's home. It bothered them, but I don't know where I would be today if they hadn't stepped in and stopped my running away and acting out. As a parent, when your child does something wrong, you feel like it's your failure. I understand that completely now that I'm a mother of several children.

The adoptive parents of Marshall (Chapter 9), who was adopted at age 14, had only a couple of years before he, after an argument with his adoptive mom, moved out on his own. Yet, Marshall (now in his early 70s) considers being adopted as an important contribution to his success as an adult.

Even when adoptions go well, adopting a 7-year-old child may allow only a decade of parental care before he or she begins to test her or his "wings." Lee's adoptive parents (Chapter 7) wisely let him move slowly into their family at his own pace. He did not call his adoptive mother "Mama" until shortly before he was married. They also let him talk about and positively remember the love and protection that his birth mother and older siblings provided—especially during his birth father's drunken rages. Today in his 60s, Lee: (a) appreciates the love, protection and care he received from his birth mother and his birth siblings as a young child; and (b) he also appreciates that his adoptive parents, his adoptive brother, and his adoptive grandparents warmly accepted him into their family and loved him as if he were "blood kin."

Encouraging Older Adopted Children to be Actively Involved in their Adoptions

Early in the 1983 interviewing process, it became clear that some of the participants were ambivalent about what had happened to them. They remembered wanting to belong to dependable and caring families, yet they feared losing control of their destinies or, as some of them said, they feared "being owned."

Years ago, some social workers at the University of Pennsylvania believed even young children could sense what was happening in their adoptions. One wrote:

> Even the child who is removed from his parents because of neglect or abuse and is placed [in a foster home] knows or comes to know that somewhere he does have parent(s), and he continues to bear their name. Eventually, he may return to them. The child who is adopted, however, will acquire a new parent(s) and a new home; but for the time between the removal of his own parent(s) as guardian and the placement for adoption, he is really on his own. [5]

Regarding choices, Angela (Chapter 5) said, "I felt I needed a new life. I had to do something with my life." She also felt hopeless. "I was told that I could make a choice, but I felt deep down that I didn't have a choice."

When older children believed that they did have choices in their adoption processes, they seemed to have less emotional turmoil. Lee (Chapter 7) exemplified such feelings as he remembered being offered several prospective adoptive families from which to choose:

> You go live with these people for a while—you don't like it—you come back. You go to somebody else's house for a while—you come back. Then the right family comes along. I guess I just fell right in with them—for no (special) reason, I don't reckon. . . . We just clicked.

How should transplantation/transfer processes be handled for older children who are being adopted into "unaccustomed earth"? Should children and youth be encouraged to talk about their original families and other caretakers?

One experienced social worker commented:

> School-age adopted children cannot emotionally accept new families simply by being encouraged to forget their original ones. They can take on new families only after they have sorted through and perceived themselves as a part of their old ones.[6]

Lee, as he often does, clearly explains how this happened in his own life:

> When my (birth) daddy would come in drunk, Momma would hide us. She was always the one that took care of us, and she did the best she could. I know she gave me good love and attention; because of that I didn't want to forget her. I carried her picture around in my wallet. She was a very, very good person. . . . From the beginning, I called my [adoptive] daddy "Daddy." I guess it was because my real daddy didn't mean a whole lot to me, but the new one did.

All but one of the seventeen 1983 study participants did contact their birth parents and other adult relatives they remembered from their childhoods. Many of the participants reported immediate interest and a flurry of visits soon after re-connecting with these birth relatives. Over time, however, the intensity of contacts tended to diminish. Some of the reasons the participants gave were:

> They did not feel at ease and comfortable with the lifestyles of their parent(s) and other people in their original families.

> The parent(s) seemed like "strangers." They had difficulty casually "talking" and "relating" to them; and the years of not interacting with them created "gaps" that were difficult to bridge.

On the other hand, the participants generally desired more closeness with natural brothers and sisters. They felt great pain when they were separated, as children. The participants frequently went to unusual lengths to locate one another. Even so, they often felt nervous and awkward meeting again after years of separation. Dana and Jason (Chapter 8) shared their experience. In Dana's words:

> Jason, you jumped out of the car and exclaimed: "Well, get up from there and give your brother a hug."

I shot back, "I haven't seen you in a dozen years and you want me to hug you?"

But we did hug. It was real warming. It just lifted me up. I really can't explain how satisfying it was. Since [our birth] Mother died, I have felt this nesting urge to get us all together, and it was happening.

The Participants as Sensitive, Caring Adults

The participants said that they are especially sensitive to and observant of the feelings of others. When asked about this, they described themselves as being able to "size people up." One reported: "I can sense almost instantly if someone is mean or if they are nice."

Is it possible that vulnerable older adopted children tend to develop abilities to quickly "size people up?" Some participants believe that they can determine, better than most people, who can be trusted and who is to be feared and avoided. Further, they believe that such qualities were acquired as self-protection measures in their childhoods.

Still, if some older adopted children develop such sensitivity and become self-reliant, one should not assume that such benefits might justify the emotional pain that these older adopted participants suffered as children. All of the adults in this study continue to carry troubling memories from their chaotic and often challenging childhoods.

The participants who have children (and grandchildren) appear to be unusually committed to them. They frequently remarked that they wanted to spare their children the anguish they themselves had experienced in their own childhoods.

During my contacts with the participants of my older child adoption study, several of their spouses and siblings voluntarily made positive comments about the thoughtfulness and sensitivity of the participants. I heard comments like, "He is a great husband/wife, or she's a great Momma/Daddy!"

Advice and Suggestions by the Participants

Since 1983 when this study began, all the participants have been given opportunities to advise professionals, adoptive parents and interested people on how to help older children cope with adoption. Their answers were forthcoming and compelling. A sampling is given below:

In a lot of situations, it's underestimated what a child takes in and understands. As young as I was, I had a pretty good idea of what was going on.

I wouldn't take them away from their real family completely. I think that hurts.

The key is wanting to be adopted on the part of children. Children should not concede to adoptions with a [birth] mother and [or] father still living unless it is clear that their [birth] parent(s) understand what is taking place and really want it to happen. I don't understand why a lot of families want to take on older children, but I am glad I was adopted.

[Advice to children who are being adopted] Just don't stay where you don't want. That's the biggest mistake anybody can make.

The child has really got to relate to somebody in the adoptive family, and [that person] got to have things in common with the child. You're not going to talk that much unless there's a person the child can really trust.

You want to provide love and care in adopted homes for children. Children need somebody they can love . . . can trust . . . spend time with. Someone they can be like, be involved with, and be accepted by.

More visits prior to adoption would've helped me.

The main thing is that there be time for social workers and other adults to sit down and really talk with the child.

All a child wants is real love and to fit in.

If a child has something on his mind or that is bothering him about some aspect of being adopted, be open with him, discuss it with him, and let him talk it out of his system.

Adoption of an older child should be a slow, gradual thing.

It'd be good if children who were to be adopted were able to talk to a young adult who's been successfully adopted.

Adoptive parents should say that they don't own you but that they just want to be there and love you.

I think parents who adopt children mean so well. They want it to work, and they kind of force it on a child.

Comments on Preparing and Supporting Adoptive Parents

Bringing children ages six and above into adoptive homes is challenging for both families and children. To make such moves easier and more successful, the participants, remembering their own experiences, felt that they and their adoptive families needed a good deal of support, preparation and coaching in the early stages of living together.

Adoption scholar David Kirk contended that community pressures and social ambiguities confuse adoptive relationships for both parents and children. He believed that adoptive parents suffer from "role handicap" and lack of "role support," because our culture fails to provide an acceptable role for them to play. In his 1981 book, Kirk pointed out that adoptive families are not given complete social sanction to fulfill their roles as a family unit. Further, he believed that to some people in the general public, adoptions appear to be "second class." For example if adoptive parents are infertile, society often sees this as not being as good as being biological parents. [7]

For professional adoption workers, this study implies that both adopted older children and their adoptive parents are far more vulnerable to the stresses of learning to live together than may be outwardly apparent. Preparation, ongoing support and emergency follow-up assistance need to be available even when surface observations may incorrectly lead professionals to conclude that adoptions are progressing smoothly.

The resilience of traumatized children is affirmed. Children and youth who experienced harsh treatment, witnessed brutality, and were denied adequate nurture have the potential to develop into competent adults, caring parents, and committed marriage partners. Although they may be able to overcome disadvantaged childhood experiences to a remarkable extent, they may continue to experience painful childhood memories.

Although additional and important information has been obtained about older child adoptions in recent years, further in-depth qualitative and quantitative research, using larger and more representative samples, will be of great value to the professional practice to child adoptions. Also, such research may be useful in better understanding the effects of divorce and the blending of families for children.

The Author's List of Findings

To assist readers, I have carefully read the manuscript many times looking for important themes that are embedded in the adoption stories. I hope the list that follows may assist readers as they think about and review how being adopted as older children impacted the lives of the people who graciously shared their adoption stories in this volume:

1. Older child adoptions can change lives in powerful, positive and long-term ways—even when adoptions are less than ideal.

2. Siblings should remain in touch with one another as they grow up unless there are compelling reasons for limiting contact. (See Sandy Cook's comments, Chapter 10.) Separating and isolating older adopted siblings can have negative, lifelong consequences.

3. Throughout their lives, the participants often wondered why birth family members, such as aunts and uncles, didn't prevent their adoptions from occurring. They also often followed up such thoughts with words such as "I'm glad they didn't."

4. Older child adoptions have lifelong and generational effects as well.

5. As mentioned earlier, many participants believe they have a heightened ability (more than they think most people possess) to discern who can and cannot be trusted. They think these characteristics were acquired, as self-survival measures, when they lived as children in unknown and dangerous places. As they have matured into middle-aged adults, their beliefs have been reinforced.

6. People who were adopted as older children often have to live in multiple worlds: (a) their birth family and pre-adoptive world; (b) their adoptive family world, and (c) the world they have created for themselves (marriage, children, careers, etc.). It is often difficult to integrate and blend these worlds, but as the participants age such issues appear to fade from conscious thought.

7. Dana (Chapter 8) expressed a sentiment, "You always feel you are running." By that, she meant that she was unsure of how solidly rooted she is in her adoptive family system. Other participants, using different words and examples, expressed similar thoughts. For example, Angela (Chapter 5) was excluded from an inheritance that distributed equal amounts of money to all of her cousins. She thinks her exclusion was related to the fact that she was not a "blood kin" relative.

8. Lee (Chapter 7) believes that successful older child adoptions are like marriages in that people should be allowed to select their partners. He advocates allowing children to pick out their adoptive parents, as he did, and also have the right to decline an invitation to be adopted by a prospective family. Adults have long enjoyed the right to select a child or the children they wish to adopt, but children's rights to choose are sometimes ignored or "glossed over." (See Angela, Chapter 5.)

9. Maynard (Chapter 6) proposes that new approaches be tried before adoptive placements are considered in situations like theirs. He, Joanne and Benny and their birth father were overwhelmed by the sudden and tragic death of their birth mother/wife. Maynard believes that a closely supervised, supported, and healing setting was needed, where they could together mourn, face reality and plan for the future. Such an experience would have prepared him, his siblings and his father to either (a) safely remain together as a family, or (b) separate as a family unit and allow the children to more easily become part of an adoptive family or families.

10. "Open adoptions" were not widely known or accepted at the time that the participants were placed in adoptive homes, but Dana (Chapter 8) and Sandy Cook (Chapter 10) believe that they hold promise for selective older child adoptions.

11. The lifelong experiences of the participants suggest that "time provides healing." Most stated that over the years they have come to

terms (or are in the process of doing so) with the negative aspect of their adoptions and moved on with their lives.

12. Contrary to conventional wisdom, although the participants experienced events that were terrorizing, abusive and lacking in compassion and love, they have become caring, loving parents and grandparents and good citizens. Their surprising resilience can become a source of inspiration and hope for other older adopted children, youth and their families.

13. One of Dana and Jason's brothers (Chapter 8), who lived for a time on the campus of the children's home and also in one of its foster homes, was never adopted. He was, however, separated for several years from his siblings. He contends, "These separations create relationship gaps that cannot be bridged." Dana and Jason agree with him, as do several other participants.

14. Many of the participants believe that God protected them at critical times in their lives, and some have made choices, as adults, to reach out and help others who are struggling and needing assistance. Jason (Chapter 8) chose teaching and coaching as a career, because it gave him opportunities to "pay back" what others had done for him—people such as his adoptive parents and his high school coach.

15. Marshall's wife (Chapter 9) believes that the most traumatic aspect of his adoption was that he remembers his birth mother "giving him away." During their interviews, other participants recalled being surprised or shocked upon learning that they were being adopted. Such childhood memories reveal an important aspect of older child adoptions. "Being given away" is a difficult and traumatic concept for children to accept, recall and "live with"—not only in childhoods, but also throughout their lifetimes. How might such life-changing news/events be made easier for the sake of children, and for the sake of birth parents who surrender their children for adoption and who are also likely to be emotionally upset by the experience?

Adoptions Can Benefit All Who Are Involved

Family relationships are a mix of volatile, roller-coaster-like emotions and stabilizing, loving relationships that range from affection to anger, from self-centeredness to thoughtfulness, and from despair to joyfulness. Amid the ups and downs of family living, it is possible for adopted people and the members of the families who adopted them to express and recognize that they are lifelong "gifts" to one another.

Not only can children benefit from being transplanted into accustomed or unaccustomed earth (from known and unknown environments), but adoptive families can also be renewed and enriched. While the design of my research project focused on interviewing people who had been adopted as older children, I believe that adoptive families also can be positively changed by adoption. David Kirk's ideas of "Shared Fate" gives credence to that notion.[8]

Madelyn (Chapter 4) expressed her belief that her adoption was mutually beneficial: "It was like I educated my (adoptive) parents and they educated me. I was there to help them, too."

Issues to Consider before Moving Older Children

(1) Can older children and youth safely remain and develop their potential—physically, mentally and spiritually—in familiar "Accustomed Earth" settings/systems?

Careful consideration should be given to the above question. Before children are removed from their original family settings/systems, skilled assistance should be offered to help strengthen, rehabilitate, preserve, and support their parent(s) and/or other family caregivers with a desire to allow children to grow physically, emotionally and spiritually within their original family systems. If a birth parent cannot provide adequate nurture, perhaps some other birth relatives can.

Many families have responsible grandparents and extended-family relatives who can supplement, and, if necessary, take on the role of parenting for children whose birth parent(s), for a variety of reasons, cannot do so.

Generally it is easier for children to be transplanted/moved into "accustomed earth" settings with trustworthy people they know —i.e., grandparents, family members, former foster parents, friends or respected adults such as Cliff and Anne Sanford (Chapter 3).

(2) If "Unaccustomed Earth" adoptions by strangers are needed to provide "roots and wings" for older children and youth, they can offer lifelong opportunities for growth and development.

If appropriate care cannot be provided for children within their original family systems or with known and trusted adults, this book's data (adoption stories) support the concept that children and youth needing permanent new families can thrive and develop in caring adoptive environments that provide fresh starts and positive growth opportunities for older children.

Desires for fresh starts and positive growth, however, do not always materialize. Could research (including shared practice wisdom) help avoid toxic older child adoptions? Could research assist professionals in developing improved ways to better match adoptable older children with prospective, emotionally healthy families? All children and youth deserve to "belong" to some adult(s) but not be "owned" or "dominated" by them. Could findings from practice-oriented research help older adopted children, with assistance from their new families, learn to "grow" roots in their new "unaccustomed earth" family systems--while at the same time honoring the positive aspects of their original families and cultures? [9]

Also in a finding that I did not expect: Even unhealthy "unaccustomed earth" adoptive settings, such as Angela's (Chapter 5), may prove to be a catalyst for growth and resilience. Such difficult-to-grow-up-in environments, however, are painful for children to live in, and they tend to leave "emotional scarring" that may require professional counseling.

Belief/Hypothesis: Over the 37 years (1983 – 2020) that I have been involved in research, thinking about, and teaching the complex phenomenon of older child adoptions, a simple belief or hypothesis has emerged for readers and future adoption researchers to consider:

The more that older adopted children and their adoptive families can appreciate that they are lifelong gifts to one another, the greater is the likelihood that both adoptive families and their adopted children will consider that their adoptions were successful.

Older Child Adoptions Can Be Amazing

In the final days of my editing this volume, I heard the following account of an older child adoption from a friend who had been my college roommate more than 60 years ago:

While we were having lunch at a local cafeteria, my wife, Elaine, saw a man, a woman with a baby in her arms and a darling little girl sitting in her own chair at a nearby table. Elaine and the little girl exchanged smiles and silent greetings. The little girl's eyes sparkled, and I followed suit by waving to her. She quickly rose, walked to our table, looked me directly in the eye and said sweetly: "I have some amazing news!"

"And what would that be?" I asked.

"I'm being adopted," she said with a smile of joy I find it impossible to describe adequately.

As she skipped back to her seat, I replied, "That is wonderful news."

I surmised the couple had tried for a long time to have a child, begun the process of adoption, and then the woman became pregnant with the baby she held in her arms. We left just after they did, and I watched as the little girl skipped gaily to their SUV in the parking lot and hopped through the door her soon-to-be Dad held for her.

That child made our day with her excitement at now finding a loving home in which to grow into a happy childhood. Elaine and I believe she was right!

Closing Thoughts

Older child adoptions should be expansive, not restrictive. This almost-four-decades-long study suggests that the ultimate goal of adoptions should be similar to successful marriages—helping all involved to show mutual respect for one another, while at the same time seeking the common good. Such a goal, while never fully attainable, can free adopted children to expand, grow and strengthen their "roots" and develop their "wings" so that they can learn to soar in their own special ways. A participant wisely observed: "A family isn't made of blood . . . it's made of love and understanding." [10]

ACKNOWLEDGMENTS

How does an author acknowledge the extraordinary assistance and support he/she has received in writing and publishing a book that has taken many years to complete? The list of people that need to be thanked is extensive, and space is too limited for such an undertaking. Even if I tried, surely my memory would not be reliable. The best that can be done is to anonymously thank one and all of the kind people who have assisted with this project. I will, however, mention a few helpers, and as I do so, may readers know that these accolades apply to many other thoughtful people:

(1) <u>Family Members</u>: Betsy, my dear wife of 60-plus years, made *Transplanted into Unaccustomed Earth* possible.

Our daughters and I gratefully acknowledge that Betsy's love and devotion allowed us the freedom to further our educations and explore our dreams as she maintained a stable and nurturing family life, including the "one thousand and one" details of daily living. All the while, Betsy earned her own graduate degree, a Master of Education, from Winthrop University (SC).

The completion of this volume, the 1985 adoption book, my doctoral studies and dissertation could not have been accomplished without Betsy's love, encouragement, intelligence, common sense, understanding and assistance. She supported my desire to better understand the complexity of older child adoptions while, at the same time, seeking to improve its practices and policies. Both goals required extensive travel and expense. She also understood the countless hours it took to transcribe interviews, to analyze qualitative data and to write and rewrite the manuscript. In short, without Betsy's love and continuing encouragement, *Transplanted into Unaccustomed Earth* would not exist. Thank you, Betsy!

Appreciation is also extended to our wonderful daughters, Elizabeth and Stephanie. Their love, understanding and encouragement over many years are gifts that sustained me as I struggled to achieve academic and professional goals that culminated in the writing of *Transplanted into Unaccustomed Earth*.

As explained earlier in this volume's manuscript, the beginnings of this book began while I was earning a Ph.D. degree from the University of North Carolina at Greensboro (UNC-G). My Greensboro family "cheerleaders" helped in many thoughtful ways during the eight years I was a (part-time) UNC-G doctoral student. My parents, Joe John and Eleanor Powell; my wife's parents Elwood and Betty Carroll; my wife's aunt, Mary Goodman, and my sister-in-law, Barbara Carroll, all now deceased, lived in Greensboro.

My Greensboro-based family made the numerous180-mile round-trip commutes from our home to the UNC-G campus safer and "doable." The Carrolls and "Aunt Mary" lived only a few blocks from UNC-G's campus. They allowed me to park in their driveways, they fed me delicious food (especially Aunt Mary's chocolate pie), and they encouraged me to take naps in their homes before and after classes.

My sister-in-law, Barbara, also provided valuable, tangible assistance. She was aware of the two-hour commutes (one-way) that were required for me to attend UNC-G classes, and she thoughtfully offered to substitute for me when I could not attend a class. Fortunately the flexible UNC-G professors graciously allowed her to do so. In full disclosure, Barbara's class notes were far superior to mine.

My parents Joe John and Eleanor Powell, lived in a Greensboro retirement facility several miles from campus. During my UNC-G graduate student days (1975 - 1983), it became increasingly difficult for them to move about. Nonetheless, they provided unconditional love and support. My mother made countless sandwiches and tasty snacks for breaks during my UNC-G classes. Throughout my elementary school years, my father patiently served, night after night, as my mentor and academic coach because I struggled with dyslexia. Yet my father believed wholeheartedly in my academic potential. Although quite ill

266

in the Fall of 1983, Daddy was extremely proud that I was about to complete the requirements, at age 48, for a doctorate (Ph.D.). In our last conversation before he slipped into a final coma, he asked when I had to turn in my dissertation. I told him it was three weeks away.

Although my father appeared to be unconscious and unaware of what was happening around him, he lived until the dissertation was completed. He died minutes after the final draft was submitted to the UNC-G faculty.

My sister, Joanna Powell Adams Burt, now deceased, her four children, and their families strongly supported my long-term graduate studies and my adoption research. While their decision was not related to the research, one of my sister's daughters and her husband adopted one of our great nephews. He has been and continues to be a blessing to our entire family.

To earn a Doctor of Philosophy (Ph.D.) degree, I needed all of our extended family's love, the support and encouragement, and they supplied it in abundance. Thank you!

(2) Academics: Rebecca M. Smith, Ph.D., Professor, UNC-G, served as Chair of my doctoral dissertation committee. Dr. Smith required her students to seek excellence in their studies. In return, she was an extraordinary teacher, advisor and fierce advocate for her students.

Other members of my dissertation committee were: Hyman Rodman, Ph.D., Excellence Fund Professor of Child Development and Family Studies, UNC-G; Douglas F. Powers, MD, Distinguished Professor of Human Development and Learning, UNC-Charlotte; and Nancy White, Ph.D., Professor of Child Development and Family Studies, UNC-G. Also Alan Keith-Lucas, Ph.D., Alumni Distinguished Professor, School of Social Work, UNC-Chapel Hill, wrote the Foreword and carefully critiqued my 1985 adoption book.

All are thanked for going far beyond their expected academic duties. These extraordinary scholars became advocates and advisors not only for my 1983 UNC-G dissertation, *Adults Who Were Adopted as Older*

Children, but also for my 1985 book, *Whose Child Am I? Adults' Recollections of Being Adopted*. Their assistance and support (along with that of many other unnamed academic colleagues) kept me "going," and indirectly led to the completion of this final research activity— the writing of *Transplanted into Unaccustomed Earth: Long-Term Perspectives of Being Adopted as Older Children* (2020).

(3) Assistance from the Host Agency: The staff of the anonymous children's agency (especially the CEO, the social workers and their long-term executive secretary) bravely trusted me to conduct research on their pioneering older child adoption program. Their assistance and trust are greatly appreciated.

(4) The Seventeen Participants: I thank the courageous volunteers who were adopted through the children's home's pioneering school-age adoption project and who participated in my 1983 adoption study. An extra bow of gratitude is extended to five of the participants who allowed their adoption stories to be featured in my first (1985) adoption book, *Whose Child Am I?* Also I thank "Angela, Benny, Dana, Jason, Joanne, Lee, Madelyn, Marshall and Maynard" for their courage, thoughtfulness and patience in allowing their long-term adoption stories to appear in this volume.

(5) Assistance of Professional Colleagues: Cliff and Anne Sanford, dear friends and colleagues, helped the older child adoption movement take hold in the United States. This volume contains their adoption story (see Chapter 3); Mary Wunder, social worker extraordinaire, a friend and colleague who carefully critiqued my dissertation and the 1985 adoption book; Professor James Campbell, an East Carolina University (ECU) close friend and colleague who grew up in an orphanage and tells about it in Chapter 2; Sandy Cook, a dear friend and colleague who shared her extensive knowledge and experiences as an adoption social worker, supervisor and as the retired Executive Director of NC's largest private adoption agency (Chapter 10); Reginald O. York, Ph.D., long-time friend and colleague who provided useful, interesting and important information for readers of this volume to consider (see "Research Notes," pages 273 to 274). I was honored that Reggie, a recognized authority on social work research, chose my qualitative

dissertation study as an exemplar in one of his research textbooks. Lena Carawan and Vicky Causby, dear friends and colleagues, are recognized for their adoption advocacy and their useful suggestions.

All of the individuals listed above and many un-named colleagues have made valuable contributions to this endeavor and their efforts are greatly appreciated. They are thanked for their kind assistance and especially for their thoughtful support.

(6) <u>Editing and Transcription Support</u>: Wendi Byas translated hours and hours and hours of audiotaped spoken words into digital typed formats. Wendi then "magically" transformed the digital verbatim words into easy-to-read sentences and paragraphs. The adoption stories she transcribed are the "heart" of this volume. Thank you, Wendi!

(7) <u>Rachael Garrity (PenworthyLLC)</u>, editor par excellence: She skillfully edited a loose manuscript into a book that "tells" important and courageous stories of how children without "roots" and "wings" have become, caring, concerned adults who are now "soaring" on their own. Thank you, Rachael, for your honesty, guidance and support.

(8) <u>Patsy Faires (BFA & MFA, UNC-Greensboro)</u>: Patsy is a long-time family friend. She and my late sister-in-law, Barbara Jean Carroll, were friends from elementary school days in Hickory, NC, close to each other as adults, and remained dear friends through Barbara's failing health and death. Although offered money for her excellent drawings in this book, Patsy refused, saying, "I want to donate the drawings in memory of Barbara (Carroll)."

Thank you, Patsy, for help making the adoption stories almost come alive with your expressive illustrations. (Note: Patsy never met or saw photos of the participants. Instead, she carefully read each adoption story and then in her mind's eye imagined each person's appearance.)

(9) <u>David Perry</u>, retired editor-in-chief of UNC Press. David is thanked for his expert suggestions that helped polish this book into a professional volume.

(10) <u>My ECU School of Social Work Students</u>: They made my life so interesting when I served as their professor. At the same time I learned so much from them. Space and memory lapses would not allow listing them all, but a few who particularly assisted with the adoption research study are: the Master of Social Work (MSW) students who were enrolled in my "Adoption Course" over the years; Sean Pumphrey, who co-presented with me on numerous occasions; Emily Earl Freeman, who critiqued early drafts of this manuscript: and Katey Bennett Valarde, former graduate assistant, who maintained the project with her exceptional secretarial skills and recordkeeping abilities while I was on medical leave. They and all my former students are appreciated for their direct and indirect assistance with my adoption research. Thank you!

The above lists are far from complete. Many more unheralded people have joined in the quest to seek to better understand and improve the practice of adoptions for school-age children.

Thank you one and all!

John Y. Powell, Ph.D. 2020

APPENDIX

ABOUT THE AUTHOR

A North Carolina native, John Y. Powell, Ph.D., LCSW, LMFT earned academic degrees from High Point University (BA), University of North Carolina at Chapel Hill (MSW), and University of North Carolina at Greensboro (Ph.D.). He was named Professor Emeritus of Social Work upon retirement from East Carolina University, Greenville, NC, and was presented the "Champion of the Family Award" in 1999 by the NC Association for Marriage and Family Therapy. Dr. Powell received the 2016 Distinguished Faculty Legacy Award from the School of Social Work, East Carolina University. He served as a member of the Board of Trustees of the University of the South, Sewanee, TN; as president of the Pitt County (NC) Mental Health Association; and as founder and editor of a weekly newspaper column, "Your Mental Health."

Dr. Powell was a part-time Ph.D. student in UNC-Greensboro's (UNC-G) Department of Human Development and Family Studies (1975-1983) during the early years of the modern older child adoption era. Aware of post-placement difficulties some school-age children and their adoptive families were experiencing, he decided to learn more about the dynamics of school-age child adoptions. This became the subject of his doctoral dissertation (*A Study of Adults Who Were Adopted as Older Children*, UNC-Greensboro, 1983), which was published in book form in 1985 and titled: *Whose Child Am I? Adults' Recollections of Being Adopted.*

Nearly a quarter-of-a century later, Dr. Powell, in retirement, was able to locate and interview several participants of his 1983 study to gain long-term perspectives on the impact of older child adoptions. The fascinating and informative results are recorded in this 2020 volume.

Dr. and Mrs. Powell have been married for more than 60 years. They are blessed with two wonderful daughters and sons-in-laws. Also they are proud grandparents of an outstanding grandson who is a university student.

RESEARCH NOTES

Introduction

John Y. Powell, Ph.D.

Reginald O. York, Ph.D., a social work research authority, used my qualitative 1983 older child adoption doctoral dissertation study, *Adults Who Were Adopted as Older Children*, [1] as an exemplar in one of his textbooks, *Building Basic Competencies in Social Work Research: An Experiential Approach*. [2] Therefore, he was familiar with the research methods used in the original 1983 study, and I asked him to write a brief summary of them for this volume. In his summary below, he explains: (1) the differences between qualitative and quantitative research objectives; (2) why using qualitative research was appropriate for this research study; and (3) what can be learned from small-scale qualitative research studies such as mine.

Research Methodology
for *Transplanted into Unaccustomed Earth*
Reginald O. York, Ph.D.

Qualitative research comes in many shapes and sizes, but all of them lack the concreteness of quantitative research that has convenient predetermined categories into which people or quantities can be placed or displayed. The advantage of qualitative research, however, is its flexibility. It provides more opportunities to learn new things. That is why qualitative methods were chosen for the study reported in this book and the original 1983 study upon which it builds.

Two of the types of qualitative research considered for this study were ethnography and grounded theory. Ethnography refers to the study of cultures within their natural settings. The purpose of ethnographic research is to discover and describe the way of life of a group or culture from the inside out. To accomplish such goals, ethnographic researchers must gain entry into groups or cultures that they wish to study and build trust with its their members. A distinguishing feature of ethnography is that the process of inquiry begins with the selection of a culture to study rather than the articulation of research problems to solve or research questions to answer. Problems and questions may emanate from the data analyzed, but they are not determined before the process of research begins. Grounded theory is more likely than ethnography to begin with a focus on the nature of the themes to be examined. For example, in Dr. Powell's 1983 study, it was known that adoptions of older children were significantly different from infant/young child adoptions, yet to increase satisfaction and success rates among those involved, more information was needed—especially from adults who had been adopted as school-age children. His study had the purpose of building on existing knowledge with the hope of further developing and refining older child adoption theory.

The original study of older adoptions, upon which the current study builds, is better classified as grounded theory than ethnography. This is because the 1983 study process began with literature on adoption of older children that suggested a set of tentative hypotheses that he hoped to refine by a specific grounded theory method known as "analytic induction." The 2007-2020 follow-up study reported in this book employs some of the basic procedures of grounded theory in that interviews were conducted with a portion of the participants of the original study with the purposes of determining if the conclusions of the earlier study should be modified and whether new lessons can be learned from longitudinal viewpoints.

REFLECTIONS ON DR. YORK'S COMMENTS

John Y. Powell, Ph.D.

Introduction

In his preceding comments, Dr. York gives an excellent summary of the research methods used in this 37-year-long study of older child adoptions. His comments do not require additions, subtractions or corrections. I shall, however, provide a few details that may be of interest to readers.

Research Goals

The goals of my 1983 University of NC-Greensboro (UNC-G) doctoral dissertation study were: (1) to gain a better understanding of how children adopted at six and older by non-related, previously unknown families coped with and were affected by their adoptions; and (2) to discover and suggest ways that the intricate process of adopting older children might be made easier and more successful for: (a) adoptable children; (b) families who adopt, love and care for them: and (c) other people who support and help sustain these life-changing and lifelong events.[1]

From a 1980s-era literature review, it appeared that we (professionals) had neglected to systematically obtain critical firsthand knowledge, from adults who had been adopted as school-age children. It would have been confusing and upsetting to interview older children and youth who were in the midst of their own adoptions. Adult "veterans" of school-age child adoptions were willing to share valuable adoption-related memories and give sage advice about their older-child adoptions.

As mentioned earlier in this book, I was unsure how to locate a suitable and unique sample of adult participants. I asked Clifford W. Sanford, Jr., (now deceased), a good friend and a University of NC-Chapel Hill faculty member, for suggestions. To my surprise, Cliff replied he had helped establish, in the late 1950s, a pioneering school-age adoption program in a children's residential institution where he had worked as Director of Social Services. Cliff thoughtfully contacted the CEO of that agency, who with his staff helped locate 21 adults who had been adopted as school-age children through the services of the agency. Seventeen of those agreed to participate in the study. (Chapter 3.)

The 1983 Interviews

Soon after both the agency and UNC-Greensboro granted approvals, interviews began. Data from the participants' adoption stories became the lens used metaphorically to "see" school-age adoptions from viewpoints of adults who themselves had been adopted as older children.

Using outlines(rather than a list of questions) to guide interviews helped the participants tell their adoption stories in flowing, uninterrupted ways and to center the data and layer it so that the participants' recollections tended to stay "on target" and be told in the same sequential order. Outlines improved both the collection and the interpretation of the qualitative data. Readers could also discern similarities and differences among the participants' adoption experiences.

Developing a Long-term Follow-up Study

Data from the 1983 dissertation (verbatim transcripts of interviews) became a base for beginning a long-term follow-up study. After a gap of 24 years, I found re-interviewing participants to be a fascinating, eye-opening way to gain more knowledge about older child adoptions.

Originally, I had planned to interview only the five participants whose adoption stories appeared in my 1985 adoption book, *Whose Child Am I?* [2] Because the re-interviewing process produced a wealth of new and useful information, I opted to add four more adoption stories (for a total of nine) to provide a wider variety of adoption experiences.

Appendix

A Group Meeting for Participants

Soon after the 2007 individual interviews were complete, a group meeting was held for the nine participants whose older-child adoption stories appear in this volume. The purpose was threefold:

(1) to give the participants opportunities to share their adoption stories with one another;
(2) to learn if there were common themes that ran through these older-child adoption stories; and
(3) to provide opportunities for the participants to offer advice to adoptive parents, social workers, policymakers and others who wish to improve older-child adoptions.

Five of the nine participants were able to attend: Angela, Dana, Jason, Joanne and Maynard.

Cliff Sanford, who developed the Home's innovative school-age child and youth adoptive program (*See Chapter 3.*), served as consultant. Cliff asked these "veterans" of older-child adoptions how being adopted had affected their lives. If an example given was shared by other participants, Cliff listed the example on a page of newsprint.

Later, Cliff asked the five participants to offer advice on how the process of older-child adoptions could be improved. They primarialy addressed their remarks to adoptive parents/families, social workers, and administrators/policymakers. This list of advice was also added to the newsprint.

The content of the newsprint lists may be of interest to some readers and also help those readers who conduct research. That content follows:

COMMON THEMES
Adoptions, while painful, improved opportunities and helped develop resiliency.

Adoption issues "dim" as we grow older, but adoption memories remain.

Devoted to our children: do not want them to grow up the way we did.

Ownership/feeling powerless/being bought-- you're owned.

Children should help select their adoptive families.

Arbitrariness: Why was my particular adoptive family selected for me?

Child's awareness of knowing what's going on.

Unique sensitivity: tend to know who can be trusted and who cannot.

Older-child adoptees can easily locate birth families and do so.

Grief and loss issues: of childhood innocence, of family caregivers and environments, of brothers and sisters, while growing up.

As an older child: "I had to leap into a new world, change my name, change my environment, change caregivers, all the while being the same person inside."

As adults: living in two different worlds--adoptive family world and birth family world.

Why was I placed for adoption and why didn't someone in my birth family keep me? Missing pieces of adoption stories.

ADVICE FOR ADOPTIVE PARENTS, SOCIAL WORKERS AND POLICYMAKERS

Have social workers check on older adopted kids throughout childhood (for compatibility, abuse, etc.).

As an adopted child you have an extra somebody who loves you, not one less that you've got to be cut off from.

A family isn't made with blood. It's made of love and understanding.

In a lot of situations, what a child takes in and understands is underestimated. As young as I was, I had a pretty good idea of what was going on.

I wouldn't take them away from their real family completely, because that hurts.

A child should not be placed unless the child is wanting to be placed. I don't understand why a lot of families want an older child. The key is a child wanting to be adopted. A child should not consent to an adoption with a mother and father still living (without giving the birth family assistance and opportunities to demonstrate that they can be responsible before parental rights are terminated).

Just don't stay where you don't want. That's the biggest mistake anybody can make.

The child has really got to relate to somebody in the adoptive family, and that person has to have something in common with the child. You're not really going to talk that much unless there's a person who you think you can put your trust in.

You want to provide love and care in the home for the children. Children should have somebody they can love. . .can trust. . . spend their time with and associate their feelings with. Someone they can be like, be involved with, and be accepted by.

More visits prior to the adoption would have helped me more.

I think that the main thing is that there be time for social workers and other adults to sit down and talk with the child.

If a child has something on his mind or that is bothering him about some aspect of being adopted, be open with him, discuss it with him, and let him talk it out of his system.

Adoption of an older child should be a slow, gradual thing.

It'd be good if children who were to be adopted were able to talk with another kid who's been adopted.

Adoptive parents should say that they don't own you, but they just want to be there and love you.

I think parents who adopt children mean so well and want it to work that they kind of force it on the child.

Remedies to Shorten the Manuscript:

As this valuable knowledge was added, the *Transplanted into Unaccustomed Earth* manuscript became far more useful for under-standing the lifelong implications of school-age child adoptions, but it soared in length. Remedies had to be developed. They included: (a) cutting redundant and non-essential portions of the manuscript; (b) summarizing, where practical, parts of the participants' adoption stories; and (c) "inventing" settings where verbatim quotes of siblings could be spliced together without compromising the project's integrity.

Chapter 6 illustrates how weaving togeether knowledge from birth siblings can shorten manuscripts and simultaneously describe how traumatic events like the sudden death of a parent can impact entire families. An example: Maynard's birth sister, Joanne, and his birth brother, Benny, graciously added their adoption memories to his recollections. The three sets of memories allow readers to gain in-depth and multifaceted understandings of the family's heartbreaking story, as they disclose how: (1) they reacted as children to the horrifying news of their mother's sudden death; (2) after they were adopted by different families, the siblings were not allowed to communicate with one another for more than a dozen years; (3) they were reunited; and (4) they now, as near-retirement-age adults, have moved close to one another for companionship and mutual long-term support.

Chapter 8 contains another example of an "invented" remedy used to both shorten the chapter and avoid repetitions, as well as to make a family's combined adoption story easier and more enjoyable to read. Siblings Dana and Jason were initially interviewed separately and their stories told in two separate chapters in early drafts of this volume's manuscript. Since parts of their individual adoption recollections overlapped, I chose to weave their individual reminiscences together into one combined chapter, by imagining (pretending) they were initially interviewed together, still using as much as possible their words, sentences and paragraphs verbatim.

In the closing portion of Chapter 8, I again pretended Dana and Jason met together with me, this time at Dana's farm. Given before and after copies of their chapter, they chose the edited version, because it was true to the spirit of their experiences and made reading their stories more enjoyable. Similar techniques have been used in several of the other adoption stories, but in all cases such changes are noted or described in the manuscript.

Three Sources Provide Information About This Study

1. The 1983 UNC-Greensboro doctoral dissertation, *Adults Who Were Adopted as Older Children*, includes individual, brief biographical sketches of the original 17 participants. The interviews were also "dissected" (taken apart and analyzed) to look for patterns that could help provide a better understanding of how the participants as children (ages 6 and older) coped with both survival and identity issues. [3]

2. A 1985 book, *Whose Child Am I? Adults Recollections of Being Adopted*, written as a popularized version of the dissertation, features five verbatim adoption stories (with minor editing). Insight and advice, recommendations and comments come not only from those five participants, but from all of the original participants.[4]

3. This 2020 sequel, *Transplanted Into Unaccustomed Earth: Long-Term Perspectives on Being Adopted as Older Children* is unique among the three publications. It is inclusive, providing information about the childhoods, young adulthoods, mid-life years, and the "rest" of the participants' lives (up to the publication date of 2020). The mostly verbatim adoption stories have been expanded from five to nine. In essence, this book provides a comprehensive overview of my long-term older adoption study and its findings in one volume.[5]

The Adoption Stories Are the "Heart" of This Book

The participants' adoptions occurred between 1958 and 1970—give or take—about 50 years ago. Nonetheless, their adoption stories yield extraordinary perspectives on how being adopted as older children changes lives—not only during childhoods, but also in the middle and later parts of the participants' lives.

The resilience of the participants is impressive. Consider Angela's adoption story (Chapter 5). Although now retired, she continues to evaluate the effects of her adoptive life: (a) her "tricked" adoption finalization at age 12; (b) her controlled, isolated, and "sentence-like" adolescent life; and (c) her long-term struggle to break free from the emotional shackles of her adoptive parents to become a respected, loving, caring mother, grandmother, business executive, and now senior citizen. Her resilient ability to "bounce back" was not a given. Like other participants, Angela has worked hard to make the most of the opportunities afforded her, and to make sense of her chaotic childhood and growing up years.

Because the participants and I had not met one another prior to the initial 1983 interviews, these interviews tended to be more formal and focused than were the 2007 and later interviews and contacts, which were more free flowing and less guarded. Both types provided important knowledge.

Dana (Chapter 8) sent an email to me soon after her 2007 interview that contained this important insight: "We feel like we are always running." Later she said that comment expressed her lingering doubt regarding whether she, as a mature woman, was truly a permanent, securely attached member of her adoptive family, or if she needed to stay actively on-guard (i.e., "running") to avoid making a faux pas (blunder) that could jeopardize her standing in the nuclear and/or extended adoptive family.

The Complexity of Older-child Adoptions

Dr. Alan Keith-Lucas astutely noted in the foreword of my 1985 adoption book that "very little first-hand knowledge [had been obtained about] what our well-intentioned [older child adoption] plans for a child really mean to him [or her] . . ." [6]

Additional and important knowledge has been added to adoption literature in the 35+ years since Dr. Keith-Lucas made his observation. Nonetheless, it appears that still more systematically collected firsthand knowledge is needed. The nine stories in this volume should help fill this gap.

Also, in this book, the participants have added "the rest of their stories," yielding longitudinal perspectives that go beyond surface descriptions. I hope this additional knowledge will encourage scholars and practitioners to look anew at how the phenomenon of older child adoptions affects individuals throughout their lives—and to a lesser extent the lives of their descendants as well.

Analytic Induction and the Development of Hypotheses

In Dr. York's comments about the research methodology used in this study, he used the term "analytic induction." A qualitative analytic induction process was used in my 1983 dissertation study to discover common patterns from the data.[7] Using what was known from a literature review and other pre-interview sources, two tentative hypotheses were formulated. Then, after each interview was completed, I re-formulated the hypotheses using the data/information from each new interview. Ultimately the following two hypotheses emerged from the interviews:

(1) Adults adopted at age 6 and older who recall their adoptive experiences tend to have a pattern of unique and characteristic lifestyles. Adults adopted at age 5 and under tend to take on characteristics of their adoptive families.

2) Adults adopted at age 6 or older, when given choice, preparation and participation in the adoption experience, tend to develop closeness with the adoptive family and reconcile painful childhood memories. [8]

The results of the 2007-2018 follow-up research support the

appro-priateness of further testing these two hypotheses using new, larger, more diversified samples of participants and perhaps additional and/or different research methods. Since my age prevents my beginning such a research study, I am hopeful that this volume will serve as a basis for additional work by other investigators.

Adding Knowledge

One cannot hope to find a simple, universal means to make all older child adoptions more successful, but sharing experiential practice knowledge and conducting appropriate research can gradually improve practices and policies. The participants of this study have made significant contributions to such a process by: (a) allowing those of us who have not experienced being adopted as school-age children to "see" older child adoptions from the inside out; (b) adding new knowledge; (c) giving sagacious advice on how to improve older child adoptions; (d) suggesting ideas for new research; and (e) raising insightful, penetrating questions.

Participants Suggest Topics for Future Research

1. Encourage and allow older children to participate more actively in their adoptions: Lee believes that older child adoptions are similar to marriages, and that older adoptable children, with appropriate support and guidance, should be allowed to choose or veto prospective adoptive families (Chapter 7).

2. Provide protections for children who are adopted/ transplanted into toxic family settings: Angela's adoption story (Chapter 5) is upsetting to read. She tells of emotional abuse; being "tricked" into finalizing her adoption at age 12; being completely isolated from important pre-adoption people such as birth siblings as well as from school friends, etc. How might the wellbeing of older adopted children be protected without excessive bureaucratic intrusion? Should the "finalization" procedures for older child adoptions be uniquely different than those for infant and young child adoptions?

It might be worthwhile for researchers to investigate how various USA states, other countries and different cultures attempt to protect older and special-needs children who have been adopted. Such knowledge could be used to compare and one would hope help improve practices, laws and policies that govern school-age adoptions.

For example, consider both "Dana's" and "Angela's" (Chapters 8 & 5) adoption stories. Would it be practical for adoption agencies to provide/require on-going guidance for older adopted children and/or their adoptive parents? Might the concepts of providing "therapy" for older adopted children and their new families be framed into new models wherein bonding and attachment issues are to be expected—such as in Dr. Sue Johnson's Emotional Family Therapy (EFT) concepts?[9] Perhaps weekend retreats might be considered to allow older adopted children and their adoptive parents to "fine tune" their interactions and relationships using group meetings or as separate family units?

3. Seek to better understand the resilient qualities of school-age adopted people: Many of the participants have managed to rebound from major childhood traumas and deprivations to become caring and loving adults. It would be interesting to investigate if other adult veterans of older child adoptions also have unique abilities to bounce back from childhood adversities such as abuse, neglect, trauma and danger. Is it possible that "strik(ing) (one's) roots into unaccustomed earth," as Nathaniel Hawthorne seemed to believe, might have a part to play in stimulating emotional growth and perhaps resiliency? (Chapter 1) [10]

4. In selected cases, consider allowing children to live, under close supervision, in protected environments with their neglectful/abusive parent(s). The purpose would be to determine if some of these families might learn to safely live together before adoptions into 'unaccustomed earth' settings are considered. Maynard believes that such a procedure might have "worked" with his family. (Chapter 6) [11]

5. Several of the school-age adults in this study wondered why extended family members did not adopt them. Since they did not, by default they were adopted by "strangers." These participants often added remarks such

as, "I'm glad they (my birth family relatives) didn't." How might older child adopted individuals be assisted with such personal, ambivalent concerns?

6. <u>How might we assist adopted children, who are school-age, as they (a) learn to identify with their adoptive families and (b) simultaneously cope with pre-adoption memories that can range from pleasant to terrifying?</u> How can we acknowledge and celebrate adopted children's multifaceted heritages in ways that honor both their original and adoptive families? Can research be of assistance in helping to develop and test ways that might help school-aged adopted children and their families with such delicate matters?

Appreciation

Will this research project provide a better understanding of and improved ways to implement older child adoptions? If so, the credit is largely due to: (1) the participants' powerful adoption stories and their sage advice and comments; (2) the assistance of professional colleagues, friends and members of my UNC-G dissertation committee, who have assisted in many tangible and intangible ways; (3) graduate students in my East Carolina University "adoption" classes who helped develop new concepts and re-framing terms like "placing" older children into "transplanting" older children into "unaccustomed earth" families; (4) a host of unidentified people who have contributed their ideas, their adoption-related experiences, their interest, their support, and their hard work; and (5) finally the love and support of my family who have traveled with me in this long odyssey of research and discovery.

A concluding belief and hypothesis: *The more older adopted children and their adoptive families can appreciate they are lifelong gifts to one another, the greater the likelihood that both families and their adoptive children will consider that their adoptions were successful.*

Advancing older child adoptions

A portion of the receipts from sales of *Transplanted* will be donated to a university with a doctorate-level social work, family studies or similar programs. The objective will be to encourage and help support school-age child adoption research. It is my desire that proceeds from this book might inspire future Ph.D. students to; (1) further investigate older child adoptions (2) improve the practice of school-age child adoptions, and (3) find fresh ways to creatively use this important area of practice on the behalf of children and families.

John Y. Powell, Ph.D., 2020

NOTES

Foreword

1. Wiltse, K.T. (1980) *Education and Training for Child Welfare Services.* (Unpublished manuscript, School of Social Welfare). Berkeley, CA: University of California at Berkeley.

2. Pecora, P.J., Whittaker, J.K, Barth, R.P., Borja, S. and Vesneski, W. (2019) *The child welfare challenge: Policy, practice and research – 4th Edition (revised and expanded).* New York & London: Taylor and Francis: 291-339.

Introduction: How This Book Came to Be

Notes:

1. Powell, J. Y. (1983) *Adults who were adopted as older children.* (Doctoral dissertation, Dept. of Human Development & Family Studies). Greensboro, NC: University of NC at Greensboro.

2. Powell, J. Y. (2020) *Transplanted into unaccustomed earth: Long-term perspectives on being adopted as older children.* Burlington, NC: John Y. Powell.

3. Powell, J. Y. (1985). *Whose child am I? Adults' recollections of being adopted.* New York: Tiresias Press Inc..

4. Keith-Lucas, A. (1985), Foreword in Powell, J. Y.'s *Whose child am I? Adults' recollections of being adopted.* (p. 9). New York:Tiresias Press Inc..

5. Personal Communication (2015). Reginald O. York, Ph.D., Professor, School of Social Work, University of NC at Wilmington.

Chapter One: A Quest to Better Understand and Improve Older Child Adoptions

Notes:

1. U.S. Department of Health and Human Services, Administration for Children and Families, Children's Bureau, Washington, DC. (2017) *Adoption and foster analysis reporting system* (AFCARS Report #24). Retrieved from <http://www.acf.hhs. gov/programs/cb>.

The U. S. Department of Health and Human Services, Administration for Children and Families, Children's Bureau, appears to have the most comprehensive data regarding children who have been adopted and those waiting for adoptive families. According to their data, as of October 20,2017, an estimated 117,794 US children were waiting to be adopted and more than one-half (59 percent) were ages 6 and over.

2. Powell, J. Y. (1983) *Adults who were adopted as older children.* (Doctoral dissertation, Dept. of Human Development & Family Studies.) Greensboro, NC: University of NC at Greensboro.

3. Powell, J. Y. (1985). *Whose child am I? Adults' recollections of being adopted.* New York: Tiresias Press Inc..

4. Ibid.

5. Ibid.

6. Hawthorne, N. (1850). *The custom house.* Boston: Ticknor and Fields.

The custom house was written by Nathaniel Hawthorne (1850) as an introduction to his classic book, *The scarlet letter. The custom house* contains the phrase "unaccustomed earth" that was used as part of this volume's title. Download *the custom house* @ <http.//etc.usf/lit2go/127/the-scarlet-letter/2264/introduction-the-custom-house>.

Chapter Two: *Transplanting Older Children into "Unaccustomed Earth"* Is Not New!

Notes:

1. Herman, E. (2008). *Kinship by design: A history of adoption in the modern United States* (p. 24). Chicago: The University of Chicago Press.

2. Downs, S.W., Moore, E., & McFadden, J. (2008). *Child welfare and family services: Policies and practices* (8th ed.), (p. 391). Boston: Pearson

Education.

3. Sorosky, A.D., Baran, A., & Pannor, R. (1978). *The adoption triangle* (p. 25). New York: Anchor Press.

4. Lindsay, H. (2009) *Adoption in the Roman world* (pp. 190- 230). New York:: Cambridge University Press.

5. Vasconcellos, C.A. (2016) *Children in the slave trade*. In *Children and youth in history*. Item # 141 <http;Chnm.gmu.edu/cyh/case-studies/141> (accessed November 14, 2015).

6. Faccett, T. [White Wolf] with study guide by Brenda Connelly (2008) *Giving our hearts away: Native American survival*. Women's Division, General Board of Global Ministries, the United Methodist Church. United Methodist Women, Mission Resources, PO Box 742349, Atlanta, GA. 30374-2349 <www.UMMISSIONRESOURCES.ORG>

7. Prest, D. (2011). *Evacuees in World War Two — The true story* (BBC) <www.bbc.co.uk/history/british/britain_wwtwo/ evacuees_01.shtml>. This is an account of how Great Britain "transplanted" a great number of children, women and vulnerable citizens from war-threatened cities and industrial areas to less dangerous villages and farms.

8. Little, M. (2015, June 21). Obituary of Spencer Millham.*The Guardian*. Retrieved from <www.theguardian.com/society/2015/ jun/21/spencer-millham.>

9. Herman, E. (2008). *Kinship by design: A history of adoption in the modern United States* (p. 24). Chicago: University of Chicago Press.

10. Brace, C. L. (1872). *Dangerous classes of New York* (p.12). New York: Hallenbeck & Thomas.

11. Brace, C. L. (1859). *The best method of disposing of our pauper and vagrant children* (p. 258). New York: Wynkoop, Hallerbeck, & Thomas.

12. Langsam, M. Z. (1964). *Children west*. Madison, WI: University of Wisconsin.

13. Herman, E. (2008). *Kinship by design: A history of adoption in the modern*

United States (p. 24). Chicago: University of Chicago Press.

14. Brace, C. L. (1859). *The best method of disposing of our pauper and vagrant children.* New York: Wynkoop, Hallerbeck, & Thomas.

15. Abbot, G. (1938). *The child and the state* (Vol. 1, pp. 164- 165). Chicago, IL: University of Chicago Press. Also noted in Downs, S.W., Moore, E., & McFadden, J. (2008). Child welfare and family services: Policies and practices (8th ed.), (p. 381). Boston, MA: Pearson Education.

16. White House conferences on children (retrieved Nov. 11, 2014) *Encyclopedia of children and childhood in history and society.* <org/childhood/ Wh-Z-and-other-topics/White-House-Conferences-on-Children. html>.

Also cited in Herman, E. (2008). *Kinship by design: A history of adoption in the modern United States* (p. 23). Chicago: University of Chicago Press.

17. Personal Communication (1983). Alan Keith-Lucas, Ph.D., Alumni Distinguished Professor of Social Work, University of NC at Chapel Hill.

18. Ibid.

19. Herman, E. (2008). *Kinship by design: A history of adoption in the modern United States* (pp. 21 - 22). Chicago: University of Chicago Press.

20. Personal Communication (2013). James M. Campbell, Professor Emeritus of Criminal Justice, East Carolina University, Greenville, NC.

The name of the children's home where Professor James Campbell lived as a child was Barium Springs Home for Children, Troutman, NC. The name was not given in the manuscript. This was done to avoid possible confusion with the anonymous children's home that developed the pioneering older adoption program that is featured this volume (Chapter 3).

21. Campbell, J. M. (2000) *Looking back to see ahead* (pp.95-102) in: Powell, J. Y (Ed.). *Family-centered services in residential treatment: New approaches for group care,* New York: Hawthorne Press, Inc.

22. Powell, J. Y. (1983). *Adults who were adopted as older children* (Doctoral dissertation, Dept. of Human Development & Family Studies), Greensboro, NC: University of NC at Greensboro.

23. Downs, S.W., Moore, E., & McFadden, J. (2008). *Child welfare and family services: Policies and practices* (8th ed.), (p. 431). Boston: Pearson Education.

24. Derdeyn, A. P. (1979). *Adoption and the ownership of children. Child Psychiatry and Human Development*, 9(4), (pp. 215-226).

25. Triseliotis, J. (1973) *In search of origins*. London, England: Routledge & Kegan Paul.

26. Kirk, D. H. (1984) *Shared fate: A theory and method of adoptive relationships.*, 2nd Ed. Port Angeles, WA: Ben Simon Publications.

27. Downs, S.W., Moore, E., & McFadden, J. (2009) *Child Welfare and family services: Policies and practices* (8th ed.), (pp. 390 - 400). Boston: Pearson Education.

28. Ibid., p. 412.

29. Goldstein, J., Freud, A., & Solnit, A. (1973). *Beyond the best interest of children*. New York: The Free Press.

30. Churchill, S.R., Carlson, B.E., & Nybell, L. M., Eds. (1979). *No child is unadoptable: A reader on adoption of children with special needs.* Beverly Hills, CA: Sage Publications.

31. Soule, F. (1982, August). *Adoptalk* (p. 1.). Washington, D. C.: North American Council on Adoptable Children.

32. U.S. Department of Health and Human Services, Administration for Children and Families, Children's Bureau.*The AFCARS Report # 24*. Retrieved from <http://www.acf.hhs. gov/programs/cb.>

The U. S. Department of Health and Human Services, Administration for Children and Families, Children's Bureau, appears to have the most comprehensive data regarding children who have been adopted and those waiting for adoptive families. According to their *Adoption and Foster Analysis Reporting System (AFCARS Report #24)*, there were, as of

October 20,2017, an estimated 117,794 children in the U.S. waiting to be adopted and more than one-half (59 percent) were ages 6 and over.

33. Herman, E. (2008). *Kinship by design: A history of adoption in the modern United States* (p. 1). Chicago: University of Chicago Press.

There are no notes for Chapters Three through Seven.

Chapter Eight: Dana & Jason

Notes:

1. Hemingway, E. (1929). *Farewell to arms.* New York: Scribner.

Chapter Nine: Marshall

Notes:

1. *Time* (2015, October 5) "Brief Milestones:" Yogi Berra: Baseball legend and accidental philosopher, p. 16.

Chapter Ten: Observations: Sandy Cook & John Powell

Notes:

1. *Model Approach to Partnerships in Parenting* (MAPP) and *Parent Resources for Information Development and Education* (PRIDE) are two curriculum-based programs that are available to: (1) help prospective parent(s) decide if they wish to pursue becoming adoptive or foster parent(s), and (2) assist those who do become adoptive or foster parent(s) to be better prepared for their important roles through professional adoption training. Many states in the USA and provinces in Canada require such training for new adoptive and foster parents. Interested readers can obtain additional information from internet sites such as: MAPP: <http://www.gomapp.com/> PRIDE: <www.cwla.org/pride-training/>.

2. Korkki, P. (2013, May 15) Filling up an empty nest. *NY Times* (p. F-1) May 15, 2013.

3. Florida sheriff's take on child abuse investigations, (2003) *NIJ Journal*, Issue No. 250, Nov. 2003 pp. 36-38.

For more information contact: Richard J. Gelles. Center for Research on Youth and Social Policy, School of Social Work, University of Pennsylvania, 370 Locust Walk, Philadelphia, PA 19104-6214, 215-898-5541, fax 215-898-5541, <gelles@ssw.upenn.edu>.

4. For information on Family Finding see: <http:familyfinding.org> or Kevin Campbell <http://www.senecacenter.org/familyfinding/ kevin campbell>.

Chapter 11: The Gift of Roots & Wings & Conclusions
Notes:

1. Cross, K. (2011, April) The last living Faulkner. *Southern living.* p. 141.

2. Ibid., p. 141.

3. Silva-Netto, B, R. (2013). (p. 368). Daily devotion from *Disciples*, Thursday, November 7, 2011. Nashville, TN: Upper Room Books.

4. Gibran, K. (1923). *The prophet* (pp. 17-18). New York: Alfred A. Knopf Inc.

5. Pile, F. M. (1946). *The role of the baby in the placement process: Helping the baby move into the adoptive home* (p. 70). Philadelphia, PA: The School of Social Work, University of Pennsylvania.

6. Personal communication. (1984) C. W. Sanford, Group Child Care Consultant Services, The School of Social Work, University of NC at Chapel Hill.

7. Kirk, D. H. (1984). *Adoptive kinship: A modern institution in need of reform.* Toronto, ON: Butterworth.

8. Kirk, D. H. (1984). Shared fate: A theory of adoption and mental health, 2nd. ed. Port Angeles, WA: Ben Simon Publications.

9. Helping older adopted children to bond with and learn from their new adoptive families' values and lifestyles--while at the same time helping one's adopted children to maintain an appreciate of their own biological and cultural heritage--is a difficult role for adoptive families

to carry out. Yet many families do so with great skill. Sandy Cook (Chapter 10) believes that adoptive families can learn to perform such difficult tasks from introductory training (MAPP, PRIDE, etc.), from "on-going" supervision, from "Buddy-Systems," etc. Practice-oriented research, could help identify effective ways for adoptive families to help their older adopted children to appreciate their "roots' while simultaneously helping them develop and become caring, responsible adults.

10. Powell, J. Y. (1985) *Whose child am I? Adults' recollections of being adopted)*. New York: Tiresias Press Inc.

Appendix

There are no notes for Acknowledgments.

Research Methodology: Introduction

by John Y. Powell, Ph.D.

Notes:

1. Powell, J. Y. (1983) *Adults who were adopted as older children* (Doctoral dissertation, Dept. of Human Development & Family Studies). Greensboro, NC: University of NC at Greensboro.

2. York, Reginald O. (1997) *Building basic competencies in social work research: An experiential approach.* Boston: Allyn and Bacon.

There are no notes for Research Methodology: **Transplanted into Unaccustomed Earth by Reginald O. York Ph.D.**

Research Methodology: Reflections on Dr. York's Research Methodology Comments by John Y. Powell Ph.D.

Notes:

1. Powell, J. Y. (1983) *Adults who were adopted as older children* (Doctoral dissertation, Dept. of Human Development & Family Studies). Greensboro, NC: University of NC at Greensboro.

2. Powell, J. Y. (1985) Whose child am I? *Adults' recollections of being adopted.* New York: Tiresias Press Inc.

3. Powell, J. Y. (1983) *Adults who were adopted as older children* (Doctoral

dissertation, Dept. of Human Development. & Family Studies). Greensboro, NC: University of NC at Greensboro.

4. Powell, J. Y. (1985) *Whose child am I? Adults' recollections of being adopted.* New York: Tiresias Press Inc.

5. Powell, J. Y. (2020) *Transplanted into unaccustomed earth.* Burlington, NC: John Y. Powell.

6. Keith-Lucas, A. (1985), *Foreword* in Powell, J. Y., *Whose child am I? Adults' recollections of being adopted* (p. 9). New York: Tiresias Press Inc.

7. York, Reginald O. (1997) *Building basic competencies in social work research: An experiential approach,* p. 263 & pp. 270-272. Boston: Allyn and Bacon.

8. Powell, J. Y. (1983) *Adults who were adopted as older children* (Doctoral dissertation, Dept. of Human Development & Family Studies), Greensboro, NC: University of NC at Greensboro.

9. Johnson, Susan M. (2005) *Becoming an emotionally focused therapist, The workbook.* New York: Routledge, Taylor & Francis Group (270 Madison Avenue. New York, NY 10016).

Emotionally family focused family therapy has become a popular form of family therapy. Many books and articles have been written about its uses and techniques. The above reference is given as a starting point.

10. Hawthorne, N. (1850). *The custom house.* Boston: Ticknor and Fields.

The custom house was written by Hawthorne as an introduction to his classic book, *The scarlet letter.* To download: <http.//etc.usf/lit2go/127/the-scarlet-letter/2264/introduction-the-custom-house>

11. Information about "family clarification" concepts can be found in the volume below. Interestingly "Maynard" (Chapter 6) on his own, thought of a similar plan,. He proposed his "pre-adoption family clarification" model to assist and test the viability for selective birth families to make a "new start" as a functioning family unit.

Keith-Lucas, Alan & Sanford, Clifford W. (1977) *Group child care as a family service.* Chapel Hill, NC: University of NC Press.